C000052704

THE VOID BETWEEN WORDS

A LIFETIME OF BEING DIFFERENT

J A CRAWSHAW

XYLEM
Publishing

Published by XYLEM Publishing

ISBN: 978-1-8383773-1-1

Author photograph by The Model Camp

Cover image by Shutterstock/Ahturner

Cover design by Michael Rehder

Editor: Helena Fairfax

For every book sold, a tree will be planted for our future generations to enjoy.

CONTENTS

ACKNOWLEDGEMENTS

This book would not be possible without the tremendous help, support and inspiration of **ALL** those listed below.

YOU. My heartfelt thank you for making the decision to read my story.

My fabulous mum and sister. The A team.

My sons. Being a dad has given me courage and purpose.

Grandad. You introduced me to the wonder of trees. I am the custodian of your passion. I miss you.

Grandma. For your sense of humour and story-telling inspiration. Miss you too.

My chestnut tree. You listened.

My oak tree. You changed my life.

Dyslexia. You had me on the ropes and very nearly beat me into submission. I'm grateful.

My fabulous editor. **Helena Fairfax.** You believed and taught me so much.

Georgina Howard. My wonderful friend and fellow author. Thank you for everything.

My computer. You allowed me to make mistakes.

INTRODUCTION

The impenetrable brick wall, otherwise known as the Introduction, was often the start and the finish of my foray into reading.

The sheer agony of wading through an introduction often prevented me progressing to the main story. Therefore, I want you to get straight into the action.

PART I

ANXIOUS TIMES

1

NEW SCHOOL

It was the summer of 1979. I lay on my back in the long grass of the field behind our house within the dappled shade of a sweet chestnut tree. My skinny body was fully stretched out, my hands behind my head and my fingers entwined in my thick curly hair. I was thinking. When I say thinking, my mind was flitting from thought to thought as I peered through the tree's vast spreading canopy. The cogs were going round, it was just that nothing was coming out. I was good at that and did it regularly. My semi-hypnotic state was broken only by the intermittent clouds racing across the sky on the brisk wind.

I pondered the planet spinning within the wider universe and me, a tiny speck, lying in the grass. How much sky was actually out there? Was our planet just a grain of sand within another larger world? Where did I fit in all this?

I didn't have any of the answers, but I could sense that nature had an immense power and energy, and although I felt small, I enjoyed being part of it. In reality, I didn't need to know the answers. I was happy in the knowledge that not everything could be explained. This enabled me to be free. Free to let my mind drift, free to explore ideas and free to just be me.

Occasionally I'd feel the presence of something else close by and catch a glimpse of a fox as he ambled stealthily along his thin, well-trodden path through the tall sedges and grass. I'd wonder where he was going, and why?

Today would be the last time the tree would offer me shelter, and it would surely be my final encounter with the fox. The bull-dozers had already moved into the lower portion of the field, and a new housing development had begun to devour my pocket of wilderness and my special thinking place.

Living on the outskirts of a grimy Yorkshire city, I was used to the clanking of heavy industry, and the slag heaps, like huge grey, acrid-smelling mountains, surrounding the collieries. These small havens for wildlife were becoming rarer and rarer as more people wanted to own their own homes.

If the bulldozers weren't bad enough, we were also moving to a new house on the other side of town. I reluctantly took to my feet, said my goodbyes and climbed over the weathered wooden gate, without looking back.

I was sad to leave, but moving house was becoming the norm. Dad had 'aspirations'. Well, that's what Gran and Grandad used to say. This basically meant that we moved a lot, and to different areas. Three moves in ten years. I would once again be leaving my patch to start afresh somewhere new.

I walked slowly back to the house. Mum was emptying the contents of a pan into the dustbin.

'What's that?' I asked.

'It was going to be tonight's tea. I'll do fish fingers instead.' She launched the entire pan into the bin and walked away.

'Mum? Do we have to move house again? I like it here.'

'Yes, John, the contracts are exchanged. We're going some-where bigger and there's a nice garden. You'll like it. Will you miss your friends?'

'Not really, other than the fox.'

'What fox?'

'It doesn't matter.'

She searched in the freezer. 'If you're worried about being shy, don't be. After a couple of weeks, you'll have forgotten all about it.'

I didn't believe her. The thought of meeting new people worried me intensely. There was one consolation – we were set to go on holiday before our move. It was booked and paid for, so we weren't going to miss the opportunity.

As a family, we were always keen to escape city life and would sometimes go to Scarborough or Bridlington for bracing seaside days out, but for our annual summer holiday we ventured further afield, and this year was no exception. North Wales it was, and off we set.

Our light-blue VW Beetle, fully laden with my sister Amber (aged nine and younger than me by one year), Mum, Dad, me, bedding, food, bats, balls and with our huge frame tent secured on the roof-rack, trundled along the road. We were campers. No hotels or B&Bs for us. It was all done as cheaply as possible and under canvas, but we kids didn't know anything else. For us, it was luxury and the ultimate freedom. We were happy to spend quality time with our parents, and our summer holiday was no better way to do it.

The journey to Wales was long and hot. The pitted plastic seats in the Beetle stuck to our bare legs, forming a strange dotted pattern on our skin that looked like a rare skin disease. It didn't help that the engine was effectively just behind the back seat, so the heat and the noise made it feel like we were in a tractor. We used the nylon sleeping bags and pillows to muffle the sound and create a backseat den.

Amber invented a game to pass the time which she called 'bob down for bridges'. You had to be the last one to bob down into the footwell before the car went under a bridge. Once under, it was too late and you'd lost, but go too soon…! You get the gist. (Seatbelts later put paid to that little nugget of travel joy.)

I sat back and listened to the ticking of the engine, trying to imagine what delights Wales might have for us. Long days, warm evenings, time to explore and time for fun. And most importantly, no school.

For the five years I'd attended school, I'd hated every single second. Well, that's a lie. We did have a trip to Temple Newsam House, where I ran through piles of autumn leaves and enjoyed a tour of the secret passages. That was a good day. Another time, the mayor came to school in all his pomp and ceremony. He had a prominent red wart, right in the middle of his forehead. When questions were thrown out in assembly, a girl raised her hand and asked what it was for, as though it might be a Hindu symbol, or some important sign of ceremony. An embarrassing silence followed. The panicky voice of the headmaster, swiftly encouraging another question to move things on, made the situation even more cringeworthy, and the sound of tittering could be heard throughout the hall.

That was an amusing day, not because of the poor mayor and his wart, but because it took my mind away from the drudgery of school life. I hated it – the walk there, the austere entrance, the teachers, most of the pupils and, worst of all, the feeling of captivity.

Amber was a fun sister, most of the time, and my holiday best mate. Mum seemed to relax on holiday, and Dad was there. I mean there in person, the real McCoy. We didn't see much of him at home. Work, football on a Saturday, and recovering on Sunday. I never really felt he was a huge presence. On holiday, and to my joy, he came into his own. He seemed to come alive, organising the trip, getting us there and pointing out things of interest along the way.

I tried to do the same in replicating his enthusiasm, in the hope he would be proud of me.

'Look, there's a kestrel,' I would shout, at every sighting of the bird of prey hovering at the side of the road.

There was something super special about the holidays. We were a family, we were united, and we were away from our normal humdrum life. It filled my heart with great warmth. I felt safe and part of a unique team, and everyone else seemed to think that, too.

We set up the tent on an open grassy campsite, which had a small, basic toilet and shower block, and a little wooded valley with a stream running down one side. Once the tent was up, Amber and I did our disappearing act and headed down to the stream. Splashing each other and dipping our feet into the freezing water, we started to make our mark on what would be our home for the week.

Wales held a charm for me, with its rugged, almost-forgotten-about feel. It was steeped in history and there was lots to do and explore. We visited castles, played on sandy beaches, took donkey rides, walked along the promenade munching ice creams or sat around our camp table in the evening. This was what a holiday was all about, and we were good at it.

The holiday flew by, as usual, and in the blink of an eye it was time to start my new school. I'd put off thinking about it right up until I was approaching the imposing gate. I felt sick and my whole body shook with fear as I dragged my feet down the drive. After our fabulous holiday, it felt such a heavy blow.

The starchy collar of my new white shirt rubbed on my neck and my 'to-grow-into' trousers caught under my heel, soaking up the water from the pavement. I scratched the itch with one hand and with the other hoyed up my trousers to my chest. In contrast to my trousers, the sleeves of my hand-me-down jumper were too short and restricted too much arm movement. There was a darned patch on the front of the jumper, where I guessed once was a hole, but Mum said beggars couldn't be choosers, and that we should be grateful the girl at number 72 had passed on the items. I wasn't grateful. Lucy had the physique of a ballerina and I knew this was just the start of clothes to come.

The kids were all playing outside before the 9am bell. I could see them through the metal fence, rushing around the playground, as I neared the point of no return.

I was taken into an empty room with a hard wooden floor, high walls, small metal windows and the distinct smell of wood polish and cleaning fluid. My new teacher showed me to my desk and asked me to place a pencil on each of the others while she went to fetch the register. The desks were stout and wooden, with lift-up lids, recessed inkwells, and absolutely covered in writing. Not an inch was left without someone's declaration of love for someone else, their favourite footy team, or swearwords, all engraved into the wood like permanent tattoos and highlighted in Tipex.

As I carefully placed the pencils, I thought about who might be sitting at each desk. I tried to imagine their faces. Would they be like me? I returned to my desk and waited nervously for the bell and my new classmates to enter. My legs shook, my palms were sweaty, and my heart pounded. Then the deafening bell filled the whole school and, one minute later, a raucous ball of uniforms, hair and bags burst in taking their respective places. I stared at them. They all seemed confident and, in complete contrast to me, blasé about their first day back.

'Hello,' a voice said beside me. 'You must be the new boy? I'm Mary.'

I looked round to see a short girl with black hair and brown National Health glasses. She was opening up her desk.

'Hello, I'm John,' I said nervously.

Mary's desk slammed shut. 'Are you sure it isn't Lucy?'

I shook my head. 'What do you mean?'

'Your jumper's on inside out. Your name tag says Lucy.'

The whole class started to laugh.

'He's wearing a girl's jumper,' someone shouted, throwing a

scrunched-up paper ball at my head. The laughter became louder and I tore off the jumper as quickly as I could.

'Is he in a skirt too?' the same voice shouted.

I looked at Mary. She was the only one not laughing, but she didn't look at me, just kept her head down, embarrassed. At that point, and to my sheer relief, the teacher walked through the door.

'What on earth is going on in here? I can hear you the other side of the school,' she shouted.

I was shaking inside. My heart felt like it was jumping around my entire body, and my legs were numb, but I tried to look as confident as I could. I wasn't going to show them I was flustered, but if I'd had the option to run away right there and then, and never go back, I would have. But this was my new school now, I had no choice. I had to just get on with it and deal with the agony internally.

The rest of the day was spent avoiding the main antagonisers and finding my way around the buildings and yards, with the aid of my new-found friend, Mary. The place seemed huge, and I thought I'd never be able to make sense of all the passages and corridors.

At break time I stood with my back against the wall, watching the boys playing football on the lower hardstanding. I was too shy to join in and, as a result of my first encounter with them, was stuck to the spot with fear. I had no idea of how to break the ice and the thought of going over there and asking to join in terrified the living daylights out of me. My summer of freedom and joy was now a distant memory, and I felt terribly lonely.

The walk home was about a mile, and I trudged along slowly, mulling over in my mind the pain of the day. I came across a stick on the ground and picked it up. The bark was peeling off, and I stripped it bare so I could feel the knots in contrast to the smooth wood. I whacked it against a tree to see how strong it was and, to my surprise, a squirrel leapt out, jumping above my head and onto the adjacent tree. I observed it, and it looked nervously back at me. I could see it was wary. Its head was twitching, and I could tell it was ready to scurry away to freedom if I made the slightest move. I held out my stick, as if offering the hand of friendship. Its ears flickered, then without warning, it darted up the trunk and disappeared into the thick canopy.

The squirrel made me smile and, as I carried on my walk, I drew my arm back and threw my stick in front of me like a javelin, then ran to chase it. It was then I remembered what mum had said about the first day being the hardest one of all.

'What doesn't kill us, makes us stronger,' she'd say.

I threw the stick again and took mild comfort from her words. Tomorrow was another day, I thought. I picked up my stick and ran the tip of it along the stone wall which led to the rear of our house, and then just a jump over it and home. The next day was likely to be easier, but the reality was, I didn't want to go back. I felt trapped and as if I had no options.

I didn't say much at home, but mum gave me some hot milk and presented me with a new scientific calculator, which I thought was cool. It helped me forget about the day as I pressed all the crazy unknown buttons. Later, I watched *Basil Brush* and *Tomorrow's World* on TV and had an early night.

The next day, I made sure I didn't arrive until the last minute. I didn't want to go through the agony of the long wait I'd had the day before.

I walked through the yard and sensed someone just behind me.

'You the new boy?' an unknown voice asked.

I looked around nervously and nodded.

'Richard,' he said. 'Sit next to me today if you want?' he added matter-of-factly, walking beside me.

'I will,' I replied, as we made our way into the building. 'I'm John.'

'Yeah, I know, I think you live near me. I could see you in front of me most of the way.'

'Oaklands Road, we've just moved in.'

Richard handed me a piece of chewing gum. 'Keep it hidden till break, we're not allowed it. I'm on Oaklands Drive, just around the corner.'

I smiled, shoved the gum in my back pocket and headed casually to our class.

The teacher issued us each with a blue-covered exercise book, instructing us to put our names on the front and then, on the first page, to write about our summer holidays. The things we'd been doing, the places we'd been and who with.

I wasn't sure where to put my name! It was just a bare cover. Not wanting to get it wrong, I looked at Richard, who was confidently writing his name in the centre, near to the top. So I did exactly the same.

The memories of our fab trip to North Wales came flooding back. There was so much I wanted to say. The details swirled around in my mind, making me giddy with excitement. I picked up my pencil and began to write.

I didn't stop writing for the next twenty minutes. I wrote about playing with Amber, sandcastles, of course, but also hunting for anything interesting in rock pools. How I'd found a piece of driftwood, silvery-white in colour. It was an actual tree branch, too heavy to lift, smooth, incredibly smooth, no bark on it and obviously weathered in the water for many years. It was a splendid find because, curiously, from a particular angle, it resembled a majestic swan, the shape of its slender neck and head as if for real, and even a knot where the eye would be, giving it an eerie sense of life. I couldn't stop touching it, running my hands along the super smooth neck and back.

My pencil never stopped as I went on to write about Amber finding a huge black crab, which we then taunted with our plastic spade, watching it scurry away under a rock. We hardly wore shoes that week and never socks. I felt free with my feet unconstrained by anything, and I felt free in my mind, too, and tried to express that in my writing. I described how there was something rather special about feeling the sand between my toes, and although the sea was cold, we splashed each other and dared to venture in beyond our waists.

I detailed the impressive castles we saw, with their high turrets and drawbridges, how we played crazy golf and consumed mountains of ice cream. Dad was always eager to kick a ball around too. He'd had trials with a First Division club when he was younger and fancied himself as a bit of a George Best. We were happy to play 'three and in goal' and to try and tackle him. We played into the evening around the tent, until mum called us for our camp dinner, which was usually burnt. It's safe to say that mum wasn't a great cook. We never needed an alarm clock at home, as we would always hear her scraping the burnt toast out of the back door, the signal it was time to get up for school. We loved her, though, and our bellies were hungry after a full day of activity, for which we were grateful.

I was keen to explain about one of the highlights, which was visiting the smallest house in Britain, in Conwy – a tiny red fisherman's cottage with rooms the size of broom cupboards and the steepest set of steps to the first floor. We tried to imagine our family living there and couldn't see all four of us huddled into one room, let alone sharing a bedroom. It had stunning views out over the harbour, though, which Mum liked, and Dad said it would be cheap to heat.

The teacher gave us a five-minute warning to finish our stories, but I still had so much to write about. I quickly sharpened my pencil in the large metal communal sharpener, which was clamped to her desk. It was the size of a small motorbike engine, or so it seemed. You put your pencil in one end, wound the protruding handle and watched the fine ribbon of wood unfurl from the other.

Back in my seat, I busily wrote about the day we set off to ride the cable-car to the top of some mountain, but the wind was so strong, it didn't run that day. Instead, we trudged against the rain and wind in our flimsy, supposedly waterproof jackets halfway up the hill and then admitted defeat and returned to the café at the bottom, where Amber and I shared a Coke and Mum and Dad had tea. Mum tried to dry her blonde hair with a tea-towel borrowed from the kitchen, and mine and Amber's feet were soaked wet in our flimsy sneakers.

It was only on returning to the campsite that the real fun started, because a ferocious wind had lifted our entire tent off the ground and deposited it, and most of the contents, twenty feet over the wall into the farmer's field, where a heard of inquisitive cows were huddled around it.

We managed to collectively shoo the cows away, straighten the bent steel poles and heave the tent back over the wall, and gather up all our belongings. That night we lay in our sleeping bags and laughed so much as the hoof marks on the side became evident in the moonlight. What a day!

'Okay everyone, that's enough time on your stories,' the teacher said, all too soon. I still had loads to put down on paper and, frustratingly, had only told half the story.

'Put them in a neat pile on my desk as you leave, and I'll mark them this evening, so we can go through them all tomorrow.'

Everyone else seemed just fine at having to stop there, but I felt I hadn't really done the holiday justice. I hadn't mentioned the choppy seal-watching boat trip or the clifftop kite-flying or the pitch and putt golf – which I won, even with Amber cheating!

Anyway, it was one of the best lessons I'd ever had at school, and it had gone fast. And I wasn't the laughing stock either, which was a huge relief.

The rest of the day seemed to drag on. Following the final

bell, I packed up my things and walked back with Richard as far as the path which split our routes. I asked him about his holiday, and he told me about a house they owned in Provence, with its own pool, and his friend Jacques who lived close by. I couldn't imagine having two houses, especially one in another country.

I told him I'd run out of time with the write-up, and he said he'd done his in ten minutes and was bored.

The following day I didn't see Richard. He wasn't at school. Our teacher quietened us down and began to give out the books containing our stories.

'I've marked your work, and I'll ask each one of you to join me to read your pieces and discuss further.'

Great, I thought. A chance to explain the bits I'd missed out.

I opened my book, and my heart sank. There was red ink all over it, crossings out, double underlinings and numbers in circles with attached comments. How could it be wrong? I thought. She wasn't there, and it was all true. I felt my shoulders drop and I slumped back into my chair as I picked through the comments, and then the final mark: 'SEE ME'.

Mary was up first and then a few others, and then it was me. I sat beside the teacher, and she peered over her glasses at me.

'John, it's lovely to have you in the class. I hope you're settling in okay?' she said, with the hint of a smile.

'Yes,' I said, not wanting to tell the truth.

She then took my book, opened it and sighed. She rested her chin on her hand. 'Wales is a fascinating place. I've been many times and loved it, but I just couldn't understand most of what you wrote.'

'It's all true, miss,' I said. 'But I didn't get chance to tell the full story.'

She scrunched up her lips. 'Hmm. Shall we just start at the beginning?'

She asked me to explain some of the words I'd used. I told

her I'd written it straight from my brain and heart, as if I was there, living it again and feeling the feelings.

'I'm not sure if the words are right, miss,' I said. 'But they feel right... and sometimes I'm not sure of the spelling, so I put all the letters that might fit, so at least some of them might be right.'

She paused for a moment, scrunching her lips up even more, then nodded her head. She explained that maybe I shouldn't rush next time. Better to get the words right and the spellings correct, than create *War and Peace*.

But I didn't understand. Surely it was about the story and the feeling, rather than the words? But I guess this was school, after all, and nothing seemed to be fair or explainable, just stuff for stuff's sake.

Before the teacher sent me back to my seat, she asked me to correct the spelling mistakes for homework and to try and make some kind of order out of it – as we would be reading the passages out in class the following day! My heart sank. It felt like it was disappearing deep within my body, never to be found again. Homework! Reading out in class! My worst nightmare. I didn't like being the centre of attention and the wave of despair continued through my body. Perhaps it was something to do with going to so many new schools and being 'THE' centre of attention. Anyway, as if being the new boy wasn't bad enough, I now had to spend the evening re-writing something I thought was really good, and then I would have to stand before the entire class and read it out the next day. School was so rubbish.

I walked home, dragging my heels. Richard was, of course, not there, but his absence did give me an idea. But my mum would never let me have a day off unless I was dying.

'You're quiet,' Mum said at the kitchen table. Amber was at her dance class and Dad was picking her up, so just Mum and me.

I pushed my burnt pork chop around on the plate and said nothing.

'Is school okay?' she asked.

'Do we have a dictionary?' I murmured.

'Of course.' She pointed over to the bookshelf. 'Oxford Concise, third in from the left. You got homework?'

I nodded. I'd never actually read a book before, let alone looked in a dictionary, and I couldn't remember anyone reading to me, either. No bedtime stories or fun children's poetry in our house. We had books on the shelf, yes. But they were just for show.

I did start reading a book once, about Robin Hood, but didn't get past the second page. Reading seemed so tedious and slow. I liked the pictures, though, and loved the way the scenes of Robin firing his bow and swinging from tree to tree were colourful and exciting.

I spent the evening at the kitchen table, painstakingly trying to correct my story. The dictionary seemed incredibly daunting.

'How can you find a word if you don't know how to spell it?' I asked Mum. It just didn't make sense. She told me it was no good her doing it for me, as I would never learn. I spent two hours just staring at the page, with my head in my hands, and I was brought to tears. The fear of the next day and the way the dictionary fried my brain just made me fall apart. It was an over-whelming feeling of despair and frustration, taking me to the point of complete breakdown.

Mum came in and put her hand on my shoulder. 'You all done?'

'No.' I said, wiping my eyes. 'Can you help me with the dictionary?'

'Of course, but you have to do it yourself, it's no good me doing it for you,' she repeated. Mum always helped, but she held the common view that school was the place for learning and that she shouldn't intervene too much. 'Parents aren't the teachers,' she would say. The thought was there, though, and she did manage to get me out of limbo and into first gear.

'How do you spell Conly Cassle? I can't find it in the dictionary.'

'Do you mean Conwy Castle?'

I looked at her, puzzled. 'Yes. That's what I said.'

Mum helped me correct a few of my mistakes and then she had to go and do some ironing. I wanted her to help me more, and just couldn't face the torment of fixing things I didn't know how to fix. And I still couldn't understand why Conly Cassle wasn't good enough, or pond-bippin. D's and B's always got me confused and ended up the wrong way around. To me, life was too short to be worrying about all that.

I didn't have the energy or the will to do any more and headed for bed complaining of an aching leg, mixed with lots of fake coughing. Mum came to tuck me in, telling me my leg and cough wouldn't kill me, and I should be fine tomorrow. My plan for a day off was foiled.

The following morning I heard the toast being scraped and lay in bed, wishing I didn't have to go into school. Life seemed so totally unfair. I looked through the window at a white cloud steaming past at a pace and tried to imagine myself riding it like a cowboy, free to explore the vast open sky, and the adventures I could have along the way, while avoiding school.

Mum shouted and I reluctantly put on my uniform and, with toast in hand, headed off to school. I caught up with Richard, who was just ahead of me at the path junction. Apparently he'd had his Grade 3 piano exam and his mum had given him the rest of the day off, as he'd had a bit of a sniffle.

He showed me his new football cards. He had Jim Holton and Ken Swain.

'Is that good?' I asked.

'Do you want to do swaps?'

'I don't have any. Where do you get them?'

Richard laughed. 'From the shop. My dad gets them for me.'

First lesson was art, and we got the chance to play around with pastels on black paper, drawing leaves. I'd done some drawing of leaves with Grandad in his garden. He showed me that oak was different to beech by the lobed edge and that beech had a slightly hairy bottom, which I always found amusing. I already knew how to identify a silver birch, apple and sycamore, because they were the three trees that bordered the path to his shed.

Drawing the leaf shapes on the paper with the pastels was effortless. My hand moved freely as I used different greens, browns and reds to create a stylised version of each leaf. I loved art, and it took my mind off English, which was to follow.

Mary was up first for her reading. We were called up alphabetically, and she was Mary Anderson. I was mid-bunch, which was regrettable, as I was understandably nervous. Extremely nervous, in fact, and under my desk I had what my mum called 'anxious leg'. I wasn't always aware of it, but the rapid shaking made the contents of my pencil case jump around on the desk.

My various classmates took it in turn to stand at the front and read their summer holiday stories. Dave had been to Skegness in his family's static caravan and been kicked in the goolies by a donkey on the beach, which was by far the funniest story as I waited. Robbo had been to his grandparents' in Doncaster and Sharon had been in the Royal Infirmary having a lump removed from her back. Someone shouted that she'd had a baby, but the teacher intervened swiftly to stop things getting out of hand. Claire talked about something in her lovely silky voice, but I wasn't listening, I just watched her lips move and was captivated by the way she flicked her hair. She was amazing.

The most exotic holiday was Fran's, who went to South Africa and saw sharks and did a safari, and heard the gunshot when someone was being killed three blocks away from their hotel. Everyone was stunned into silence. Who could possibly follow such a story as that?

Well, me. Typical.

I grabbed my book and headed to the front. I was aware of everyone's eyes watching me, and my anxious leg was making me walk funny. I skulked to the front and froze on the spot.

I looked at the teacher, and she nodded that she was ready. My leg started to shake even more, and my head felt very hot. I looked at my page, which I was gripping so much it creased, making the words go out of focus.

'I went to Wales,' I said. But there was something wrong. Something very wrong. My brain, mouth, lips and tongue blurted out the words, but my ears heard nothing. I tried again, but my voice had completely gone. My lips became dry and my tongue even drier, like when you've licked the inside of a banana skin.

I tried to swallow, but couldn't. A wave of anxiety consumed my entire body, starting in my feet and then along my bones and veins, like a plague of locusts moving their way to my heart.

Someone giggled and then someone else. Someone threw a rubber, which hit my arm and ricocheted onto the teacher's desk.

'Where did you go, John?' the teacher asked.

I looked at her, turning my head, my feet welded to the floor and unable to move.

'Where did you go, John?' she repeated calmly.

I just stared at her. The whole class now laughing.

'He went to mime school,' shouted evil Billy Tranter, and the entire place erupted into more laughter.

I could feel my lungs breathing out, more than in. I licked my lips. 'I – I – I've been to Wales,' I said to the teacher, not daring to look back at the class. I knew my burning red face would instantly give away my embarrassment and the shame that I couldn't tell my own story.

'Quiet, everyone,' the teacher said. I felt relieved that she seemed to understand my plight and was ready for her to send me back to my seat, so I could escape the hideous embarrassment. I turned to face my desk and then...

'John is going to carry on, so quiet everyone. John.'

The world suddenly stopped turning. It was like Muhammad Ali had just walked straight up to me and given me his best right hook straight in the face. Twice.

I looked individually at each and every person in the room. They surely would have some compassion and let me go. But their eyes seemed even more intent on making me carry on than they had been before. There was complete silence. A deafening silence.

I looked at the paper again. The words moved in front of my eyes, jumping all over the page. I could see red. There were red lines all over the place. I gripped the paper tightly, clenched my toes and forced it out. 'I went to Wales.'

My breathing was rapid and shallow, my heart exploding with fear, but I'd done it. Got it out. Got the ball rolling.

The class was still silent. Mary smiled, which gave me some encouragement. 'I went to Wales,' I said with joy.

The teacher nodded, raising her eyebrows, suggesting I carry on. I looked at the page and tried to focus. 'Erm... erm... Me, my mum, dad and sister went camping in Wales,' I blurted out. I actually knew that bit off by heart, so I didn't have to read it. The next line wasn't so easy. We went to... Con – Con – Conly – Cassle.'

Someone laughed again, and I froze.

'He can't read,' shouted Billy and went into uncontrollable laughter as he rocked back in his chair. 'He's as thick as two short planks.'

It was then, unusually, I felt the debilitating anxiety slowly filtering out of my body, to be replaced with a coldness that filled my core. My heart was hardly beating, as if it were frozen. It was a lonely coldness. The hairs stood up on the back of my neck, and a shiver ran through my entire body. I was numb, numb to the bone and I was alone.

Billy was right, I couldn't even read my own writing. I *was* thick, and I was stupid, and I hated school, and I hated them. I threw my book on the floor and stormed out of the class, to complete uproar.

2

THE SWITCHEROO

In the summer of 1981 our beloved tent stayed in the garage, and we became the proud new owners of a gleaming red, Bedford campervan. Second-hand, of course, and a little weathered, but to us, it was about to change our camping holidays forever. It had a fridge and a little two-ring gas cooker, and the roof lifted to reveal hammock-style beds for Amber and me. We couldn't be any more excited. The best thing was, the inevitable family arguments about which pole went into which socket, and who wasn't holding their corner high enough, were long gone. We could just pull up on site and start exploring straight away.

That year we set off enthusiastically to Cornwall, feeling like royalty as we sped along.

No sooner had we got on the road than a campervan passing on the opposite side flashed its lights, and we could see the occupants waving like crazy.

'Shit! There's something wrong,' Dad said, checking the dash for warning lights. 'We'd better pull over and have a look. Maybe it's the roof.'

We pulled into a lay-by and Dad gave the van a once-over. At one point we just saw his legs poking out from underneath.

Amber looked at me with horror on her face. She didn't need to say anything, I knew exactly what she was thinking. The tent might be coming out of retirement. Oh, joy. Flange A to socket B, and all that jazz.

After a few minutes, Dad jumped back in, and to our delight we carried on our journey.

'Did you find anything?' Mum asked.

'Nope. It all looks good.'

The warmth came back into Amber's face and she regained her smile. She hated doing the tent. I quite liked the adventure and technical aspect, but for Amber, the tent was tedious, and the van meant 'easy'. She was bone idle when she wanted to be.

We continued on our journey, and Amber started setting up the table. There were no seatbelts in the back, so we had the freedom to walk around and, yes, play games. She assembled the table and then out came 'Operation!'

Now, if you've ever tried to remove someone's Charley horse with minute tweezers in the back of a rattling van on winding roads, you'll know it's just about impossible. The buzzer buzzed and the patient's red nose lit up like there was no tomorrow, much to Amber's frustration. I managed to skilfully extract his water on the knee by scooping the bucket's handle onto the tweezers and flicking it into the air.

A little further along, another van flashed its lights and the occupants waved frantically.

'Are you sure you checked the roof?' Mum asked Dad. He remained silent, but you could feel the cogs grinding in his head as he stroked his Tom-Selleck-style moustache. He was an engineer, so we trusted his judgement, and the van seemed to be progressing well, so we returned to our game and Mum pulled down the sunshield and put some lipstick on in its mirror.

At the roundabout to get on the motorway, a campervan came around in front of us. We watched with complete amazement as a whole family in the front (there must have been six of them) waved and smiled and beeped their horn. It was then it dawned on us. A code between campervans we'd never known about. A friendly code of acknowledgement between others who'd found freedom from poles and heavy canvas. We found ourselves in a club, a campervan club, where acknowledgement on the road was the rule. Well, to say we were all relieved was an understatement, and you could hear the four of us all sigh simultaneously.

The biggest excitement was when we did OUR first wave. Another Bedford van approached on the opposite side, and we waited and waited until it was close enough, and then we all waved frantically. The two elderly occupants and their dog gave us a fantastic smile and the driver a thumbs up. We were in the club.

Cornwall was a hell of a journey from Yorkshire. Dad kept saying, 'We could have gone to bloody France in the time it's taken us to get here.' Mum wore her hair up in a headscarf to stop it blowing uncontrollably in the wind as the camper negotiated the narrow Cornish lanes, and Amber and I cemented our close relationship further, teasing each other and playing more games.

For a lot of the journey, we listened to Dad's tape of ELO's *Time* album, and I almost became fluent in the lyrics to *Ticket to the Moon*. It seemed like absolute freedom to be jetting off to another planet, and I stared up into the sky, wondering what it would be like to do just that.

We lived in one pair of shorts each, demolished most of Cornwall's cream teas – jam on first, obviously – and I tried crab for the first time, which instantly became my favourite thing to eat. The van took us to a new camping level, and although it was a bit of a logistical scramble into various beds, it was warmer and infinitely more comfortable.

One evening a van came to the campsite selling hot Cornish pasties. Mum instructed me to go up and get four for dinner. I didn't want to go as I'd never bought anything from a van before, didn't know what to say, or even what a Cornish pasty was, but mum thrust a £10 note in my hand and told me to have a bit of confidence and get on with it. I now know it was her way of beating me out of my shyness, but it seemed like the end of the world right then. I walked slowly to the van. There was a queue, so I waited in line. I tried to read the little sign, with the options and prices, but got a little confused, because Amber said she wanted one without onions and there didn't seem to be that option.

My turn in the queue came, and the man told me that they all come with onions, like it or lump it. I didn't dare ask what else was on offer and nervously placed my order for four. The man said something which I didn't really understand and handed me the pasties, which were hot and difficult to handle. I handed him the money, and he smiled, a really big smile, so I smiled back and headed to the van, while almost literally juggling the burning hot pies.

Mum relayed them inside, and we all sat around the table in anticipation.

'Where's my change?' Mum said jovially.

I looked puzzled. 'There wasn't any change.'

Mum looked straight at me with a wry smile. 'Yes, there was.' And held out her hand.

'There wasn't any. It was £10,' I insisted.

Mum turned from a lovely tanned brown colour to white as a sheet. '£10! They're 50p each, I saw it on the poster in the loos. It should have been £2.'

'Oh,' I said sheepishly.

There was an eerie silence, and then Amber laughed. 'Did you get me one without onions?'

Well, that seemed to be the start of my new best trick. Misreading things, getting confused and getting into a state of mild panic, and making a mess of everything. No wonder the pasty man had a smile from Land's End to Boscastle.

Mum looked at Dad, who was shaking his head.

'You'd better get yourself back up there and get the change, the robbing... you know what,' he said in his deep Yorkshire accent.

No way. No way were they asking me to go back up there and confront the man, in front of a queue of people. No way. I was far too shy, and I knew I wouldn't be able to speak.

'Go on, we're not eating these until you've got your arse up there and sorted this mess out. £10 is a lot of money and there'll be fewer things to do for the rest of the holiday.'

Fear struck me straight in the stomach. It turned my whole body inside out. 'I can't do it, Mum,' I said, with a tear in my eye. 'I can't do it.'

'What have I said about your shyness, John? Get up there and sort it. Now!'

I tried to hold back my tears and slowly made my way out of the van, hoping they would change their minds, but they didn't. What I would have given for Dad to offer to sort it for me, or Mum to just let it lie. Speaking to strangers made me anxious, and asking for the money back seemed like nothing short of pure hell.

I made my way slowly and tentatively up the grassy hill. The pasty van was lit up with fairy lights and there were people milling outside.

My tears were now in full flow. I was desperate and out of my depth, and I was shaking like a leaf. I could see the man through the serving hatch. He had bulging muscles and a beard like a pirate. Another man went up to the counter, so I hid behind a bush and watched. Still shaking, I tried to tell myself it was okay and to be brave. I waited till he'd been served and then boldly walked halfway to the van – and promptly diverted to the toilet block as the pasty man clocked me.

I sought refuge in one of the cubicles and sat there shaking and staring at the back of the door in the cold. I felt trapped. My sobbing became uncontrollable and my anxious leg was going ten to the dozen. I waited for some time – I don't know how long, it could have been five minutes, could have been an hour – I didn't know, and I was cold. Then suddenly I heard whistling and a mop came under the door. The camp supervisor was doing his cleaning round.

He tapped on the door. 'You okay?' I remained silent and waited a few seconds before unbolting the door. Then, while he wasn't looking, I made my escape. I resumed my original position behind the bush and waited for a gap in the customers so I wouldn't have to stand in the queue.

The steam from my breath was bound to be giving my hiding place away, so I calmed my breathing and tried to compose myself. I straightened my back, took a deep breath and walked purposefully to the pasty van and then, with about fifteen strides to go, I diverted back to our van. I was snivelling as I opened the door to the eager faces of my family inside.

'Erm... He'd gone,' I said, under my breath.

Mum said nothing and just nodded in a disappointed manner. Dad was reading the paper and didn't look up, and Amber had half a pasty in her mouth.

No one spoke. Mum laid a pasty out for me, and I slowly munched my way through it, still partially shaking and still snivelling. I think she knew the truth – well, looking back, I know she knew.

She pushed a mug of hot milk towards me and said, 'I used to be shy, you know, and your grandad was too, but it never did us any good. You'll get walked all over if you don't stand up for yourself.' I just looked at the table and nibbled on the pasty.

At twelve, I was beginning to find my freedom, and the new silver racing bike I received that Christmas was my pride and joy. No one else was allowed to ride it other than me, and I promised myself I wouldn't throw it on the floor, like all the previous bikes I'd had. I loved that bike, and I was determined to look after it. It took me on adventures within a few miles of home, which usually involved calling at the shop for a bag of sweets with a 10p that had been burning a hole in my pocket. If I got the quarter-penny and halfpenny chews, it amounted to a worthy bag full. I didn't mind going in there, as I didn't have to speak to the shopkeeper – just stuff your bag and pay. Sometimes he tried to communicate, but I just kept my head down and then ran out.

The one thing I was confident about was riding my bike. I was instinctively a good rider, and it looked smart. Smart enough, I hoped, to impress Claire from my class. She was the most beautiful girl I'd ever seen. Long brown hair, which she often wore in a ponytail, high cheekbones and incredible lips. They were juicy, not like lips I'd seen on any other girl.

I first fell in love with her when she played *The Entertainer* on the piano in our music class. We were all accompanying her on recorders. Well, I was meant to be, but I couldn't stop staring at her lips as she concentrated on the piece. I just pretended to blow and mimed the finger bit.

I found out from a mate where she lived, and me and the Silver Dream Machine would cycle past her house, in the hope she'd see me and come running out to proclaim undying love. Claire lived in a little cul-de-sac, so there was no other reason to be going up there other than to see her, which, looking back, must have seemed odd to the neighbours. The bike almost seemed on autopilot the number of times I slowly rode up and down, but she never appeared. The truth was, Claire never knew I existed. All my attempts at school to be near her in the tuck shop queue or on the same table at lunch were futile. She never acknowledged me, and I never got an opportunity to speak to her, although if I had, I probably would have frozen anyway.

I knew another girl at school who liked me. Janice was perfectly fine, friendly, a nice smile and long legs, but she wasn't for me. I was holding out for Claire, and no one else.

One evening Mum cut my curly hair, and after my bath I headed to my bedroom, where I played with a gadget for embossing letters onto a thin, sticky strip, which was all the rage in the 1980s. I turned the dial to form each of the letters of her name, Claire Baker, and punched them out onto the strip. I then peeled the backing paper and stuck her name to the underside of a poster I had of *Mork and Mindy*, my favourite TV show, which was stuck to the wall. Somehow there was something thrilling about printing her name out and having it secretly hidden in my room.

I thought many times about writing Claire a note in class, but my nerves always got the better of me. Even though I wrote a few out, I never delivered them.

But that Christmas, the school announced there would be a seasonal postbox, for us to post cards to our fellow classmates. It was the perfect solution. I managed to pluck some courage from somewhere. I 'borrowed' a Christmas card from my mum's selection, wrote my seasonal greetings to Claire and signed it. I printed my name too, underneath, just so there was no doubt it was from me, and slid it stealthily into the box for delivery.

The following day the representative 'postboy', Will from 5C, arrived at our class and gave out the cards. I got one from Richard and one from Mary, but I was more interested in what Claire was about to receive, and what her reaction would be. I squirmed in my seat, watching her out of the corner of my eye, while pretending not to look. I kept looking over and then away, when I thought she might see me.

Claire Baker, the postboy shouted. He handed her seven cards. Very popular, I thought, and one was bound to be mine. I kept my eye on her as she opened each one, expecting her to look over at any time. I watched her thank various people in the class, but she didn't acknowledge me. I kept looking over, but she didn't look back.

I sat back in my chair. Perhaps my card might still be in the 'sorting area' and would arrive the following day. In a way, I was relieved, as it meant I wouldn't have the awkward confrontation that I so badly wanted, but was so massively scared of.

The class ended, and we exited into the hallway. Claire came up beside me. I could sense her just on my shoulder, and I could smell her girlie, soapy scent. My legs felt a bit weak and there was a sort of cramp in my stomach. Halfway down the corridor, she got a little ahead of me and turned.

'Thank you for the card,' she said.

All I could see were her lips making the words. I smiled nervously. 'It's okay.'

'You spelled Christmas wrong.'

Instantly the blood drained from my face, arms and legs, and the cramp in my stomach twisted, like I was dying inside. Crippled with total embarrassment, I caught my shoe on a drain cover and stumbled to the ground, scuffing my knees and grazing my palms. I regained my feet, and when I looked up, she was gone.

Who knew Christmas had an H in it? Or a T, for that matter?

For the next four months I continued to admire Claire from a distance. I knew she was still the girl for me. Our brief but to-the-point conversation had made me feel like we had a connection, even though she was more interested in her piano and flute lessons than me. Anyway, May of that year proved to be an interesting month.

Four distinct things happened. Firstly, I pooled all my sweet money 10p coins and bought some football cards. Two packs. Everyone was swapping at school. There was a game whereby you competed against your opponent, flying your card against the wall. Whoever got their card nearest to the wall scooped both cards. You had to hold the card between your index and middle fingers and do a sort of flick, so that the card skimmed and rotated in the air and – hopefully – just landed up against the wall. The skill was to play your least favourite card, in the hope of winning something new for your collection. I had to be a part of it.

On opening my brand-new shiny packs, I soon realised I had two Don Massons. I didn't know who he was, but Dad told me he was pretty well-known and a good player. I paired them together in my bag and slid the rest into my back pocket. I wasn't going to risk the Don Massons in a throw-off.

The next day I joined in the fun and challenged someone to a game. My opponent threw first. His card landed about six inches from the wall, then it was me. My card flew through the air to float and drop about two feet away from the target. He'd won. I gracefully conceded, and we positioned ourselves for another round. I threw first. This time my card hit the wall before rebounding back towards me, almost landing at my feet. I lost that one too. My opponent picked up his winnings, and we nodded, to indicate we were up for another shot. I carefully placed the card between my fingers, drew back my arm and gently but purposefully ejected it. It flew up to the wall and seemed to stall, before floating down to rest on the ground, leaning up against the wall. It was the perfect shot. You couldn't get any closer. My opponent's only chance to win was to try and knock my card out of the way, with a fast and deliberate hit, which was risky, but he had no option.

He blasted his card towards mine with such force, it missed my card and rebounded back towards us. I'd won. I'd only flipping well gone and won. I strolled over and calmly picked up my winnings. And there it was. A Don Masson. I now had three.

Later that week, I played against some of the kids from the lower year at cross-country training, and although I lost three cards, I managed to triumphantly claim another Don Masson. The four identical cards, after that, never left the house. I thought it was fate and I was on a winning streak, although it was to take me another six months to amass my prize collection of nine Don Massons.

It was only in my mid-twenties, and on telling of the story to some friends, that I became aware that the aim was to collect the whole team, and not just one player. And I now understand why everyone at school was so despondent at not being able to complete their collections, because there were no Don Massons in the whole area. I still have them in a box in the loft.)

The next distinct thing to happen was, I suddenly had hairs. My legs were the first to become carpeted. I had a few stragglers on my chest, but by far the most impressive were my pubic collection. I looked strange in the mirror – a pale, white, skinny boy, with a mop of dark hair on his head and a manly mop lower down. I had spots all over my face, and my voice at certain times went very squeaky. I was turning from a boy into a man.

Thirdly, and to my completed surprise, I found a new skill and it's not what you think! I was hovering over the fruit bowl one day, deliberating whether to have an apple or a tangerine. My hand went for the small orange and then I changed my mind, as the thought of having to peel it put me off.

I fancied the taste of the tangerine, but the apple was easier to eat. In my deliberation, I picked up both. I threw the apple into the air and, before I caught it in the other hand, threw the tangerine up to a similar plane and caught that, too. It felt good, so I did it again, and then again. There was a rhythm to it, which I liked, and I soon forgot about being hungry and kept going with the fruit, from one hand to the other. After a few minutes, my eye was drawn to another tangerine in the bowl. I picked it up and, instead of repeating the pattern of two, I threw the third into the mix and promptly dropped it. But, here's the strange thing: I knew next time I wouldn't. Instinctively I could see the pattern in my head, and as I threw the apple and then the tangerine, I waited for it to fall before releasing the next tangerine and... dropped it.

I picked the fruit up and, bending my knees slightly and keeping my back straight, I went through the moves in my head, to the tune of 'The Entertainer', courtesy of my favourite girl in the whole world. If I could pull this off and juggle all three, it could be a one-way ticket to winning her heart, I thought.

The tune played out again and I started with the apple, high into the air, and then the tangerine, and waited... then launched the third and... caught it. Yes! 'The Entertainer' definitely helped. It felt great, so I did it again, and this time I kept it going and going. What the hell was I doing? I'd never seen anyone juggle – well, not properly. Charlie Cairoli did daft juggling on TV, but I'd never seen it done for real.

So, there I was: a juggler, instinctive and natural. A skill I hoped might win the heart of a girl but, realistically, a skill which was pretty useless. But one aspect of this new-found skill was the feeling I had in my head. It felt weird – like total concentration, but without the thinking, involving acute peripheral vision and the inability to think or focus on anything else. That was very strange indeed.

The fourth thing to happen was a mass date. Yes, five of us – Dave, Spider, Robbo, Smiler, all new mates from my form class and me – managed, somehow, and I think through Robbo's twin sister, to arrange a date with five girls. I, of course, declared my undying love for Claire, which was to everyone's amazement, and through tough negotiation and grossly embarrassing liaisons the plan was hatched and executed. We would meet the girls outside school on Saturday afternoon and go for a walk. There was a ruined castle up on a hill about half a mile away from the school, with stunning views over the city, and it seemed like the perfect romantic scene in which to court our dates. The main plan was to hold hands and walk and chat. I contemplated taking some tangerines but, realising they may look compromising in my trousers, thought better of it.

We all met up at Robbo's house and made our way to the rendezvous point. We larked around and tried pushing each other into the road. Spider ripped his trousers on a metal hook protruding from the wall, and we laughed at how daft he looked with his pale white leg showing underneath.

Secretly I was nervous, but I guessed the other boys were too, hence the mucking about. I couldn't believe Claire had agreed, but I reckoned my perseverance had finally paid off. Plus it was a group thing – safety in numbers, and all that. We waited impatiently for the girls to arrive and Smiler offered everyone a chewing gum.

'You need fresh breath, lads, with all the snogging we're going to be doing.' He smiled, which is what he did constantly. He had a mouth which was permanently turned up at the ends, a bit like the Joker, but not quite as menacing. Smiler had an older brother who imparted all his words of dating wisdom to him, and he was happy to be our font of knowledge. 'And if any of you boys, get lucky,' he said, chewing his gum and slapping his lips, 'I have one of these.'

He reached in his pocket and produced a condom. At that point, the girls came into sight, casually walking up the road. He rapidly stuffed the condom in his pocket. I counted, and there were five, and there she was, second from the right, wearing skinny jeans, a white t-shirt and a leather jacket. She looked incredible. I moved the chewing gum around in my mouth to get maximum benefit and took a deep breath. They came closer and the five of us just stood, rooted to the spot. Even Smiler didn't look so cocksure, although he was still smiling.

One by one the girls, who seemed to know exactly what they were doing, paired off with their respective guy, and they immediately held hands. Claire came up to me and gave a little smile.

'Hi,' I said enthusiastically, and then off we set in a line, up towards the castle.

I didn't have a clue what to say. I could feel my heart pounding and sometimes missing a beat. My mind was consumed by one simple fact: I had skin to skin contact with the most beautiful girl in the whole world, and it felt amazing.

Our heads down and in silence we headed up the road to where there was a bend in the path and the entrance to the castle. There was no entrance fee – it was open to anyone, with pathways and endless scrambling potential on the exposed ruined sandstone walls. As we approached, I spotted Janice on the opposite side of the road. The girls all waved, and she came over to talk to Claire. I was hoping there wasn't going to be a catfight over me, so I stood firm and gripped Claire's hand tight, to show she was safe with me, and I was in control.

But then a very strange thing happened. In fact, one of the most puzzling things I have ever experienced. Claire suddenly let go of my hand and moved closer to Janice. They whispered in each other's ears, which I remember thinking was a bit strange as they never really seemed like friends at school. Anyway, what did I know? I was a boy, and girls were almost like aliens. They seemed friendly enough with each other, though, and I was relieved there wasn't going to be a scene.

Then Janice came in close and grabbed my hand and, to my complete surprise, Claire walked off, coolly and calmly. I watched her go further and further until she disappeared around the corner. I felt the tight grip of Janice's hand and I looked at her.

'Are we heading to the castle?' she asked, as if nothing had happened.

'Yes,' I said, in a complete daze. The switcheroo had taken place right under my nose. It happened with such stealth, I just accepted it. The element of surprise didn't give me a chance to question it, and there we were, walking along, Janice gripping my hand like a heavyweight wrestler and Claire nowhere to be seen.

I don't remember anything else about the date, other than feeling betrayed and rejected, but what I do remember is it made me even keener on Claire than ever before, and even less keen on Janice, who seemed to view the whole escapade as a green light to move in on me. She even managed to secure the seat next to me in art class. To be fair, she was a good painter, so we shared tips and helped each other. Janice was a camper too, with her family, so we shared ideas from our holidays and incorporated them into our work. She did a painting of a tent by a river in the Lake District, and painted herself standing by it with me by her side. I said it looked out of proportion, since the sheep looked like cows and my nose wasn't that big. Janice was easy to get on with, but she wasn't Claire. She didn't have that air of class, the feminine shoulders, lips and long neck that I admired from afar. And I'd never heard her play *The Entertainer*.

3

TEAMWORK

'I'm proud to present this trophy for the new school 1500m record holder to... John Crawshaw.'

Everyone started to applaud as the headmaster called out my name. I didn't want to get up from my place on the floor of the assembly hall. I was grateful, of course, but my shyness had become worse and worse. I didn't feel worthy of such an official award. I'd won it because I was a fast runner, not because I was anything special. And the last thing I wanted was the whole school watching me walk up to the front. I was self-conscious about my long lanky legs, my spotty face and the patches of hairs on my chin. I'd developed a strange kind of walk, which was predominantly on my toes. It involved bobbing up and down a lot, and always received maximum ridicule. My anxiety at school was at an all-time high, and at any hint of being watched or being in the limelight, the walk would kick in – and the more I thought about it, the worse it became.

The headmaster called my name out again, and my teacher glared at me. So I slowly took to my feet and tried to negotiate the line of my classmates' crossed legs. I caught someone's shoe with mine and tripped, and had to steady myself with my hand on their head. The entire school cried out with laughter, and then I headed towards the front to collect my prize. The blood was pumping thick and fast through my temples, and my face was on fire. I felt crippled inside, and there were knots of anguish twisting my stomach.

I did my involuntary lolloping walk to the front and could feel every eye concentrated on me. I approached the headmaster's lectern and nervously shook his hand. With the other hand, he handed me my engraved trophy, to mixed laughter and applause. He also handed me the school colours' tie, which had a double gold stripe instead of just the single, and was a sign you'd done something good. I'd already made the decision not to wear it. It was too much of a statement and might draw unwanted attention, so I stuffed it into my pocket.

For the rest of the assembly I just looked at my name engraved on the silver cup. My name on the top, with the previous record holders below me. Running my finger over it, I could feel the clearly defined edge of each letter and how permanent they felt.

When the assembly finished, the trophy was swiftly taken from me, and the secretary placed it inside the glass cabinet in the entrance hall, next to the office. All the school trophies were kept in there, to show to any visitor that we were a school of champions. I walked past the cabinet every day for the rest of that year, just to check my name was still on the trophy and just to check, well... just to check, you know... nothing more than that. Just to check.

I also won the cross-country race that year. I'd gone from never having anything in the cabinet, to having two trophies, side by side. The cross-country trophy wasn't actually a trophy, but a wooden shield, with tiny metal, engraved badges stuck to it. It looked impressive, though, and my heart sang every time I went to check it, which was once a day and sometimes twice.

You would have thought that two great accolades such as

those would have increased my confidence. But instead of sharing the glory, I kept it all in. I never gloated and never mentioned it to anyone, except Mum and Dad. Mum said, 'That's nice,' and hurried off to finish her sewing. I don't think she really understood how brilliant it was. And Dad patted me on the head and then droned on about his football trials and some medal or other that he'd won. The thing was, I was a good runner, inherently good, long-distance of course, and my legs were getting stronger. I didn't feel like a champion, though. I'd just won because I was the quickest. By complete contrast, I couldn't kick a ball for toffee, much to my father's dismay. Well, I could kick a ball, but never in the direction I was aiming. As a runner I should have been good on the wing, but instead my default position was in goal because, frankly, no one else wanted to be there. Where's the glory in that?

I hated the dreaded team selection line-up, the captains each taking it in turn to pick their best players. Me, I was always last to be chosen. Well, sometimes second to last, because Timothy Trimble had a false leg. Literally a wooden leg, which meant his kicking ability was slightly worse than mine. He was off school on a regular basis on medical grounds. We never actually knew what that meant, but needless to say he somehow managed to make me feel a little bit better about myself when he was there.

(He's probably got a carbon-fibre leg these days and become an Olympic athlete, or something equally brilliant. Well, I hope so. He was a decent guy.)

Anyway, I might as well have had a wooden leg and wooden arms, with all the goals I let in. The truth was, I wasn't a great team player. I'd given Scouts a try, and on the first session there was a sponsored silence. I was playing snap with two other Scouts and one of them cheated by looking at his card before he put it down. I immediately and diligently flagged this up by shouting 'Cheat!' very loud. Needless to say, I was disqualified from the whole event and spent a very boring two hours on the sidelines, in complete silence, watching something I was no longer part of. I made the decision Scouting wasn't for me.

But dropping out of Scouts meant that one half-term, while Amber was at Guide' camp, I had the luxury of having Gran and Grandad all to myself for the week. I liked staying at their house. Gran's homemade cream cakes and hilarious tales of what happened at the Women's Guild were just the best, and Grandad took time and showed an interest. It didn't really matter what we were doing, he just spent time with me, and I loved it.

Anyway, there we were, Gran, Grandad and me, as Gran told the story of the time she wanted Grandad to take her to the village dinner dance, and he wouldn't go because he'd lost his false teeth. Gran had bought a new dress and was excited to be going, and had even collected the tickets, but Grandad was too ashamed of his exposed gums, so it looked like it was off the agenda. But then Grandad did what he did best, and, as usual, it took place in his shed. Under great duress, he took an old walrus-tusk ashtray and whittled and carved and glued and chamfered it, to produce a gleaming set of walrus-tusk gnashers, which he wore with pride, as he gallantly accompanied Gran to the ball.

'You should have seen the vicar's face when Grandad gave him his fabulous smile,' she said. I loved hearing that story. It always had us in side-splitting, jaw- and stomach-aching hysterics as Gran embellished it every time.

The giggling declined as we started to argue about who should take the largest slice of cake. Then Grandad announced, 'Tomorrow, we have a very important job to do, and I need you to be my right-hand man.'

'What is it?' I asked

'You know that sycamore down by the shed?' he said, stroking his chin.

'The one with the old crow's nest in it?'

'That's the one. The roots are lifting the shed, and a branch fell off last week and nearly killed your gran.' He looked at her and nodded. 'So, we've had direct instruction to remove it.'

'Wow! What do you want me to do?' I couldn't contain my excitement.

'I need you to climb up and tie a rope in it so we can drop it between the shed and next door's greenhouse. Your job is to pull like hell.' Grandad was a true Yorkshireman, so obviously there was only black-and-white and no fuzzy middle ground. Fell tree in one, possibility of near-death, just miss two vulnerable obstacles on the way down. No messing. Simple!

'How long's the rope?' I asked nervously.

'You'll be alright son, it's long enough.'

Well, I could barely sleep that night. I worked through in my head my pulling strategy, and my getting out of the way strategy, too.

The next morning Gran shouted me for breakfast, but I wasn't interested. Grandad was outside preparing the tools and I dashed out to offer my help.

We deposited the gear at the base of the tree and looked up its long, long trunk into its mass of branches. It looked huge.

'It's about fifty foot,' he said, looking at me. 'It'll come down with a right old clatter, so once it starts to fall, run like hell towards the house. Right?'

I nodded.

'First of all, tie this rope around your middle and I'll hoy you up to the first branch. Then climb up halfway and tie this knot I'm going to show you. Got it?'

I nodded again.

I felt like Sherpa Tensing as I put the rope around my waist and clambered onto Grandad's back. I locked my hands onto the first branch and then started to climb, branch by branch. They wouldn't be doing this at Scout camp, I thought to myself.

'Am I halfway?' I shouted, as my arms began to tire.

'No lad, keep going.'

My leg started to shake.

Grandad laughed. 'Have you got disco leg?'

I wasn't laughing, I could feel the tree moving backwards and forwards. I managed to get a little further and then I looked down. It felt mighty high.

'Am I halfway?' I asked again, my voice shaking as much as my leg.

'No, not quite, but put it in there, it'll be fine.'

I locked my foot into the V-shape junction of a branch and, with one hand, grabbed the end of the rope. Then there was a problem.

'How do I tie it with two hands and hang on to the tree at the same time?' I shouted.

There was silence, but I could tell he was thinking.

'Hmm, didn't think about that.' He stroked his nearly worn-out chin. 'What about your teeth?'

At that point, I started to lose grip. I couldn't hang on much longer.

'I'm going to fall, Grandad. I'm scared,' I shouted, in a trembly voice. The disco leg was jumping up and down, my arms were tired, and my head for heights had just about given up.

'You need to be a man about it, lad. Lock your arm around that there branch and get the rope around as quick as possible.'

'Okay.'

With a bit of trying different arm positions and a whole load of goodness-knows-what from deep inside, I did just that. I passed the rope around the trunk and started to go through the rhyme out loud. 'The rabbit comes out of the hole. That's right, isn't it, Grandad?'

'Yes, that's it.'

'Then around the tree and then back down the hole.'

'Just get the bowline in as quick as possible,' he shouted.

I pulled it tight and then used the rope to gradually lower

myself down. About ten feet off the ground I couldn't hold any more and just let go. I guess that's what a free-fall parachutist feels like as they jump out of the plane door.

Suddenly I felt Grandad's arms around me, and I don't know how he did it, but he caught me. He flipping well caught me. Not bad for a man in his seventies.

'Good lad,' he said. 'Now the hard bit.'

Grandad used his trusty panel saw to cut a notch in the front of the trunk, and I assumed my position on the end of the line. I didn't have much strength left, but I didn't want to let him down, so I gritted my teeth and summoned some more of that thing from deep inside.

I stood firm as he started cutting from the back, and then I pulled like crazy. The rope cut into my hands and began removing the skin. Then, suddenly, without warning, I heard a loud *crack.* and Grandad shouted, 'PULL! PULL IT!' at the top of his voice.

Well, you've seen that show on TV, *Toughest Loggers*, or whatever it's called. That was me. Bleeding hands, weak legs and arms, and sweat running down my face. I instantly understood how tough they were.

The rope went slack, and the tree came straight towards me, and fast, so I turned and ran towards the house. *Crash!* it went as it hit the ground, and a powerful gust of wind blew me off my feet. I crawled and then turned to look back. The tree lay still, about two feet away from me.

I gained my feet, and Grandad and I both stood in our respective places, hands on hips, looking at each other, and feeling very happy with ourselves. That was teamwork. He needed me – him on the saw, and me on the rope. It felt like something real, something which needed to be done, and not some stupid game of football.

We only smashed two panes of the greenhouse, which Grandad said were probably loose anyway, and the shed luckily was unharmed. A large branch, though, had put a crack in the paving right where I was originally standing.

Gran called us in for tinned salmon sandwiches and some milk, and we gladly accepted. We all assembled around the kitchen table and Grandad and I gave her a blow-by-blow account. Grandad said I'd done a brilliant job and he couldn't have done it without me, and he handed me a slice of Battenberg.

The next day we set about chopping the tree up and, best of all, we assembled some paper and small sticks and built a fire to burn the branches. The larger pieces Grandad said would be cut up later, and he'd use them for carving and making things.

I had a go on the saw, but it was for sawing dried workshop timber, not freshly felled logs, so Grandad gallantly took on that role while I dragged the branches around the back of the shed and loaded them carefully onto the fire. It was at that point I learned that you can't rush a bonfire. No, no, no! Loading on piles of branches just doesn't cause it to burn, so God knows how concrete buildings catch fire.

Under Grandad's supervision I rebuilt the fire using some scrunched-up *Daily Mirror* and the smallest of small twigs. Grandad tipped a little bit of petrol around it to give it a helping hand and threw a match on it. There was a blaze of glory, and then it settled into a small smouldering base, which I was instructed to keep loading with small pieces.

'You have to kindle a fire,' Grandad said. 'Treat it with respect and don't rush it. Start slowly and build gradually, just like I had to do when I was courting your grandmother,' he added with a chuckle.

So I did just that, and before long there was a mass of orange flames and smoke billowing across all of the other back gardens. Gran came out to collect next-door's washing off the line. I heaved and dragged every bit Grandad chopped off and felt more and more confident supervising the fire. At one point it was so hot, I had to stand back and just marvel at the patterns the flames were making, and how the wood oozed sap, and how it cracked with the occasional *pop*.

Later on, in the afternoon, the fire seemed to have burnt out in the middle. I tried kicking the wood further in, but it was too hot. I could feel the intense heat on my face. I shouted to Grandad, 'I think the fire's going out!'

And he shouted back,' Just throw a bit more petrol on it.'

I'll never forget those words or the smell of the few singed hairs I had left on my legs. Later, and for years afterwards, we laughed about it, but the whole shed going up in flames was a sight to behold. Grandad had paint in there, and weed spray and the like, and the fireball apparently could be seen in Halifax. The fire brigade were brilliant, though, and I got to sit in the engine and wear a helmet.

We were banned from starting fires after that.

4

THE VOID

A fter that summer, the cold, foggy September brought about another brand-new school. The evenings were starting to draw in, and there didn't seem to be much light in my school days, either. My area had the middle-school-system, so we went up to the high school in our thirteenth year, until the age of sixteen.

The high school was an intimidating place, with industrial metal fencing along its perimeter. The graffiti on the old History-block wall, with the word 'Spunk' etched in silver spray paint, gave the place an edgy and unkempt feel. The building was the remnant of a school of a hundred years ago, with the addition of a super new science block and art rooms. There were acres of corridors and too many little dark corners, with the potential for an ambush by some bullying scumbag to steal your dinner tickets.

Dinner tickets were paper raffle tickets which were given out at the beginning of the week, with one ticket for each meal. Mine ended up down a deep, rank-smelling drain on the second day, thanks to a blatant pincer attack near the tennis court performed by two menacing and very tall upper years. After that I secretly made sandwiches, so Mum wouldn't find out, and took those in for the rest of the week.

Fights and scuffles were a daily occurrence, and the teachers didn't really do anything to remedy it. Bullying was rife, too. If you did flag it up, you became an even bigger target, so most of us kept our heads down and avoided any conflict we could. One boy in my year was hanged from a tree by his tie and only narrowly avoided death, thanks to the quick actions of a groundsman who was cutting the grass.

My overriding feeling at that time was one of sadness. I didn't like the conflict and I didn't like feeling I had no choice other than to walk through those austere gates every day, into academic and social captivity. So I drifted, and I existed, and I did the minimum to survive. At break times I would often walk, on my own, along the perimeter fence, wearing a little worn path, just like a caged tiger at the zoo.

There were a few 'no go' areas within the complex: the quad-rangle, which was notorious for dinner ticket raids; the upper years' corridor, for obvious reasons; and the rear of the sports pavilion, unless you were a smoker, or on a death wish. But there was another place, which was far more daunting for me. A place where the air was thick, thick with the dust of academia and the eerie silence of expectation. I'm talking about the school library. Why would anyone want to go in there? There was an intimi-dating quietness and the librarian, dour and judgmental, never took her eye off you, so if you dared to enter, you certainly had to leave with something profound in hand.

We had a compulsory tour of the library not long after starting at school and were issued with four library tickets. We were instructed not to take any more than four books out at a time. I thought this must be some sort of joke. Anyway, we had to take our first book out on that visit, and I had no idea what I was going to choose. On entering the room, I immediately spotted Claire at the counter, signing out four books. All I could see was her immaculately brushed hair from the back, but knew it was her. I tried to act cool, pretending to browse the shelves and scratching my chin, like I was spoiled for choice. She was ready to leave, so I darted to the door and opened it for her with a smile. She walked straight past me as if I were a ghost.

The feeling of rejection, tied with the pressure of having to choose something, made me start to shake. Faced with a myriad of meaningless, hemmed-in vertical book spines, my eyes glazed over and the whole wall of books turned into a hypnotic kaleidoscope of fear.

Our teacher pushed us to make a choice, and that's when the panic truly set in. What would I choose? I knew not one single author, and I didn't feel drawn to anything, either. I felt my anxious shaking and burning red face must be becoming obvious, and my fight or flight instincts were telling me to flee – flee to the hills and burn those tickets.

'Come on John, have you chosen a book? The next class will be here in a minute.'

'No, miss. I... erm... don't really know what to choose.'

At that point the teacher was distracted by a girl who'd fainted by the Greek Classics section, which I thought was a brilliant get-out ruse, and I gave her full credit. I sat on the arm of a wooden chair and looked blankly at the spines again. And then my eye was drawn to one book among the hundreds. It was yellow and black, like a bee, and I reached out and touched it. I ran my finger down the spine and looked around to see if anyone was watching. They were all still distracted by the now recovered girl, who was fine and sipping water. So I took the plunge and pulled down on the top edge, releasing the book into my hand. *The Butterflies of Britain and Europe.* Suddenly it felt like the one and only perfect choice. I flicked through the pages quickly and was astonished to see how many different and brightly coloured butterflies there were.

Later I studied the pictures closely with Grandad. The

sketches seemed like absolute art to me. There was hardly any writing – mainly pictures guiding you through the species and how to identify them. Grandad loved them too.

'That's a Brimstone and this one is a Painted Lady. You can see why,' he said, as we sat in front of the fire admiring each and every one of them.

After a few months we had to choose our subjects for 'O' Level. English, Maths, one science and one humanities subject were compulsory, and then four more, of our choice. I went for Art, Drama, Geography, History, Biology and Home Economics. I enjoyed cooking at home, and with Mum's cooking, this was often a matter of survival. Geography was okay, because I liked maps, and I'll never forget my Geography teachers saying: 'A picture or diagram can speak a thousand words.' Now that was my kind of subject.

History wasn't a strong point, and neither was Biology, unless it was nature related. Art was a no-brainer, since all of the pieces I'd done so far could be submitted, and I was scheduling a B. Drama became a bit of a revelation. My form teacher was the drama teacher. She told me they didn't have one single boy in the group, and would I give it some serious thought? I said yes immediately. Claire might be doing Drama. Enough said.

The start of the new term saw me with a new vigour for school. My options were chosen, and it seemed as though I had a direction, for once.

First lesson of the day was Drama. Me and thirty-one girls. What could go wrong? Miss kicked us off with a few 'warm-up' exercises. Firstly, throwing a ball across the group and shouting out the name of the person you were throwing to. Claire was my first recipient, but as I threw, the ball span off my thumb and ended up hitting her on the knee, before rolling behind the stage curtain.

Then we stretched and grew like a tree from the ground and did some growling, like wolves. I was liking Drama.

Miss then announced that we were going to be working on a play with a kissing scene in it, and although there was no pressure, she was looking for the main parts and the potential chemistry. I thought I'd died and gone to heaven. Me and Claire. It was obvious.

'John, I want you to pair up with... Karen,' miss insisted.

'But miss, it should be me and –' I didn't get a chance to finish.

'Right, everyone, happy?' she asked, without expecting an answer.

Karen came over and sat right next to me. Karen was – to me, anyway – a bit intimidating. She already had boobs, and she had other curves too, which were quite evident in her tight skirt.

'Okay, John, obviously you're going to be in demand here, but I want you to say the two lines leading up, and then execute the kiss. Got it? Okay and action.'

I looked at the first line and gulped. 'You – You – You –'

'Okay, stop there! What's wrong, John?'

'Sorry, miss. I don't know how to say the first line.' I didn't dare look up from my script.

'Just say it as you mean it.' She gave an impatient huff. I felt completely out of my depth. How come every time I wanted to read anything, the words would just jump around the page?

I cleared my throat.

'Ready?'

'Ready.' I gave a gulp.

'You... are... Sorry... are the most beautiful woman. I – I've waited all my life for a woman like you.'

'Kiss me.'

Karen came close. I could feel her bosom pushing against my chest. She smelled of strawberry soap. We hesitated and then she kissed me. We're not talking a peck on the cheek here. This was a full-on lips-to-lips kiss affair. She pushed her lips tight against mine and then started to move them around. I could taste cherry lipstick and... Wow, what was that? It was like we were eating each other, and I loved it. Eventually she pulled away and looked into my eyes. I was simply paralysed. Where did she learn that? I thought, wanting to go in for another rehearsal.

'Perfect, that's just what I'm looking for. Karen, maybe let John take the lead next time, but other than that, it felt like there was a real chemistry.' Miss thumbed through the script.

No shit, I thought, when do I get to do that with Claire?

'Oh, and John, please learn your lines for next week.'

The following day we had History, and to be honest, it was fascinating learning about the history of medicine and Hippocrates and drilling holes in people's skulls. The teacher called it a 'lecture'. He said it would prepare us for going on in education. What that basically meant was we had to listen to him and write copious notes in our exercise books.

I started off enthusiastically. Fortunately, he'd written 'Hippocrates' on the board, but I soon started to wane. I struggled with the whole lecture-style ears-to-brain and brain-to-pen thing and soon gave up with the notes, optimistically thinking I could remember it all.

Next was English, where we had a new teacher. She had grey hair and a moustache. I couldn't stop looking at it. It wasn't a full bush, but patchy grey and black, more obvious when she peered over her bifocal glasses.

'Good morning, class. Today we're looking at comprehension, and I want you to turn to the beginning of our story on page three...'

I looked at the page, but my mind quickly became distracted by her moustache. I imagined there was really a mouse hiding there and began concocting a story in my head of the adventures of the mouse that lived on her top lip.

She caught me gazing at her. 'Crawshaw, page one, please.'

I tried to focus, but couldn't see the point of 'comprehension'. Why did he do this, or why did she say that? I stared blankly at the page. The voice of the teacher was beginning to sound like a faint LP record, playing at slow speed in a deep monotone, and the more I looked at the words, the more they didn't make any sense. My vision started to blur, and each letter on the page became just a shape without meaning. My mind relaxed and, just as I had done in the field behind the house, I let my peripheral vision capture the whole page. It was if I were staring using another eye, a central eye. The white of the page began to get whiter and whiter, and my vision began to sharpen. I relaxed further. My shoulders dropped, and all I could see were bright white patterns before me. No words, no letters, just the gaps in between. The regimented black of each letter was now the restricting border of each white shape. I stared deeper into the page and an impressive galleon in full sail came into view, chasing a bear with five legs, who was eating Italy. As I moved further down and twisted my head, my eye was drawn towards the Sicily bit, and a river with a vast delta, many streams flowing into one, and then down some stairs and into a white cave – no, not a cave, more like an emptiness, a nothingness, a bottomless void.

I felt myself being sucked in as the black, repressive walls of print opened up further, drawing me deeper and deeper inside. I felt tiny, like a speck of dust disappearing deeper into the whiteness. I experienced an acute sense of scale, and everything in my life seemed to be behind me. Not just my class or my school, or my city even – the whole planet was behind me, on top of me, crushing me, as if I were in a hole looking back out of the ever-shrinking entrance. The more I descended, the more helpless I became. A wave of fear washed over me. I was starting to disappear.

'Crawshaw. *Crawshaw*! Have you finished?'

The sound of my teacher's voice brought me instantly back into the room, but instead of feeling a jolt, as if I had just woken, I felt calm. Surprisingly calm. I looked at her feeling I'd been on a journey. A journey to God knows where, but a journey I was never going to forget.

'CRAWSHAW!' she shouted.

I blinked. 'Yes, miss?'

'Are you listening?'

'Yes, miss,' I said convincingly. I didn't know whether two minutes had gone by or two hours, but I knew I'd been to another place, a place which seemed familiar, somehow. And although very unnerving at first, it was both exhilarating, and yet extremely calming.

The following week, we were put into subject sets.

Set one for the boffins, set two for the clever ones, set three for the could-do-betters and set four for the thickies and the idiots.

My form teacher handed me an envelope with my placings, and I opened it slowly.

Maths CSE - Set 4
English CSE - Set 4
History CSE - Set 3
Geography 'O' Level - Set 2
Biology CSE - Set 3
Drama 'O' Level - No Set
Art 'O' Level - No Set
Home Economics 'O' Level - No Set

The table confirmed your allocated set and whether you were expected to get an 'O' Level or the substandard Certificate of Secondary Education, or CSE. For Art, Drama and HE, we were all in together.

I looked at it and decided, in the right light, and on the face of it, it looked like I could get four 'O' levels. Mum would be proud, I thought, as I stuffed the table into my bag.

It stayed in my bag for three weeks, until Mum questioned me about it when she was looking for my PE kit to wash.

'Are you happy with your sets?' she probed.

'Yeah.' I shrugged.

'Maths and English look a bit poor. Do you think you need to pull your socks up?'

'Yeah,' I replied, and that was it. There were no more socks to pull up and nowhere I could go for help. I was, officially, thick. Stupid, lazy and an underachiever. In fact, I'd known it for a long time. It didn't come as a shock.

The streaming into sets affected my confidence even more, and I took a downward turn. I started to become more reserved. It was easier to stay quiet than risk looking an idiot. I was often overwhelmed by my feelings of inadequacy. Biology had been vaguely interesting, but I couldn't keep up and it became tedious. Geography maintained my interest, just, because my teacher was such a laugh and I was interested in maps. Art was easy. Drama was cool and, as the only boy, my kudos with the female school population increased exponentially, and so did my kissing skills.

Home Economics was great. I loved making stews, and my Swiss roll got a B. But I struggled in History to keep up with the lecture-style approach.

Maths and English were a joke. I was with a class of complete nutcases, Billy Tranter being one of the main ringleaders. He usually created some kind of distraction to learning, often by jumping out of a third-storey window, or bringing his air-rifle into class. One day, our Maths teacher went into the store cupboard in an emotional rant to get some new blackboard chalk, and never returned. I think the classroom taunts gave him a nervous breakdown.

Dave was my saviour. He was 'normal', and like me, whatever that was. Anyway, we sat together, managing to keep our heads down most of the time and dodge the main protagonists. We did, however, become aware of an apparent bonus to all this, and that was that being in a class of school bullies meant you automatically had status with them, and that the other more 'swotty' kids tended to be more of a target. Hence Dave and I were safe. Well, at least we hoped so.

Dave was not your average guy. He lived with his grandad, somewhere miles away, and caught the bus into school. He's probably the kindest person I've ever met, to this day. He'd obviously had some hardship to be living with his grandad, and I never discovered the reasons for it, but I did think that he probably had a right to be a bit angry or selfish. But no. He was as solid as a rock, a hundred percent dependable, and as funny as hell. I'd thought Gran was the sharpest wit I'd ever encountered until I met Dave. Dry and quick, with impeccable timing. We laughed about everything – the teachers, the disruptive idiots, and whatever else came into Dave's overactive brain.

One freezing cold February afternoon, we had rugby. Just after finishing our dinner. (Actually, this is the perfect time to mention and put straight once and for all that in Yorkshire in the early 1980s dinner was at dinner-time, with dinner ladies, at 12 noon, and tea was at tea-time, 6pm. Lunch didn't exist, and there certainly wasn't any brunch, trunch, elevenses or afternoon tea.

Anyway, Dave and I headed for the playing fields to recce the frozen solid pitch – and yes, it was as we thought. Muddy ruts filled with ice and razor-sharp ridges, and not a blade of grass in sight. We were going to have to deploy our best 'get-out-of-rugby' ruse.

Dave suggested he play his back-injury card, from when he'd slipped getting off the bus two days earlier, and that I pretend I'd mistakenly only brought one boot, and therefore wouldn't be able to play. The plan was hatched, and we headed confidently to the changing rooms, while Dave kept batting on about not revealing the true contents of my bag to Mr Strictland.

Mr Strictland was not a guy to be messed with. He was a Scotsman, thin, with a pale face and ginger hair. He was a hard man and didn't take no for an answer, and I never saw him smile. In fact, I don't think he had a compassionate bone in his body. He'd caned a boy in the previous year with his shoe for 'giving him lip', so I was a bit nervous. Dave hobbled in, holding his back, and he was instantly sidelined. He looked at me and winked as I began to put my kit on. I rummaged in my bag, over and over again.

'Sir,' I shouted confidently 'I've only brought one boot. Must have fallen out, or my mum didn't pack it.'

He turned and gave me a hard stare. So I smiled, knowing it was a clever ruse.

'Are you sure?' he said. 'Have another look. Here, let me help.'

'Er, no, sir, it's definitely not here.' I waved one boot in the air. The other was stuffed under my jumper and the books in the bag. I was enjoying acting confident in front of him, because it felt like a game, like in my acting class.

Dave gave me a thumbs up from across the room, but I pretended not to see him and so potentially give away our cunning plan. Everyone else had changed into their kits and they were all out on the pitch. I started to take off my rugby shirt and stuffed it into my bag.

Mr Strictland went all official on me. 'Did you look properly, laddy?'

'Yes, sir, it's strange. I'm sure I had both this morning.'

He looked at me with one of those knowing looks, so I knew I must sound convincing.

He gave the hint of a smile. 'Okay, well, that's unfortunate,' he said, in his Scottish lilt. 'You'll have to play in just one boot.'

I nearly dropped dead. 'One boot, sir?'

'Yes. Now get a hurry on, everyone's waiting. I'll have to put you in the scrum.'

Have you ever felt like your world has just completely caved in? One boot and the scrum! This could not be happening.

I reluctantly put on my shirt and then one boot. I chose the right one as that was my strongest, and I figured I could stand on it for longer than the left. I was in psychological agony. I looked into my bag and contemplated putting on the other boot, but I didn't. The pitch was frozen, but what could I do? I couldn't just 'find the other one', not now.

Mr Strictland came marching in. 'Crawshaw! On the pitch, *NOW!*' he screamed.

'Yes, sir.'

I limped across the tiled floor and out onto the rutted pitch, where everyone was warming up. My sock was soaked before I'd even got into position. As I joined the others, I could see Dave huddled in blankets and kit, keeping warm on a bench by the pavilion. He waved, and I stuck two fingers up at him.

For the first five minutes I managed to avoid the main thrust of the game, and then a scrum was awarded to the other side. Heads down and pushing with our shoulders, we gripped each other's shirts, and my foot basically became the ball. Everybody had a go at stamping on it, even my own team. We stayed locked in position, moving across the pitch like a man-crab.

Mr Strictland kept shouting, 'Come on, you bunch of girls, I've seen better footwork down the old folks' home.'

I could have gone over there and stabbed him. Anyway, I never 'forgot' my boot again, and I nearly rammed it down Dave's throat when I caught up with him later.

5

HIGH ANXIETY

It was pitch black and I was struggling to find the door. I scrambled around, my hands fumbling, my body pressed hard against the wall, pushing to break through to what was beyond, but I just couldn't find an opening, and the harder I tried, the harder it became. Panic took over. I flailed my arms, hoping for a gap, a crack, a handle or knob, a hinge or a panel, anything or something to tell me where my escape route was. It was there somewhere, I could sense it. I was lost in the repressive darkness, and frustration was trapping me, pinning me down, preventing my escape. There was no hint of light and no way of telling exactly where I was, but I wasn't going to give up, I wasn't going to be crushed...

Suddenly I became aware of a bright light, a dazzling light, blinding me. I tried to open my eyes, but I felt dizzy. I put my hands up to block it.

Then, the calming sound of Mum's voice. 'John? Are you alright?'

I couldn't reply. I was disorientated and confused. As my eyes began to adapt to the light, I could see her in the doorway in her dressing gown.

'John, are you alright? I heard something and thought it was a burglar.'

I looked down at my cold bare feet. I was standing among the power and aerial cables at the back of the TV in the living room.

'Come to bed now, John. I think you've been sleep-walking. Everything is okay.' As she spoke, she came close and, with her hand, guided me into the open room and cuddled me. I didn't speak. I couldn't. I felt her arms around me as she escorted me to the stairs and back into my room.

I woke to the sound of toast being scraped and lay in bed, staring at the ceiling as my mind drifted in and out of conscious thought. Although I couldn't remember everything, I was aware I'd been on some kind of frustrating and anxious, sleep-induced journey. It had left me feeling scared but also intrigued. I stared at the ceiling and began to unfocus, just as I'd done in class. Slowly my peripheral vision became acute, and it was as if I were looking once again from another eye in the centre of my head. I could feel the uncomfortable, anxious feeling of searching for an escape which I'd felt in my sleep, and I saw swirls of orange and purple. They became more intense and again I began to feel small and insignificant.

The smell of burnt toast filled the air. It was the weekend and I could lie in, but instead, I threw on my faded blue jeans with the worn knees and went downstairs. As I walked past our sage green telephone, which stood on a little table by the frosted glass front door, it started to ring. I was petrified of the phone. I never knew what to say, and it might be someone I didn't know, which was even worse. I hid in the cupboard under the stairs. As I crouched amongst the shoes and coats, I heard Mum shouting me to answer it. I stayed hidden and then I heard her walking down the hall. I tried to listen to the muffled conversation. I heard my name mentioned a couple of times, and then the call ended. Mum called me, but I stayed where I was. She waited a minute and then shouted again, so I exited the cupboard, clutching the Hoover, and made up some story about going to clean my room. I don't think she believed me. As I was lugging the bulky machine to the top the stairs, she announced that Richard's mum had just phoned, and I was invited to his house for the whole day, to play on his ZX Spectrum and then stay for tea.

I wasn't sure about going around there. I'd been feeling a bit low and wasn't in the mood for socialising. Richard was a good friend, but he was a bit posh, too. I didn't really want to leave the house. I hadn't even been out on my bike or to the shop for weeks. Anyway, I felt like Mum needed me around at the weekends, so I told her I wanted to decline Richard's invitation.

Mum told me she'd already said yes, and it would be very impolite to back out.

Immediately I felt nervous and anxious. 'What if I can't find his house? What if they have a big dog? What if I have to join in with his piano lesson?'

Mum didn't listen, she just thrust my jacket into my arms and shoved me out of the door.

I turned the corner into Richard's road. It was very different from ours. The houses were all detached and had long drive-ways, with manicured open front gardens, some with topiary. All the houses had names. His was Beech Croft. It had a huge garden and an imposing tree in the lawn. The drive led to a double garage and there were frosted windows on either side of the front door.

I thought about turning around but knew mum would just send me right back out again, so I tentatively walked up to the door and rang the bell.

Richard's mum answered. She seemed lovely and gave me a friendly smile as she welcomed me in. I spotted a downstairs loo, through a door off the hall. I'd never seen one of those before. Richard's mum showed me into a vast lounge, where Richard was sitting on a large sofa. She offered me a Vimto. I didn't know what she was talking about and declined, then wished I'd said yes when I saw Richard drinking his tropical looking purple drink. I was too embarrassed to ask for anything else and felt parched for the rest of the morning.

We didn't have exotic drinks at our house. We were allowed a can of lemonade once a week, when we helped mum at the supermarket. Oh, and a packet of crisps. Coke was for Christmas or holidays, and we never had anything like Vimto. To be honest, I'd thought it sounded like a class A drug, and wondered if that's why Richard was always so perky.

The ZX Spectrum lay on a little glass-topped coffee table in front of the TV. It had a bulky silver cassette player next to it. I couldn't take my eyes off it and marvelled at its sleek design and the dazzling colour flash across the corner.

'Wow, the keys are –'

Richard butted in. 'Yes, they're rubber. Don't you think rubber is going to be the future?'

'Yes,' I said, 'and what's magenta?'

'It's a colour,' Richard replied as we took our seats beside it. He picked up a magazine and explained that all we had to do was type in this text from the mag and amazing things would happen. We got straight to work, firstly me reading out the words and Richard inputting, and after an hour we swapped, because I could tell Richard was getting a bit frustrated with my slow reading, and then after two hours we finally completed the whole text. We hesitated over the enter key, in anticipation of seeing what we'd created. If anyone had seen the sheer excitement on our faces, they would have thought were about to launch a space rocket. And then it happened. Richard plunged his finger on the button and... boom!

His name in four different colours went zig-zagging up the screen. We looked at each other in silence. Should we be ecstatic or bitterly disappointed? After a minute of bewilderment on both parts, Richard announced he had a game on cassette called 'Asteroids'.

At that point, his mum came in with ham and cheese sandwiches and, glory of glory days, I said yes to a Vimto. We stuffed it all down and prepared to load the game. We had to connect the tape recorder to the Spectrum, and press 'Load' and 'Enter' and then 'Play' on the tape machine.

Things were just starting to happen when Richard's cat, Treacle, suddenly dashed between us and the TV, quickly followed by his sister, Anna, who tripped over the power lead to the recorder. The whole system ended up crashing on the floor. Richard went crazy. He leapt up and stamped his foot, throwing his half-empty Vimto glass at Anna, who started crying.

Thankfully the Spectrum was okay and still functioning, but the tape recorder appeared to be defunct. Richard frantically pressed each and every button to try and get it working, but to no avail. He stormed into the kitchen and there was an almighty row, and more crying. I had an uncomfortable few minutes sitting in isolation on the sofa, wishing I wasn't there, but while the whole family shouted at each other, I quietly removed the plug from the wall.

I opened it with the small knife that had accompanied our sandwiches, and there was the problem staring me straight in the face: the live and the earth wires had been pulled out of their mounts. I quickly set to work securing the wires back in their respective places.

Richard walked back in, flustered and still fuming, his face all red. 'What the hell are you doing?' he asked anxiously.

'The earth and live wires had been pulled out. I think I've fixed it.'

Richard flicked the power switch and the machine sprang into life. He looked at me in complete amazement. 'How did you learn to do that?'

'My grandad showed me. This is simple. You just have to

know which wire goes where, or you'll probably blow the whole house up. The hardest thing I've done is take an electric motor apart. That's pretty tricky.'

Richard looked puzzled. 'You're not thick, are you?'

I shrugged.

'Why are you in all the lowest sets at school, when you can do things like that?'

I shook my head. 'Dunno.'

The following week at school was the usual agony of getting left behind more and more. The best thing, though, was that I bought another two packs of football cards, and suddenly life was on the up. I added another Don Masson to my collection.

The next Saturday I'd agreed to meet up with Dave, Smiler and Robbo in the city centre. This would be my first solo voyage to the city, and on a bus. There was a cool hangout called the Ark just behind the outdoor market. It was a tented/disco/roundabout kind of set-up. Well, when I say cool, it was a bit tacky, but nevertheless, it was the place to hang out.

We were meeting at 1pm, and by 9.30am I'd already backed out. It wasn't the thought of the Ark which put me off – that was intriguing, and I thought Claire might be there. It was the whole getting-on-the-bus malarkey which frightened me to death. My anxious leg had kicked in quite aggressively. It annoyed Mum constantly when she saw it out of the corner of her eye. 'Stop that twitching!' she would shout.

I was chewing on a dry and overdone crumpet when Mum came and sat opposite me at the table.

'Look, love, I know you're nervous about getting the bus, but remember what I said about being shy. It leads to nowhere. It will do you good to go and meet your friends. It's one bus there and one bus back.'

'What if I get on the wrong one? Even if I don't, I don't know what to say to the driver, and how will I know when I'm there?'

She put her hand on mine. 'It's simple. It's the 126 to the city centre and 126 or 127 back. They both go the same way. You can't go wrong. The bus stop is right by the shop, and you get off in the bus station, and then everything in reverse.'

I wasn't convinced. The fact that there were two potential buses on the way back completely put me off. 'But what do I say to the driver?'

She gave me an encouraging smile. 'Half return to town please, and give him the money. It's as easy as that.'

The big problem here was that Dave didn't have a telephone, so I had no option except to be there and not let him down. I spent the next couple of hours in turmoil. The more I thought about it, the more times I went to the toilet, and the conflict of wanting to see Claire, mixed with complete fear of the process, made me feel mixed up inside. All my organs were grinding together, like rocks in a cement mixer.

Mum was great, though. She said all the right things and, somehow, she managed to turn my negativity around. I summoned a bit of courage and set off down the road to the bus stop. I rehearsed the words in my head, 'half return to town please,' again and again.

I had to cross the busy main road to get to the bus stop and got stressed that it hadn't come before I'd even had the chance to get over, and then felt concerned that I'd arrived too late and missed it.

'126, 126 to town,' I kept saying in my head. Then suddenly there was a bus approaching. Its number was X10. Mum hadn't mentioned the X10. Had they changed the numbering since Mum last travelled? And was this now the one I had to catch? I didn't want to miss it, so stuck out my hand. The bus approached, slowed down, and then sailed straight past. I felt hugely embarrassed in front of the other people at the stop, with my arm out, fully stretched. I didn't dare ask them if it was the right one, for fear of looking uncool. I just pretended to wave at a friend and then scurried around the back of the shelter to hide. Two minutes later I saw another bus approaching.

'126', it said on the front. Was mine 126? I'd suddenly forgotten, and the more I said it in my mind, the more the numbers got muddled up. 162? Half return to town, 261? My head started to explode with the worry. The bus slowed down. I got into even more of a flap, because I didn't know whether I had to say where I was getting off on my return. My leg started to shake, and my mouth became very dry. I let the other people get on first and then walked up the steps to the driver.

'H – Half return to town, please,' I said and handed over my money.

Then something very strange and totally unplanned happened.

The driver spoke to me! That wasn't part of the plan.

I froze to the spot. I could hear words, but they had no meaning, so I remained frozen solid, not daring to move, and then he spoke again. The words appeared totally unrecognisable – not helped by the driver's broadest of broad Yorkshire accents. I heard the sounds and the rhythm and subconsciously locked them into my brain, then turned and ran down the bus to the back seat, to hide behind a guy in a white t-shirt with broad shoulders.

The bus pulled into the bus station. Through the window I could see Dave and the boys, waiting under the clock tower. They met me with a smile and a pat on the back.

'I thought you might not come, seeing as it's a bit of a journey,' Dave said.

'I wouldn't have missed it for the world.'

The Ark was heaving with kids when we arrived and Dexy's Midnight Runner's *Come on Eileen* was thumping out of the speakers. Lots of flashing lights, red, yellow and green, and lots of older kids, fifteen to seventeen, smoking. The guys in leather jackets and the girls in tight jeans.

The Ark itself was a roundabout, but no ordinary roundabout.

This one was fast, and instead of little cars or horses to sit on, it was open, with the exception of three fake motorbikes, strategically placed on the floor, which went up and down in waves. It looked like a death trap. Dave jumped on and rode the floor like a pro surfer as each wave peaked and fell again. It looked like he'd been on it before.

'Come on,' he shouted, so I tentatively approached and jumped onto it, trying not to look fazed.

The undulating floor and flashing strobe lights caught me off balance, so I reached out and grabbed the nearest thing to me, which wasn't a good move. A guy was chatting up a girl on one of the motorbikes. They must have been around seventeen. As I reached out, I grabbed her bottom, before sliding down her legs to the floor and hanging on around her ankles.

After what seemed hours, Dave thankfully came to my rescue and picked me up, just as the guy started to look handy. I flung my arms around him, and he shouted, 'Get off me, gay boy.' Everyone looked around to witness Dave and me in what looked like an embarrassing passionate embrace.

What an experience. I was the uncoolest person there for sure, and the uncoolest person who had ever gone there, but I was just glad I hadn't broken anything. Claire wasn't there to see my maiden voyage, either, thankfully, and as we walked back to the bus station, I felt like I'd achieved something. Awkwardly, yes, but loads of people in our class had never been to the Ark, so inside I felt cool.

I managed to catch the 126 back home. The 127 left twenty minutes earlier, but I felt safer on the 126, and so I waited nervously. All journey I couldn't help reliving the episode when I'd got on the first bus, and what the driver had said to me. I went over the sounds in my head.

When I got home, Mum asked me if I'd had a good time. I nodded and said, 'What does watsupladasriggamorticesetin mean?'

She smiled. 'In what context?'

'It's what the bus driver said to me.'

She nodded. 'It sounds like he just wanted you to take your seat, as the bus was about to go.'

It was years later I found out what rigor mortis was, and was mortified.

The following week at school, we couldn't stop talking about the Ark and how cool it was. We must have looked like peacocks, strutting our stuff around the place.

But very soon after, things weren't so good. Dave was off school, and he didn't return for two weeks. I heard that he'd found his grandad dead in the doorway when he returned from school one evening. Very sad news, and he was devastated, but the bonus was, he was back with his mum. I could see it had hit him hard. His usual humorous jibes almost vanished and he was often late for school, or not there at all. I offered to help and talked about another trip to the Ark, but he just needed time to recover.

School was tough without him on those days. The more I learned, the less I seemed to remember. Lesson after lesson would be filled with these wonderful yet devastating descents into the void between the words as I pretended to be reading. I dived into adventure after adventure, but what was becoming increasingly apparent to me was that the journeys I went on, although fascinating and enthralling, always ended in tragedy. They were becoming more and more sinister and unnerving. The void had no physical ending. It felt like an infinity of insignificance. The further I went down, the smaller I became. Just a dot floating in a nothingness. There was never a way out, just like my nightmares.

At school we had tests in every discipline, and my results were poor. In fact, they were awful. I told my mum I'd done okay, but that there was room for improvement. She accepted this, and it was then I realised I was actually quite convincing, a bit like an actor. I decided it was easier to pretend to be who I wasn't, than actually be me. Over a short period I developed a persona who was seemingly doing okay, who was confident and handling everything well and being a good kid. The reality was, of course, that I was flunking out. I was putting on an act, and I was covering my tracks. Bizarrely, I found with my adopted persona I was able to speak quite intelligently to people. I could not only hold a normal conversation with my peers, but with adults too, and convincingly at that. It had taken a while, but I'd learned to hide the fact I was virtually illiterate with a verbal smokescreen. It became a game of distraction. Hide the turmoil inside and look like you've got everything under control. Talk and lie myself out of tricky situations and never, ever write anything down or read anything out loud. That was a one-way street to my cover being blown. I called my new alter ego Jonny. I gave him a name because he seemed like a totally different person to me, and I needed to be able to summon him, whenever I needed him. The real me was able to hide behind Jonny and his 'hold-your-own' conversation style. Jonny had the ability to protect me from what was really going on inside, and I started to use him more and more.

When I didn't have to blag my way out of situations, I would keep my head down and be as quiet as possible, not draw attention to myself and remain silent. Occasionally I would sit on the back wall at home and think about the world. I regularly questioned the purpose of human existence, because, at that time, I couldn't see a reason for it. Why were we on this planet? Why was there so much anger and trouble and anxiety? So many countries seemed to be at war. Even my own country was in conflict. The troubles of Northern Ireland. Troubles! They were bombing each other all the time, in the name of religion, both Protestants and Catholics. People in the same streets, breathing the same air and with the same voices, hating each other. What was the point of that? I couldn't understand why they just didn't get on with each other. The irony for me was that they both believed in religions which said loving thy neighbour was paramount and in which forgiveness was at the heart.

The bombing wasn't just confined to Ireland, it was over in England too, and I saw things on the news that frightened me. We had a cold war with Russia, and the threat of nuclear war. Yugoslavia was looking unstable, not to mention my own parents. Conflict and aggression seemed to me to be totally unnecessary. I had enough going on inside me and I had an inherent dislike of it. The whole thing worried me.

6

CONKERS

I lay there motionless under my Union Jack duvet, my eyes open, but staring into nowhere.

I spent the next minute with my toes curled up and tightly gripped, as if holding back the sheer agony of what was or wasn't about to happen. I then simultaneously did the same with my hands and face, even my eyebrows and mouth, thinking hard about which day of the week it was. If it was a Saturday, I would release all the scrunched-up tension and let the calm and tranquility of it not being a school day fill my entire body with joy, before thinking eagerly about how I was going to fill my free time.

If it was a Monday, Tuesday, Wednesday, Thursday or Friday, I would use the energy of the scrunching to try and force the day to be a Saturday. Although I knew it wouldn't work, I had to try with all my might. I hated the anxious, painful feeling, which I knew I would have all day, and l wished it would all go away. The thought of leaving the warmth and comfort of my bed and venturing into a cold, wintery day of despair made me shiver with fear. The days were getting shorter and darker, and a darkness was starting to infiltrate my mind.

At school I was still in the lowest sets and struggling to keep my head above water. One day I was enduring a Biology lesson, trying to copy down from the blackboard into my book, when Dan Withenshaw displayed two stink bombs to the class behind the teacher's back. Everyone tried to ignore him. The bombs were in glass tubes, and when you smashed them, the noxious odour would escape, choking everyone around.

The teacher sensed something was afoot by the tittering. She couldn't put her finger on who or what was distracting the class, but kept a wary eye on everyone. It was only when she bent down to pick up her chalk that Dan threw both of the bombs towards the front. One smashed in front of her desk, and the other landed on top of my bag, which was situated on the floor by my chair.

The smash of the glass startled everyone, and the liquid leaked out onto the floor, releasing its foul stench. The teacher turned and clocked the debris and literally went crazy. She walked up to the mess on the floor and then looked at the class, scanning her eyes over each and every one of us. I knew the other one was on my bag. I could see it out of the corner of my eye and I didn't want to get caught with it, so I nervously waited until my best opportunity to grab it and hide it in my pocket.

'*Who* in their tiny, stupid, moronic mind thought it would be a good idea to throw glass at their teacher? I shouldn't have to spell it out, how completely and utterly dangerous this is, and how angry I am that one of my pupils would act with such irresponsibility. No one is leaving this class until I find out who has done this.'

She looked once more at the steaming pile of glass. It was then I decided I wasn't going to get caught with the other bomb and I started to undertake my manoeuvre. I quickly and stealthily reached down with my arm, while still facing the front, and grabbed the unbroken bomb, gripping it tightly in my hand. As I did, the teacher looked straight at me.

'Crawshaw! What is that in your hand?'

I instantly froze and said nothing, still clutching the glass container.

'*Crawshaw!*'

'Nothing, miss.'

'Was it you who threw this?' She pointed to the glass on the floor.

'No, miss, I promise.'

'Then you won't mind showing me what's in your hand, will you?'

I shook my head and wished for some piece of a miracle to get me out of the situation.

'If I don't find out who the idiot is who did this, you will all stay behind after class until someone owns up. Do you understand me?'

The whole class nodded simultaneously, and as she fleetingly looked around the room, I tried to get the container in my pocket, but I fumbled it, and it fell on my lap, where it started slowly slipping down to the floor.

'CRAWSHAW! What are you doing?' She'd spotted me out of the corner of her eye. 'Stand up and come to the front. NOW!'

Scared and shaking with fear, I grabbed the container tight in my hand and slowly took to my feet. She never took her eyes off me as I painstakingly walked to the front with my hands behind my back.

'Do you have anything to show me?'

I didn't dare speak or move.

'Show me your hands.'

I looked at her and kept completely still. I could feel the container in my hand, but I wasn't going to show her.

Someone shouted 'Miss. There's been –'

'Quiet! I've asked no one else to speak. Crawshaw, show me your hands right now.'

I had no choice. What could I do? I started to bring my hands towards her.

'Miss… You haven't –' The same voice tried to interject.

'SILENCE!' She shouted, with so much force I took a step back, and then continued to offer my hands to her, revealing the canister.

Her eyes moved from my face to the offending article and back to my face. Then she nodded and scrunched up her lips.

'Well, well, well. Crawshaw, you're a coward, and nobody likes a coward. Do you realise how dangerous it is to throw glass in school?'

'Yes, miss.'

'You're a no-hoper, Crawshaw. You're an idiot, and there are no prospects for people like you, especially if you try and get attention like this. It's the dole queue for you, lad. Right. Headmaster's office. Now!

I narrowly avoided the slipper, as it was my first offence.

After this, I couldn't see any light at the end of the tunnel. I withdrew my respect for teachers, and I withdrew my faith in truth and fairness. I was spending less time with my friends, and some break times would go and sit alone, just wishing the day to end. I didn't go back to the Ark or round to Richard's, despite numerous invitations. I was happier on my own, and I was happier absorbing myself in my only solace. Nature.

When I mean nature, I mean wildlife, trees, fresh air, the openness of the sky, just like I'd enjoyed back at the old house. Grandad, with his love and fascination for trees, had opened my eyes to the natural world, and I felt safe there.

We didn't have a tree in our garden, but there was a mature Horse chestnut in the grounds of a large house at the end of our road, which I was drawn to. I'd exploited a weak section in the chain-link fence to create my secret entrance. I would sneak in by carefully parting the wire, so there was enough gap to crawl through, and then I'd silently scurry to the base of the tree, hoping not to be spotted. My entrance was partly concealed by undergrowth and by the pendulous bow of a rowan tree, which created a subtle archway. There was never anyone around, though, and the tree was far enough from the house to feel remote. Although I was on private property, I didn't feel like I was invading someone's privacy, or that I was really doing anything wrong.

It was a bit of a scramble up to the first branch. The roots flared out at the base, giving a handy first step up, and the bark was rough enough to get some purchase with my sneakers. With a leap of faith, I was able to shin up and get a foothold on a huge branch that ran parallel to the ground. From then on, the branches opened up like an arboricultural staircase, almost right to the top.

I'd found the tree when out searching for conkers one afternoon, and it was by far the best supplier of championship-standard ammunition in the neighbourhood. In the late summer, every branch became stuffed with large, green, spiky husks which, when opened, presented a gloriously shiny chestnut-brown treasure. I felt an incredible sense of optimism when opening them up. I'd marvel not only at the colour of the conker but also at the delicate grain. This is easily missed, but if you look closely, the intricate lines can be seen, defining the unique shape like contours on a map. Of course the main thing on my mind then was whether the conker was going to be a winner. I didn't bake them or soak them in vinegar, like others claimed they did. I let nature do the talking. A large and round specimen, with a solid and intact exterior and a glossy veneer, was always the standard. Just a fine hole straight through the middle and secured with a shoelace, and that was it.

Climbing the tree was exciting and challenging, but gradually I got to know her every bump, lump, crevice and strong foothold. After climbing her many times, the route became second nature, and I learned to respect and trust her. She was mighty, strong and tough, her bark rough and gnarly. I marvelled at how she was able to survive in all weathers and, what was most incredible to me, at how she changed through the seasons. In the winter she stood proud, her skeleton fully on show and her true height and spread unveiled. Her only sign of life then were the large, brown, sticky buds and the horseshoe mark on the twigs, where last year's leaf was attached. I guessed this is how she got her name.

The tree's limbs seemed healthy – strong enough to support me and strong enough to withstand the harshest of weathers. One day I happened to see her swaying in a gale-force wind, and she almost appeared to be dancing. Her limbs and mighty stem reacted gracefully to the force, yet she was rooted strongly within the ground.

In spring she was one of the first big trees to burst into life. The new leaves in their vibrant green were almost entirely and perfectly formed, but as they emerged from the bud in miniature, and as I examined in detail their delicateness, I wondered how nature managed to produce such an incredible feat of engineering and design. Their appearance was the epitome of new life and of optimism, and in my mind they were art.

In summer the tree was out in full leaf, and the leaves were huge, the size of dinner plates. From my usual and familiar position, well within the maze of branches, I could make out the tiny young conkers, starting their journey to maturity. The dense canopy of leaves formed the perfect den, and I naturally positioned myself in a U-shaped branch junction, which was securely attached to the trunk. I could sit comfortably there and observe everything around me, whilst remaining hidden. It was my own secret crow's nest.

In autumn the leaves began to turn brown, but as they did so, the tree revealed her mass of green husks in all their reproductive glory. They say that the older a tree becomes and the closer it is to death, the more abundantly it reproduces. My tree was definitely a veteran. I had no idea of her age, but she certainly did produce a plethora of seed, and I had access to most of them.

So that was my secret den, my place of solitude, and a place where I could think and try and put things into perspective. For some reason – maybe it was the quietness or the direct access to nature, I'm not sure – my hidden spot opened my mind to thinking about life.

I'd be up in the tree for hours, and I began to realise she had the ability to listen, because there were times when I spoke to her that she spoke back to me. So now you're thinking, this guy is crazy, and you're right, I was crazy. Crazy with all the different feelings about life, school, family, friends, learning struggles and anxiety. This was the only place I felt safe. I felt at one with the tree, and that felt mighty special.

One cold, grey, windy day at home, there was a great feeling of unrest in the house. My parents rowed constantly, but this was the kind of row which festered all day. Doors were slammed, and the mixture of shouting and heated but whispered discussions (so that the kids couldn't hear) was starting to unnerve me. Wherever you went in the house, there was tension. Even when I went in the shed to tinker with my bike, the Silver Dream Machine, I could still feel the anger in the air.

At one point I heard mum screaming and went to investigate. She was crying in the kitchen and Dad was leaning over her.

'Mum… Are you okay?' I asked.

Dad turned to me with an angry look on his face. 'Get out of here, this has nothing to do with you.'

So I did. I grabbed my coat, and I ran as fast as I could to my tree. The late afternoon, early autumn sun still had some warmth as I climbed up onto the first branch. I made my way speedily to my crow's nest perch near the top.

It wasn't the first argument recently, and it was beginning to get on top of me. Amber was out at her friends, so I couldn't talk with her. Not that I would have, anyway. So I talked to the tree. I didn't come straight out with it. I sat for a while and watched a blackbird on the ground below, struggling to pull out a worm. He pulled and pulled and pulled, then hopped around to get better purchase, and then pulled some more. I must have watched it for a good five minutes until, finally, the sizeable juicy worm came free. The bird almost looked proud of himself as he grasped it in his beak. At that point, another blackbird swooped down and startled the first, who immediately dropped the worm in surprise. The interloper then snatched the prize and flew off.

How unfair life was. Even in nature, things weren't fair. The poor blackbird, after all his efforts, had his glory and meal taken away. My parents arguing and pushing me away didn't seem fair, either. Being a teenager didn't seem fair, and school definitely wasn't fair. I stared way down below me and contemplated jumping and hitting the ground. How fair would that be? I might die, or end up with a broken back, but would anyone care? Probably not.

I shuffled in my seat, so I was barely in contact with the branch, and leant forward, shifting my weight as if I were a bird about to take flight. The stony ground below appeared to beckon me. I loosened my grip and envisaged the freedom of falling. I was going to do it. It felt like it was the right thing to do. I would set myself free. Free from all the anxiety and fear within me, and free from the constraints of life. I was going to do it, and the time was now. I didn't want to go home and I couldn't survive up a tree in freezing conditions. The only option was to launch myself out to fly. My mind was filled with how it might feel to be soaring high above the trees and houses like a bird. Free to explore, free to be yourself and free to liberate your mind of all the toxic trappings of day-to-day normality.

I loosened my grip a little more and leaned out, so that my arms were behind me. Only my toes and fingertips were in contact with the tree. I leaned further and imagined again how I was that bird, an eagle about to flap its wings and take off.

I felt the tree move as the breeze became a little stronger. She seemed to twist as she gently swayed backwards and forward, and I was moving with her. For a moment, I was part of the tree, part of her structure, but also part of her being. At that point, I felt something extraordinary. I wasn't sure what it was at first, but it seemed to enter my body, like a small electric shock. It tingled in my hands, and then filled my entire being. My heart did a little kick. Whether it lost a beat or gained one, I don't know, but something happened, and it felt energising and positive.

I let go completely with my hands and began riding the tree's every movement as she swayed and twisted. The wind began to pick up speed, yet I felt safe, and I felt secure. With the wind in my face, my mind finally began to feel free of all the anguish and confusion I'd been holding in. I was free, like a bird. I screamed at the top of my voice as I leaned out further. The tree pushed back into the wind, resisting its force, not only protecting herself but protecting me, too.

My short-lived feeling of security ended with a twist and a lurch forward. I lost my balance, grabbing onto the tree with both hands and pulling my body in close to her stem, where I felt reassured and safe. I spent the next couple of hours up there, just being, just relishing her strength and support. Somehow, I felt different. The tree didn't speak any words, or say things like, 'Come on, John, pull yourself together.' But she gave me something. An energy, a sign. Whatever it was, it was something huge, it was real, and, with a jolt of positivity and of optimism, it had entered me and consumed me. I was touched by an incredible force which seemed to come from a combination of things: her ability to withstand the elements; her secure connection with the earth, which I felt rising up through her entire structure; and the haven she provided within her strong body and arms.

I sure as hell wasn't going to waste this new-found energy. I climbed down from my perch and headed to the gap in the fence in the moonlight. I caught some of my hair in the chain-link fence as I squeezed through, but I didn't stop. I was heading home, and I was going to sort my parents out. Tell them to belt up and stop arguing. I stomped along the road and in through the front door.

'Where the hell have you been?' shouted Mum. 'I've been worried sick. You've been gone for hours. I thought you'd run away.'

I stood in the hall and looked at her with an air of confidence. 'Where's Dad?'

'He's gone out,' she said defensively.

'You two need to stop arguing. It's driving me mad.'

She just looked at me, and I could see by her forlorn face all was not well. There was a sadness in her eyes. I ran up to her and wrapped my hands around her and squeezed her tight. I didn't have the words to put things right, but I wanted to pass on some of my new gift. Surely that might help?

7

NUMB

A few weeks went by. After a period of calm, Mum and Dad had a massive row in the kitchen. The worst row they'd ever had. Amber and I were watching *Multicoloured Swap Shop* in the lounge. Mum was shouting at the top of her voice.

Dad slammed the front door and I heard him frantically trying to get the car out of the garage. Mum was crying, and we ran out into the front garden to see our red-faced dad backing the car onto the drive. The tension in the air and his sense of urgency was strange and disconcerting. He wound down the window and looked straight at Amber and me. He paused for a moment, looked down at the ground and then lifted his eyes to meet ours.

'Look, kids... I'm leaving,' he said. Just like that. 'I'm leaving, I'm sorry.' He wound the window up and drove off, leaving us on the drive, bemused and shocked. I was rooted to the spot, standing barefoot on the frozen winter ground. I turned my head and looked at Mum. She was sobbing in the doorway, her arms folded tight to her body. Amber went over and hugged her, but I stood and watched the car disappear out of sight. Then I waited a few minutes in the hope he would turn around and come back, but all that happened was my arms started shaking, and I began to feel the numbness in my toes.

Our world fell apart that day. It took months, for it all to fully sink in and for the full brunt of the shock to hit us face on. He'd gone.

Mum cried for many weeks. Amber stuck to her like glue. And me? I just felt cold. Ice cold, empty and numb. My newly gained energy and positivity were destroyed in an instant. It didn't make sense. Mum didn't have the answers to my questions, so I lay awake at night, thinking about why he'd want to leave us. I came to the conclusion it was because of me. He'd never really played with me. He showed more interest in Amber, and she used to go and watch the football with him sometimes. I was an embarrassment to him, I knew that. I didn't like football and, as you know, couldn't kick a ball, which used to frustrate him. He never appeared interested in what I was doing, and I couldn't remember having a conversation with him about anything. Dad was fun on holidays, I remembered that, but always as a family, never just with me. I'd tried so many times to get his approval by copying him. His mannerisms and the way he ate and the way he always touched his nose when he was speaking. His attention was never forthcoming, which made me crave it more and more.

I didn't sleep well for the next month or so, which left me exhausted at school. I wasn't even enjoying Drama. It was impossible to concentrate, and I fell asleep many times in class, which got me into loads of trouble with my teachers. As usual I continued to struggle with English, and my work always seemed to be wrong. We would have to read things in class to ourselves, and although my classmates weren't the brightest bunch, they always finished ahead of me. I tried to discuss it with my teacher, but she just said I had to concentrate and stop daydreaming.

So that was it, I was a daydreamer.

I was worn out, shredded, blank, empty and disillusioned. I was increasingly visiting my parallel world, within the void. It wasn't as if I particularly wanted to, but I just couldn't see the words any more. I couldn't help it. My eyes would unfocus, see the white and not the black, my mind would relax and I would enter a state of calm, such as I rarely experienced in real life. During my trips into the void, my eyes would relax until it felt like I was opening up the void with a central eye. My breathing would slow to a point where it felt like I wasn't breathing, and then the deepening of the senses would start. My peripheral vision would become extremely acute, and as the void opened in front of me, I would crawl in. Once inside, I felt free to discover and free to escape my normal life, but I always felt small, like the smallest thing in the universe, like a speck of dust. As I went deeper and deeper, I was always concerned I might disappear altogether, but I couldn't help myself.

I became a frequent visitor to the void in my classes and I began to go there in my dreams at night, too. The bizarre thing was that I could never remember dreaming and thought I didn't dream at all. On waking in the morning, I would have no recollection of a dream, its contents or meaning, but I would have an overwhelming feeling of having been somewhere. It was an uneasy feeling, as though I'd done something profound, but didn't know what.

What was even more disconcerting was that although in the morning I would have no recollection of a dream, as I drifted off to sleep the following night, there became a point where my mind would often be sharp with the visual and sensory map of the previous night's dream, like a recap. It was only then I would be able to see and feel it. I would be there, slap bang in the middle of it, but the next day I would again only be aware of feelings of insignificance and overwhelming anxiety. The vastness of the void in my dreams became a very scary place, where

I had no control. I couldn't stop myself becoming smaller and smaller, and as I tried to claw my way out of the vast whiteness I would usually wake suddenly with a jolt, or with Mum gently talking to me, as she mopped my brow.

8

STRUGGLING FOR WORDS

L ife definitely changed after Dad left. Every day seemed harder and harder, and the three of us got by as best we could. Christmas morning was strange. I woke early and did my usual staring into nowhere thing, then Amber came in to get me up. She was excited about what might be under the tree. She tried dragging me out of bed, but I didn't want to move. Christmas wasn't going to be the same without Dad.

Frustrated, she disappeared, and then a few minutes later came bounding in again with a small but perfectly wrapped present, which she shoved in my face.

'It's for you.'

'What is it?'

'It's for being the best brother.'

I looked at her. She was smiling. I hadn't seen that for some time. She pushed it into my hand. 'I love you.'

'Yeah,' I said, looking at the present. She'd never said that to me before. 'I'm not getting a big one this year, then?' I added with a grin.

She looked despondent.

'Only joking. What is it?'

'And I hate you.' She started to laugh, which in turn set me off, and we enjoyed a moment of happiness we hadn't experienced for quite some time.

The present was wrapped in gold and silver paper, and a tiny tag in the shape of a reindeer had 'John x' etched in glitter pen. I opened it slowly to reveal a red casing and shiny steel edges.

'It's a penknife. I thought you could use it for opening conkers and for keeping us safe, now Dad's not here.'

I glanced at her, and then back at the knife, and for a moment was struck dumb. There was an expression on Amber's face I'd never seen before. I could see she meant it, and she was relying on me not to let her down. Her words struck me straight in my gut, but instead of feeling emptiness, I felt her pain transfer into my body. At the same time her face seemed to light up with optimism and joy.

She jumped straight up and darted for the door, gesturing to me to follow downstairs. 'Come on, there's more under the tree.'

I put on the dressing gown I'd received the previous Christmas, now barely fastenable, and the sleeves too short, and ventured downstairs. From along the hall I could see Mum was busy in the kitchen, so I went in and gave her a kiss on her cheek.

'Happy Christmas, Mum.'

She gave me a hug. 'Happy Christmas, love,' she said, with a hint of sadness and a smile.

Amber was already underneath the tree, examining the parcels. Mum had very little money to buy presents and other festive treats, so gifts were thin on the ground, but we enthusiastically and gratefully unwrapped our few presents. Warm socks and gloves seemed to be the main theme, and I also got a few Woolworth's record tokens, which later blown on the Christmas number one, Band Aid's *Do they know it's Christmas?*, and Madonna's *Like a Virgin*, in all their twelve-inch splendour. I played them relentlessly on my old Alba record player. The record player was in a blue-covered wooden box. It had a central metal spike on which the records were loaded, to be released one by one onto the turntable. I loved it.

Gran and Grandad came over in the afternoon. Gran unloaded bags full of wrapped goodies, and Amber's eyes came out on festive stalks. Grandad fiddled around in the boot of his car for a while and produced a small wooden house, which he'd built himself. It was so big, he struggled to get it out of the car and in through the front door. It was half-timbered, with cotton-wool snow covering the roof and front garden, a tiny picket fence, a solid wood front door and electric lights which glowed yellow through the tiny leaded windows. A snow-capped chimney finished off the miniature building – the essential feature for Father Christmas to be able to carry out his duties, and he hadn't let us down. The house was filled with presents, which Gran said we could open after dinner.

Mum had put the turkey on before Amber and I were up, and the sprouts followed soon after. To our relief, Grandad assumed the role of chief turkey supervisor, and Gran produced her home-made Christmas cake. This was a rich fruitcake with marzipan and white icing, and in good old Yorkshire style we would eat it with a slab of crumbly Wensleydale cheese.

We opened Gran's presents, which consisted of more warm items of clothing, and chocolate-related treats. I got a brown tie and some second-hand grey shoes, which were two sizes too big. As usual they were to grow into.

We sat patiently in anticipation of our Christmas dinner and eventually out it came, steaming and smelling divine. Thankfully, after putting the turkey in the oven, mum had left the responsibility to Grandad, and the piping hot bird formed the centrepiece to our festive table. The sprouts had boiled dry and tasted burnt and metallic, but we were used to it and didn't complain, just nibbled one and then left them.

It was turning out to be one of our best Christmases, and to top it all, after dinner, we raided the mini house to find little packs of cards, intriguing metal puzzles with pieces you had to twist and disconnect, rubber bouncing balls, chocolates, and even a slinky. But we saved the best to last. Our Yuletide tradition and never-to-be-bettered game of 'The Ring is Going'.

So far in life, I have never met anyone else who plays this game. For us, it wouldn't be Christmas without it, and we still play it to this day.

Oh, yes, the rules. You thread a ring onto a long length of string and fasten the ends to each side of the fireplace, or each side of a chair, or to anything else suitable. Everyone sits in a semi-circle, holding the string with both hands, apart from one person, who stands in the middle. The person in the middle has to locate the ring as it's secretly passed along the string, hand to hand, by the others. Deceptive and distracting moves, all welcome. The accompanying song goes:

'The ring is going, I don't know where.
The ring is going, I don't know where.
The ring is going, I don't know where.
The ring is going, I don't know where.
The ring is going, I don't know where.'

We sang each line in a different tone to prevent it from getting monotonous!

In later years, Gran introduced that old classic *She'll Be Coming Round the Mountain*. But we only ever knew the words until the pink pyjamas bit, and so we defaulted back to 'The ring is going...'

So, it was a strange Christmas. Not one I'd been looking forward to, but it turned out pretty good. We seemed to stop taking each other for granted, became united in our love for each other and, ever so slightly, grew stronger.

There were times when I missed Dad, which was funny. I never really remembered him being interested, so that wasn't the thing. It was that suddenly he wasn't there. People would ask,

'Where's your dad?' But I couldn't answer. I internalised the pain and the stigma of being in a single-parent family. We were no longer normal, we stood out from the crowd, and once again I felt different and insecure.

One particularly dark and bitterly cold January morning, I woke early to the sound of the icy wind battering my bedroom window. I was wrapped tight in my duvet and could see my breath in the air as I exhaled. The thought of leaving the warm comfort of my bed was not a great prospect. To make things worse, I had the worst day of school ahead. Tests in just about every subject, and I was filled with dread.

Faking illness was never going to be a winner with Mum. Running away seemed a very inviting proposition, but I had no money and nowhere to go. After much agonising and no plausible get-out plan, I levered one leg out into the cold and then the other, until my feet felt the full brunt of the freezing draught from beneath the bed. I sat on the edge, staring at the scrunched-up pile of school clothes on the floor and started to think about exactly what my purpose in life was.

Why did humans even exist? What was our purpose? Why did everyone in the world seem to be in conflict with each other? The Protestants and Catholics, Labour and the Conservatives, police and miners, Russia and America, black and white, North and South, school bully and the vulnerable, and Mum and Dad. I was bewildered and confused. The whole world seemed to be unhappy and I was disappointed we couldn't all live in peace, and that there was so much hardship. The problem was, I couldn't see where I fitted into such a mixed-up world.

I thought long and hard but couldn't come up with any positive reason for my existence. I felt the coldness from my feet slowly extend throughout my body.

I knew I wasn't destined for any kind of further education, and that meant I had to find work. Unemployment was at an all-time high, and the traditional industrial jobs which were the mainstay of the North were being lost by the day, as the government at the time waged war on manufacturing and heavy industry.

What was a hopeless case like me ever going to do with his life? I felt pretty useless, had nothing to offer the world, life was a struggle and I just couldn't see a light at the end of it. Without a purpose in life, I was irrelevant and dispensable.

Out of the corner of my eye I spotted my new penknife on the floor. I leaned over to pick it up and opened up all the individual tools. There were so many different and clever implements for various jobs, but the most prominent, not only in size but for its usefulness, was the knife itself. I ran my finger along the blade and it sliced straight into my skin. Blood oozed out, so I put my finger into my mouth. There was something weird about tasting your own blood. It tasted savoury and yet sweet, but also metallic, and it felt wrong that I was effectively drinking my own blood. Overwhelmingly, though, it felt liberating and comforting.

My thoughts turned to the fact that it didn't hurt, and I pondered how it was possible to release so much blood without pain. I withdrew my finger from my mouth. The blood oozed into my fingertip and I watched three drops fall, almost in slow motion, onto the bedsheets.

Maybe the knife was my way out. Maybe I could end my confusion about the world and my place within it. I could do it. I sensed I could do it. Things would be easier that way, and I was fed up with the overwhelming turmoil inside. I'd seen a TV program where they'd killed a goat by slicing its neck. It seemed painless and quick.

I tasted the blood one more time, stemming the bleeding with my tongue. I removed my finger and pressed hard against the wound with my opposing thumb, and as I did, the blue vein close to the underside of my wrist rose to prominence. With the knife still in my other hand, I slowly bought the blade to the vein and pushed it purposefully against my skin. One cut would be easy and painless, and it would solve everything. I braced myself and closed my eyes. I was going to do it. I'd had enough of all the anguish.

My breathing became shallow, but my heart was pounding so strong, the vein bulged and throbbed. I rested the knife on my leg and then took a grip on it as if I were holding a dagger. It felt dangerous and aggressive. I drew back the knife and, with all my force, stabbed it. Stabbed it and twisted it hard. Forcing it in deeper.

I let go in shock and lurched backwards. At first I couldn't look, but out of the corner of my eye the handle was visible, protruding from the mattress. I stared at it and froze. I couldn't move, just stared. Then I felt disgusted and ashamed that I could even think about harming myself. I pulled the penknife out of the mattress and tossed it onto the floor.

Amber's words resonated in my mind. The knife was for protection, not for harm. I'd scared myself, and I was shaking. Using my foot, I kicked the knife further away and then started to cry uncontrollably.

In that moment, the knife brought me to a profound conclusion. It was for protection and I had a responsibility and a job to do. I had to grow up to be a man and be strong for my family.

So there I was, promoted to head man of the house, a new role of responsibility and at last, a purpose.

I never told Mum or anyone else about my brush with the blade. It was a personal thing and I felt ashamed. I passed off the blood as a nosebleed and assumed my new position. I was given new man's stuff to do, like putting out the bins, mowing the lawn and trying to control Amber – because overnight, my lovely best mate and sister had somehow turned into the Devil. Mum called it hormones, but she was simply the Devil in my mind. She'd definitely gone off the rails. No one knew this except me, but she was the hidden face behind the neighbourhood's secret washing-line cutter. Armed with a pair of scissors, she would sneak around the area cutting people's washing-lines in half. It was obviously some kind of anger release for her, and it didn't last long, but I secretly respected the ingenuity of her style of retribution on the world, and I laughed internally at the vision of people trying to tie knots in their lines and getting frustrated there wasn't enough slack to accomplish it.

Mum could obviously have done all of those jobs around the house. She was very capable, but she just needed a bit of help here and there, now we were a team of three. Amber took a bit more galvanising than Mum and me, but underneath I could feel she was on board. I gave serious thought – yes, I actually thought – about what a family needed and the roles within it, and my view of women changed. I actually became one percent less self-ish, and my mum went up greatly in my estimation. Not Amber, though. The strops, attitude and reluctant participation in chores sometimes made it hard work. She thought she'd become the boss overnight, and I wasn't going to put up with that. No, she needed a bit of management, and Mum needed a man.

So, approaching the age of fourteen, I did kind of become a man. I had duties, and I had responsibilities, and I rose to the challenge.

Dad engaged in half-hearted contact and started picking us up on Fridays. We usually went out for tea somewhere, which was a treat.

After a few weeks of this, Amber and I went over one day to Dad's new house. He was living with his new partner, June, in a little house in the mining village he grew up in. It took us a while to get there as the whole road was blocked with striking miners in a stand-off with the police. Rows and rows of police in riot gear, with shields and batons, stopped us going any further, so we parked up a little side street, and Dad took us away from the main thrust of the protest. As we climbed the hill and reached the junction at the top, we could see the miners brawling with the police below. A car was on fire and miners were throwing bricks and lumps of concrete, while the police beat their riot shields with their wooden batons. A group of lads brushed by us in a hurry. I could smell petrol and saw they had milk bottles full of it, and one of them had a large stick which was burning at one end.

I could feel the tension in the air, the very sky was black with rain clouds and smoke, and the streets were black with police uniforms and the sound of the miners chanting 'Scab, Scab, Scab'. The scene was to leave a long-lasting impression and it consolidated my intolerance of any kind of violence or abuse.

Dad encouraged us to move on with all speed, and we eventually arrived at the house. Amber was shaking, and I was trying to be brave and look unflustered.

Dad wasn't a miner. His father was and his grandfather, but he had different aspirations, selling nuts and bolts out of a van instead. 'Workshop consumables', he called them. We loved that they had a soda stream, and we calmed our nerves with a sweet fizzy fix. We had deep-fried onion rings and chicken Kievs for tea, followed by Viennetta, which seemed very posh and very different from being at home.

Dad told us they'd been broken into by burglars. They stole the microwave oven and a bag of frozen chicken legs. Probably a miner trying to feed his kids, he said. The microwave was found abandoned in the field behind the house, but the chicken legs were never seen again.

Dad's house didn't feel like it was our home, and it never did. We didn't have any of our stuff there or a bedroom which was ours, and I always felt like a visitor. To me, our visits seemed to be out of duty rather than anything else, and although Amber appeared to be a little more attached and always liked going over there, I felt uneasy and unsettled. I had to take off my shoes at the door and had no room to disappear to.

One Saturday, I helped Dad load his van with the various

consumables. 'I saved a goal in football today, Dad. A header from a corner.'

'Make sure you get all the right components in the right boxes,' he said.

I nodded and reached into the back of the van. 'Yes, saved it with my stomach at full force.' There was no response, so I turned my head, but he'd gone.

I was losing faith in him more and more. Rejection from your father is not an easy thing to deal with. All I wanted him to do was hold me, or laugh with me, or even just acknowledge I was there.

At school there was a massive downside to being part of a single-parent family, and that was free school meals. A real bonus for Mum, but for me it involved claiming my free tickets, which were a different colour to the 'normal' ones. Green for 'normal' and red for 'abnormal', and once again I was singled out as being 'different'.

So what was hard about that? The red tickets had to be collected in a classroom on the second floor, every Monday at first break. You had to somehow fight your way to the desk and shout out your name. A tick was put in the register and you were issued your five tickets. Easy.

Not quite.

I just wanted to get in, grab the tickets and get out of there, but frequently the teacher would be late, and that's when things got out of hand. There was no orderly queue or polite discussion among the kids about what food and beverages they might exchange for their tickets. The atmosphere while we waited was more like the wing in a maximum-security prison.

One morning I was heading secretly, as always, to get my tickets. I never wanted to cause anyone to suspect I might be an underprivileged kid. I reached the bottom of the stairs and saw

Claire at the Secretary's office window. Going up those stairs, and at that time, would mean only one thing, and putting one foot on the first step would instantly give the game away. I couldn't handle the embarrassment of Claire realising I was a 'free dinners loser' and risk the chance she might diss me forever. I casually carried on walking towards the main door and my escape. My plan was to wait outside around the corner until she'd gone, and then re-enter and covertly claim my tickets.

Claire was chatting to the secretary and, so far, hadn't seen me, so I tiptoed past her. Just as I was about to exit the building, the dinner-ticket-issuing teacher came bounding through.

'Crawshaw, you're going the wrong way. Shouldn't you be going upstairs?' he boomed.

Claire looked around and I froze to the spot. 'No, sir. I have to collect something from the secretary first.'

I joined the queue behind Claire.

'Do you want to go in front of me? I'm waiting for a message from my mother,' she said politely.

'Erm... no. I'm just... erm... collecting... erm... a...' I was trying to think on my feet, but the words just weren't forthcoming. 'I'm... waiting for a message too. Yes, a message. I can wait.'

'No, please.' She gestured with her hand for me to move forward. So I did. I had no choice.

'Yes?' said the secretary, as Claire stepped back from the window. 'Oh... yes... erm... Is there a message for me?'

'What's your name?'

'It's John. John Crawshaw.' I daren't look back at Claire as I could feel my face burning and knew it would be bright red.

'No. No message. Were you expecting one?'

'Erm... yes, from my mum,' I said unconvincingly. I felt my anxious leg start to throw me off balance. I was now late for the ticket issuing and Claire would inevitably see me for the loser I truly was. Panic started to set in and I just wanted the ground to swallow me up. I was an anxious wreck and I felt trapped.

'Hold on a minute, I'll check if it came in earlier.' She picked up an envelope. 'Claire, this is for you.'

I moved slightly to give Claire access to the window but didn't dare look at her. The secretary handed her the note and I tried to control my legs, which were both shaking.

'See ya,' she said and skipped off towards the door. I nodded and kept my face hidden.

As soon as she'd gone, I burst out, 'I've got to go!'

Without waiting for a reply, I dashed as quickly as I could to the stairs. As soon as I reached the top I heard the raucous screams and intimidating hum of adolescent voices from the dreaded room.

I entered to see Dean Stoker, otherwise know as *The Stoker*, dangling a kid out of the window by his ankles, and the teacher in stealth negotiation mode, just like on TV, when the policeman is trying to coax down a suicide jumper. Apparently the kid had refused to tie The Stoker's shoelaces and this was his punishment. The Stoker wasn't the sort of guy to mess with. He had a reputation, and one for destruction, at that. I couldn't tell you how many fires The Stoker had started, but one was reportedly the old science block. And he'd also punched a teacher once.

I waited by the door until the situation was resolved. Stoker was sent to the headmaster and the ticket issuing began.

'J – J – J – John C – C –' When it was my turn, I couldn't say my name. No matter how hard I tried, I just couldn't form the words. This was the time and the place where I would develop a stutter. It usually revolved around saying my name, but it could happen at other times, too, when I was particularly anxious. The trouble was, I really enjoyed my dinners, and didn't want to lug one of Mum's carboniferous packed lunches around all day, so I had to endure those Monday mornings for the rest of my schooldays.

So there we are. School was a living hell for me. I had gang warfare to deal with, and the threat of being dropped out of a window at The Stoker's whim. I battled relentlessly with literacy and numeracy, and for most of my classes I was in with the school's disruptive idiots. I had a debilitating and embarrassing stutter, and the girl I loved thought I was some kind of freak.

9

FAMILY

For my fourteenth birthday, Mum brought home a Chinese takeaway. Amber had beef with mushrooms, but I was feeling a little more adventurous and went for sweet and sour pork. I was very excited. Sweet and sour wasn't a new taste for me. Mum's homemade lamb casserole often had a hint of sour in it, but I don't think it was intentional.

Amber made me a card that said 'To the Best Brother in the World'. It had a flower on the front. Mum gave me a record token and I blew the whole thing on an album. *True*, by Spandau Ballet. Over and over, I scrutinised the front cover with its arty silhouette of a man in a hat. I thought it was kind of cool, although it made no sense at all. The contents were entirely different, though. What an album. I played it on the old Alba until it was nearly worn out.

The day after my birthday was a Saturday. Mum gave us free rein of the house in the evening, and Amber and I invited a group of friends to a snog-fest party. Mum said no alcohol, but people secretly brought cans of Double Diamond and Carling Black Label and became drunk very quickly. I was mainly in charge of music, and Amber topped up the nibbles and organised the snogging. I did have a little smooch with Jane from down the road, but this was short-lived after she threw up all over the carpet. Mum wasn't happy, and I spent most of Sunday in rubber gloves, 'making it disappear'.

On Sunday evening, Dad and his partner June took us to Lou Cabrachi's restaurant. Lou introduced himself with typical Italian flailing-armed exuberance.

'Good evening and welcome to my restaurant. You ladies are looking extremely beautiful tonight.' He summoned a waiter to take our coats. I rolled my eyes at the blatant flirting, but Amber and June seemed to love it. 'I have a very special table for you tonight, in the window,' he said to Amber, as he pulled out her chair. 'Here the light will catch your beautiful hair.'

He was starting to get a bit creepy now and it made me feel a little self-conscious. I didn't want some old guy moving in on my sister.

We all sat around the table and perused the menus as the waiter poured sparkling water into our glasses.

'Dad, you know Don Masson collection?'

'Hang on a minute, John.' Dad spoke to the waiter. 'Can we have the wine list, too?'

I paused for a minute. 'Yes, you know Don Masson, well –'

'Amber, what do you want to drink?' Dad said.

'Can I have an orange juice and lemonade?'

'Yes of course. And you, John?'

'Oh, yes, well, I'm doing really well, with my collection. Guess how many–?'

'John, what do you want to drink?' he said abruptly.

'Oh... erm, Coke, please. Anyway, you know my Don Masson's? Well –'

Dad cut me off again. 'You know you can get Cherry Coke in Florida?' he boomed.

'You can get that here, too,' Amber and I said simultaneously.

'It was hot there, though, wasn't it, June?' he went on.

June nodded and smiled.

'Did we tell you we're just back from Florida? Disney World and Universal Studios were amazing. Weren't they, June?' She nodded again. 'It was too hot to enjoy it, though. A hundred degrees it was in the shade. You'd love it there, all the Coke and ice cream you can eat, and burgers. The burgers were massive, weren't they, June?'

She nodded and illustrated how big with her hands.

'Sounds great,' I said.

'Oh, we got you a present. Here it is.' Dad reached under his seat and produced a white plastic bag.

'What is it?'

'Open it,' he said, nodding eagerly. Instantly my mind went into overdrive. It's a load of Don Massons, I knew he'd listened to what I had been saying. I unfolded the bag and pulled out the contents.

'It's a Busch Gardens t-shirt. Busch Gardens was incredible, wasn't it, June? Lions, tigers and giraffes just walking around. They only had medium, so to grow into, probably. Unless that's the one for our Tony?'

'Who's our Tony?'

'June's daughter's boyfriend. He's a medium, isn't he? June nodded and then Dad reached under his chair again, 'Here's one for you, Amber.' This time he brought out a black plastic bag. When Amber opened it, out dropped an Epcot Center t-shirt with a huge scientific-looking ball on it.

I could feel my leg shaking and my mouth drying. 'Erm... remember my Don M –?' I stopped to get a sip of Coke.

'Don what?' Dad said, as if he didn't know.

'Oh... nothing. It doesn't matter.' I reached out for my drink. But instead of clasping it firmly in my hand, I knocked it clumsily and the sticky, fizzy contents ran straight across the table and swashed onto June's lap.

'*John*! We can always rely on you to ruin a party.'

On the way back to Mum's, it didn't feel like I'd had a birthday. The whole evening had left me feeling flat, and although I'd enjoyed my garlic mushroom and chicken pizza, the disappointment and sadness within me grew stronger.

Dad dropped us off and Mum greeted us with a smile. 'How was it? Did you have a good time?'

Amber went straight in for a hug and I just headed upstairs to my room.

The following day, after school, I made my way up to my tree. I needed some thinking time. I squeezed through the chain-link fence, which caught my school tie and yanked me back. I removed the tie and stuffed it in my pocket, then clambered up to my high perch. The tree was in full leaf and I was completely hidden from the world around me. For a moment I sat still and completely silent, and then the mighty tree moved. Not hugely, just a slight sway in the breeze, and then I heard a creak.

It's alright for you,' I said, as if answering her. 'I don't know where I am, or who I am any more.'

The tree creaked again.

'You know what to do. You grow your leaves, supply the conkers and sway around a lot. I'm lost, completely lost.' I paused and listened to the leaves rustling. 'I feel like I'm a good person, but I'm not sure. I'm not much good at anything and I always make a mess of things. I feel useless, like no one's interested. I wish I were a tree like you.'

The tree swayed a little more, but I felt safe within her branch-like arms.

'Do you ever get sad? Do trees feel sad when nothing's going right?'

10

ALTER EGO

The summer holidays, as usual, flew by. We'd camped in North Yorkshire on the coast by Robin Hood's Bay. I usually loved waking in the morning to the sound of birdsong and the sun warming the side of the tent. I even enjoyed venturing up to the toilet block and collecting water from the tap in the middle of the field on my way back, but this year I felt subdued and apathetic.

I half-heartedly took pictures of the wildflowers and butterflies, when I could get close enough with my bulky Box Brownie camera. I only had eighteen shots on the film, so couldn't afford to waste one on blurry images of a butterfly flying out of shot.

Conversation revolved around my final year at school.

'Do you think you'll pull your socks up this year, John?'

'I don't really want to talk about school, seeing as we're on holiday. Can we talk about going to a pub tonight for tea? I fancy a huge steak and chips.'

Mum's cooking was always a bit hit and miss on camping trips. She swore by tinned boiled potatoes and corned beef, which made it feel like we were on an army survival course.

'We're camping, John. I've got some Vesta rice for tonight, or there's corned beef.'

I rolled my eyes.

'Anyway, what grades do you think you'll get?'

'I'm hoping all the teachers will get a disease and it will all be called off.'

'Don't be stupid, it's an important year. There's massive unemployment and you need to be ahead of the game. What about Art? That's your favourite subject, isn't it?'

I sighed. 'Yes, Art is a done deal. I've done a couple of Rembrandts and a lino print, so should get a B.'

'Stop messing about, John. What about the other subjects?'

'I'll be fine, Mum, stop nagging, I'll get a job. There's a new supermarket opening opposite school. Anyway, Amber, do you fancy a big fat juicy steak tonight?'

Mum glared at me. 'John!'

'Okay, Vesta it is. Yum!'

On returning to the high restraining fences and time-table shackles of school for my final year, I knew I couldn't break free from my lessons, but I dared to break free from the constraints of my starchy uniform. I decided things were going to be a bit different and wore non-regulation skin-tight trousers, a thin black leather tie and hair gel. My confident air of rebellion was instantly dampened when I was ordered to the headmaster's office on the first day and told to wear the appropriate uniform. I didn't have a regulation tie with me, so I stuck it out for the rest of the day, and then the next day I thought I'd try my luck again, and no one seemed to care. No one seemed to bother, because that year was the year of the teachers' strike. Yes, not only were the miners holding out, the teachers were demanding something, too. I wasn't sure what, but it meant that for half of the school day, there were no teachers to teach us. Some people thought the strike was damaging and unnecessary. For me, it was a gift – a gift of freedom – and I was fully behind their plight, whatever it was.

There were many afternoons with no classes, and we would simply doss about on the playing fields and venture to the chippy for chips with bits. Bits were the crumbs of batter left in the fryer, but with a splash of salt and vinegar they were a real treat. We also hung out at various people's houses if they lived close enough. Mum had no idea, and it was only when we caught the bus into town one afternoon, I had a real shock. I was positioned on the downstairs back seat of the bus. It was actually the emergency exit, and the glass window was floor-to-ceiling. The bus pulled up at traffic lights and, while stationary, I looked at a car crossing the junction directly opposite. It pulled up to a halt about ten feet away from me. The car seemed familiar, very familiar, and the driver even more familiar. Mum was suddenly looking straight at me, and I was looking straight back at her, and, with nowhere to go, I was stranded, caught in the act of skiving off and going to be in big trouble.

As soon as I got home, I dashed out on my bike. I thought I'd have an amble up Claire's road. I hadn't been up there for a while and I wanted to keep out of Mum's hair as much as possible.

Claire was obviously doing homework or revision or something equally swotty, because I didn't see her, and on arriving back home, Mum greeted me with silence at the door. She gave me that look. The one which was more powerful than a point-blank shot from a revolver.

I set the table for tea and the eerie silence continued well into our meal.

'Amber is at the same school as you now, John, and she managed to stay there all day. Why was it so difficult for you?'

I looked at Amber who was gnawing on a crozzled sausage. 'Hardly any of my teachers were in today because of the strike. It's not my fault.'

There was nothing Mum could do. She was disappointed, obviously, but more often than not, we just didn't have any classes, and she had to work and couldn't sit at home with me. Alternatives were in place to prevent us from sloping off, like library time or project work, but I didn't want to be there, anyway. After a few stern words, Mum seemed to begrudgingly accept my absences, as long as I promised to be there as much as possible.

Drama was always in the morning and the strike action usually in the afternoons. This meant we always had Drama. It was the class I always attended, and I enjoyed all the female company. I found it an outlet for my shyness and, bizarrely, forget about my inhibitions. You'd think it would be my worst lesson, having to read plays, but it was the opposite. On stage I did find I had an ability to act, as long as I could learn the lines and remember them, which wasn't my strong point. My technique was to try and picture the words, to feel a sense of them in my heart. My stutter only happened in the real world, when I was super stressed or worried I might make a mistake, but it was never a factor when I was immersed in a role. There was an escapism element to it all and, again, I felt like I was free and able to hide behind whoever I was pretending to be.

It was at this point, and I guess this was another part of my rebellious phase, that I became more reliant on my alter ego, Jonny. I could hide behind him, conceal my inner feelings, cover my inadequateness and deflect any attention away from my low self-esteem. Jonny was much more confident than me. Just like being on stage, he could walk into any room, and he was at his best when thrown into the deep end. He wasn't cocky or arrogant, but he could throw himself into any situation, and I wanted to be him. Well, I was him, but he wasn't the real me, of course. I could never do what Jonny did, but it did help that I could just flick the switch when I needed him. After a while I could tell that, other than my family, no one suspected the real me was the complete opposite to Jonny, and no one had any inkling that I felt so incredibly insecure. I could turn Jonny on and off. I just said the words in my mind, like any other film director. 'And... *action.*'

Offstage, I kept myself out of trouble where I could, but when forced into a social situation, or in my official family capacity, out came Jonny, the confident, smiley, charmingly friendly and responsively articulate young man.

So I started to bluff my way through life's struggles, Jonny seemed to have it all sewn up and he embraced life to the full. He became my number one tool, and a brilliant strategy for coping with my despondent attitude to life.

Sadly, even as Jonny I never got the opportunity to kiss Claire and those incredible lips. To be honest, I'd just about given up on her after years of being overlooked. Anyway, remember Karen? Well, something had been brewing between us since our encounter in that first Drama lesson. I hadn't had the courage to ask her out, but every time I was near her, I felt something like a magnetic pull. She'd often share some chewing gum or a slug of Coke with me, and I got interesting tingles in my tight trousers.

I was scheduled to get a grade D in Drama because my play-writing and my ability to read plays out loud let me down badly, but I did enjoy the practical sessions, which were forty percent of the grade.

Art was my favourite subject. All continuous assessment was based on our practical work throughout the two years and I was mighty proud to be in line for a B. Yes, a B! A proper 'O' level grade B.

Cooking was okay. I enjoyed getting stuck into making something worthwhile and something I could actually take home and eat. That seemed to make sense to me – something tangible and useful. Our bread-making assessment was a complete flop, though. Literally, I swear someone swapped my teacakes for theirs after they saw theirs were not rising. Anyway, mine came out more like rock buns than the light and fluffy rolls I'd hoped for. I'd missed quite a few lessons due to the strike, so I wasn't holding out for anything, really.

The rest of the subjects were not looking good. English was no exception. My reading and writing were still a completely agonising chore. I was slow, tediously slow. My writing was scruffy, punctuation non-existent, and spelling often just a random set of squiggles to make it look like I'd attempted it. The feeling of simply wanting to get any writing over and done with filled me with despair and a loathing for words.

I sat in an English lesson one day looking at the void and thought about the differences between Drama and English. Drama was about pictures, meanings and feelings. English seemed to be about writing words and reading words, not creating fun out of them. I attended English, but stopped partici-pating. Many times, distracted from what I should have been doing, I would make up my own stories in my head. Like little plays, sometimes just short scenes or comedy moments. Exploring the world of drama and plays had opened my mind to the visual elements of a story, rather than the written. I could visualise a scene, the people and the action, and I just messed around with silly scenes, like boy meets girl in an awkward situ-ation, or brother and sister superheroes. Once home from school, Amber and I would re-enact them and present them to family and friends, with mad costumes from anything we could find around the house.

English lessons became my favourite time to delve into the unnerving and hypnotic white world of the void between the words. It was easier to go there than battle with reality. One morning, we had English first lesson. I was looking forward to getting lost and letting my mind wander freely in my semi-hypnotic state, when to our complete surprise a new teacher opened the door and marched in with a purpose that commanded all our attention.

He took the time to look at each and every one of us and then introduced himself. 'Good morning class, I'm Mr Hooray'.

Well! Was that meant to be some sort of joke? A celebration of our underachievement? Honestly, I thought about going on strike at that moment, too. But instead of the class erupting into its usual chaos, everyone settled and eventually became silent, except Billy Tranter, who coughed a swear-word under his breath.

'Right class,' he said, in a calm but commanding manner. 'I don't take any bullshit. So if you want to act around, I'll enrol you with Miss Harding in Drama, and you can put your acting ability to good use.'

'You mean like little Miss John over there, sir?' shouted Lee Bickerstaff. He pointed at me and everyone laughed.

'Lee, isn't it?' sir said, as if he knew him. 'If you want me to take you down there right now, I will gladly do so.'

Lee shut his mouth immediately. Everyone pointed at him and laughed under their breath, and then abruptly stopped as sir gave us all another of his looks.

It was weird, as though he had some kind of secret magical power to control kids with just a look. He wasn't the sort of teacher who sat down, either. In fact Mr Hooray was a leaning-on-the-desk-with-both-arms kind of teacher, a strolling-around-and-mingling teacher... someone who came to look at what you were doing! This was potentially my worst nightmare and my guard was up.

'Okay,' he said, leaning further into class. 'Let's think of this as more of a boot camp than a lesson. We're not going to focus on the things you should know, but instead, on the things you don't know. There's no embargo on asking those questions you've previously been too embarrassed to ask, let's get everything out in the open.'

'What's an embargo, sir?' Shaz Birstow shouted.

'Well done, Sharon, that's exactly what I mean. Nothing is out of bounds in this class as long as it stays respectful and strictly no swearing... Lee!'

Everyone nodded.

'I'm going to release your interest in learning, an interest you probably didn't think you had, and you are going to prove to yourselves that you are worthy students.'

I looked around. Everyone was sitting upright, with elbows on desks, looking like they were paying attention. He was the first teacher I had ever seen with the ability to get everyone listening. I couldn't believe it. He sounded like he wanted to help, rather than just bat on regardless, whether you understood or not. It did feel a bit late in the day, though. Our final exams were only a matter of weeks away, and most of us had almost completely given up.

'So, who doesn't understand comprehension?'

There was silence.

'Hmm... Eccles, what do you think it is?' He pointed at Sarah Eccles. Sarah always had a love bite on her neck and chewed bubbly.

'I don't know, sir,' she said, slapping her chops. She then blew a bubble, which popped.

'Cook. What about you?'

Steve Cook was like me, a normal kid, but he was a sportsman, not an academic. 'It's boring reading, sir.'

'And you, Peterson?'

I couldn't believe he knew all our names. We'd never met him before, so how the hell did he know?

Susie Peterson was a punk. Bright pink hair in a Mohican and a stud through her nose, and more leather on her than I was prepared to dare.

'It's like reading and trying to make sense of it, sir.'

'Very good, Susie. So, I'm going to show you some tips on

how to do it. A kind of masterclass for you bright bunch of young people.'

I was glad he hadn't come to me with a question, and I looked at him curiously and wondered, who was this Lone Ranger? He was a maverick, alright. He seemed interested in us and didn't treat us like kids, and he was on the ball. Oh, yes, he was on the ball, and knowing everyone's names was freaky. Anyway, I was interested.

He then took both guns from his holster and hit us with, 'Who's ever heard of Shakespeare?'

'There's the Shakespeare Inn round the back of the market. My dad practically lives there, sir,' said Jimmy Armitage, making a supping gesture with his hands.

'Excellent, Jimmy. I've probably met your dad in there at some point. No, I'm talking Romeo and Juliet here, the greatest love story ever written.'

'Oh, yeah,' shouted Jimmy. He started making kissing noises with his lips on the back of his hand.

'Shakespeare is difficult to understand. I struggled at first, and I still do sometimes, but essentially it's the story of two people, a boy and a girl, and their attempt to be together against all the odds. A bit like you and Susie.' He gestured at Jimmy with a wry smile.

'That's out of order, sir,' said Jimmy, a serious look on his face. 'Everyone knows she's a lezzie.'

'Look, if I show you how to understand Shakespeare, then you can understand anything. There are only four things to know. It's simple. Number one: where is it taking place? Two: who is taking part? Three: what's happening? And four: why is this important to the story? It doesn't matter if it's Shakespeare, Enid Blyton or the *Sun* newspaper, it's the same. No one writes something in a story unless it has a meaning and it moves the people along in the story.'

I found myself nodding. I did a double-take at myself and

realised I was actually agreeing with him. It was a revelation. Was that it? Was it as simple as that?

I wanted to know more. Sir explained that Romeo and Juliet were madly in love but couldn't be together. It sounded just like Claire and me, so I sat up and tuned right in. He explained about the feuding families and how in one scene they planned a suicide pact and how that affected the story, because later there would be a mix-up. Boom! No one had ever put it in such simple terms and made it real. It was obvious. Who? What? Where? And why?

How come no one had ever explained that before?

As the weeks went by, English lessons became a little more bearable. They seemed to be more relevant, but I'd already decided I'd leave school at the first opportunity I could after my sixteenth birthday. My plan was to start work, and this plan involved anything but more 'learning'. I couldn't wait, and to ease myself in gently I persuaded mum to let me have a paper round.

Being up at the crack of dawn and nosing up people's drives and entering into places I never knew existed was thrilling. I even delivered to the big house where my tree was located. The tree looked different from the perspective of the house. I worked out that the house was probably inhabited by elderly people, and that's why I never saw anyone. There was a ramp to the front door and grab handles, and they took a copy of the *People's Friend* magazine and *The Financial Times*. I'd never seen that newspaper before.

One of my houses further along the road had the dog from hell. I swear it could smell me coming before I was anywhere near, and the second I thrust the paper through the door, it was immediately snatched. Through the frosted glass window I could see and hear the paper being ripped into a thousand pieces. It made me wonder if the people there ever got the chance to read it.

I loved that paper round, and although the earnings were no way reflected in the number of papers I had to deliver, the job gave me a purpose. It also meant I had a bit of money in my pocket, and so I went and bought my first double album by the Electric Light Orchestra. Wow, what a record! And the double album sleeve of *Out of the Blue* was literally, out of this world. It had come out in the late '70s, so it wasn't new, but it was new to me and it blew me away. I'd first listened to it at Richard's, and my favourite track was everyone's favourite, *Mr Blue Sky*. I played it over and over again.

Within a few weeks, I was hungry for more work, and I managed to secure another round delivering the free paper on a Thursday evening. I earned £1.99 for what seemed like 1000 papers, but that meant I was on about £5 per week, which wasn't bad, seeing as you could buy a seven-inch single for 99p and an album for around £2.99.

The other bonus of having some cash in my pocket was that it enabled me to take Karen out. Of course I still had a thing for Claire, but Karen was much more available. We went for a walk around the lake, which led to a little café. I showed Karen how to skim stones, and she showed me how to kiss properly – and I mean properly. She nearly ate me alive, and it felt amazing. I could feel her bosoms pushed tight against my chest and I knew that I liked her. In fact, every part of my body liked her. We walked hand in hand and kissed a few more times. I even pushed her against a tree for a kiss, and she squealed.

So, at fifteen I had a girlfriend. Not the girl I'd been chasing for years but someone with a completely different set of attributes. I never asked her if she could play *The Entertainer*, but to be honest, I was interested in other things now, and she was eager to please. She was a little older than me by a few months, and her sixteenth birthday was certainly one to remember.

Karen was going out for dinner with her family at a local pub restaurant, and I was invited. It would be only the second time I had met her parents. I'd briefly said hello when I called for her a few weeks earlier, but the celebration meal would mean spending time in their company for the whole evening – something I wasn't looking forward to at all.

I wore a new white shirt and a tie. I felt the occasion warranted it. It was one of those shirts that had a metal bar between the collar tips, and a chain dangled over the front of the tie. I felt smart as we walked into the pub. It was busy and noisy when we arrived. Our table for five was a round table in the centre of the room. I sat next to Karen, who sat next to her sister Tracey, and her parents were opposite me. I felt nervous, not only being in the centre of the bustling restaurant, but also the in the immediate glare of her Mum and Dad. As usual, I tried to hide my anxious leg by fidgeting in my seat. As we perused the menus, Karen's mum asked if I was okay. She was a teacher, and that freaked me out even more. Teachers never seemed like normal people to me. She had that friendly smile which camouflaged the 'I know your game, laddy' look in her eyes.

'I just have a bit of cramp,' I said nervously.

'Oh! Do you need to go outside and stretch it?'

'No... I'll be fine, thanks.'

'What will you be ordering, John?' she asked.

The menu wasn't easy to understand. Lots of fancy names, like something Florentine and devilled something else. Two things to stay away from, I thought.

'I'm going for the chicken,' I said, playing it safe and going for what I knew.

'*En papillote?*' she asked, looking down her nose.

I had no idea what she'd said, so I nodded, and Karen gave my leg a secret squeeze under the table.

'And you, Karen?'

'I'm having the duck à l'orange.'

'Rather you than me,' I said with a laugh.

No one smiled, and my self-consciousness shot to an all-time high.

Out came my chicken and it was wrapped in pastry. It looked like the puff pastry Gran sometimes put on the top of her pies. This was followed shortly by Karen's duck and the other meals.

Mine took some cutting through with my knife, but I sawed it vigorously, while Karen's dad told an embarrassing story about when the family had all got food poisoning on holiday in Turkey, and Karen had thrown up in a plant pot.

'Dad!'

'Sorry, Kaz. I thought John might like to know that you're not a hundred percent perfect.'

She rolled her eyes. I gave her leg a reassuring under-the-table-squeeze and smiled.

'Have you been to Turkey, John?' he asked.

My mouth was full of pastry and it was tough going. I mean, really tough. I gnawed at it and chewed until my mouth was so dry, I couldn't swallow it. I shook my head and continued battling with the feeling I wanted to spit it all out. Eventually, I managed to break through, and slowly digested the driest pastry and chicken I had ever had. Mum's pastry was easier to eat than this, I thought. I kept quiet and let the family engage in conversation and continued, mouthful by mouthful, to get through it. I embarked on tackling another piece and consumed half a jug of water in the process. I could feel my face burning, and I was crippled inside with the anguish of not participating in the conversation or even asking Karen if her meal was good.

I was overwhelmed by both not wanting to leave my food and risking looking ungrateful, and keeping going and nearly choking to death. Anyway, I progressed through three-quarters of it, and while Karen's sister handed me some more water, she said, 'Isn't *en papillote* wrapped in greaseproof paper?'

I stopped chewing and immediately looked at my plate, and then at everyone around the table, all looking at me.

The following day I invited Karen around to my house, timing it for when Mum and Amber were out shopping. After some vigorous kissing, we quickly set to it. We'd done a few practice sessions down by the old railway sidings, so I had a basic sense of direction. Our passionate kissing took us into the lounge and onto the shag pile carpet and then awkwardly up against the bottom of the sofa. Anyway, it was amazing, but it didn't last long, and to me, it felt a little rough. I don't mean hard and dangerous, but bristly and chaffy. It worked for me, though, but I felt Karen was a little underwhelmed, by here despondent face.

That experience has led me to wonder whether I lost my virginity to my girlfriend or the gap between the sofa and the shag pile carpet. To this day, I'll never know, but I did a bit of growing up that day, that's for sure, and no children were brought into this world as a result. We did use contraception after that, and my positioning technique improved with time.

One thing I discovered about having a girlfriend was that it didn't come cheap. It wasn't that we didn't share paying for things, it was just that we started doing lots of things that required money, and my two paper rounds were not quite as lucrative as I'd hoped. I mentioned it to Mum and one day she announced that the milkman was looking for help. It was Saturdays to start with, and then the possibility of moving to weekdays, too. Saturday was a double drop, as the deliveries covered Sunday, too. This was back when everybody had milk delivered, so it was a big round.

The milkman told me he'd pick me up at 4.45am. I was never awake at that time, let alone ready. He would wake me by throwing gravel at my bedroom window, and I would dash down with barely my shoes on. Once up and in the van, we called at the dairy to load up, where there were crate after crate after crate of heavy glass bottles, all with neatly clamped coloured foil lids.

We loaded up and embarked on the skilful art of doorstep

milk delivery. This involved me and the two other guys we picked up after the dairy clinging to the back of the van, while standing on a little wooden footplate. At first I'd needed Jonny to give me confidence with the communication needed and the teamwork with the other lads. They all knew what they were doing, but I was the newbie. We each had a wire-framed basket that could hold ten bottles. We would load up on instruction from the milkman, who was driving. You knew which house number you were starting at and how many bottles to drop for the next four to five houses, and the van never stopped moving. You had to load the correct amount, drop the bottles safely and securely by the front doors, and then hotfoot it back to the moving van for your next load, not forgetting your report back to confirm whether they'd been left the correct delivery or whether there was a note.

A note could throw everything out of the window. No milk today was fine, you could just hop on to your next house. An extra pint was okay, because we always carried a spare. Two extras meant a dash back to the van or else give them what was due further on and hope they didn't want any. It was a skilful art of planning, execution and memory. I haven't even mentioned the cream, yoghurts and fizzy pop we used to do, too. Jonny enabled me to gain confidence in remembering the sequence of deliveries, reporting back any changes, and feeling like I was part of a team, but most of all he loved riding on the footplate at the rear of the van, and he had an assured way of hopping on and off the moving vehicle.

We called normal full-fat milk with the silver cap 'white' milk. Hardly anyone drank semi-skimmed then. Maybe half a dozen on the whole round, and probably twenty percent had gold top with full cream.

The 'white' and 'gold' milk used to attract the blue tits, who would break through the foil lid to nibble at the cream which was always at the top. I knew that because I delivered to my own house, and when I'd finished the round, the tits had always had a go.

So there I was, a six-days-a-week milk boy, up at 4.45am and dropped at the school gate for 8.55am. My last drop before school was two white, one semi, one gold and a peach yoghurt, which was for me. I ate it with my finger as I walked in the school gate, right on the bell.

11

THE LONE RANGER

The Easter of 1985 and my sixteenth birthday signalled the start of our final 'O' level exams. I had totally lost interest by this time and did absolutely no revision whatsoever. I couldn't even read my own writing, so all in all, a pointless exercise. I was also exhausted from working every morning. Anyway, I felt like I was already a working man and it felt good. Besides the milk round, I'd also managed to secure a job on Thursday evenings at the Ponden Mill shop in town. I basically was the muscle, who unloaded the delivery van of all the bedding and curtains, etc, and took them up three flights of steps to the storage rooms. It paid quite well, and although it was seriously hard work, I saw it as an opportunity to build some strength and muscle on what was my spindly and very un-muscly body. An additional, yet exciting, part of the job was cleaning out the air-conditioning extractor fans on the roof. I had to climb out of a little hatch, crawl along a thin ledge, and remove the extractor housing without dropping it into the pedestrian walkway some five storeys beneath. I would then hoy the filters, one by one, back into the building, where I would wash them in a sink with soap and water. I left them to dry while I manhandled the linen, and then before the end of my shift, I would climb back out and reinstall them. The water that came off the filters was black, and no matter how much washing I did, they always came out the same. Anyway, the great thing was, from the rooftop I could see all the backs of the shops with their little seating areas, and some even had gardens. It was like looking at a giant map of the city, and if it wasn't for my work, I could have stayed up there for hours, working out all the passages and secret ginnels and snickets. The sloping roof and slippery tiles were unnerving in the rain, though, and occasionally the gusty wind caused me to lose balance. But it wasn't school, it was exciting, and I was starting to enjoy working for a living.

My exit strategy, therefore, was to find work, qualifications or no qualifications, and in the meantime all I had to do was go through the motions at school.

There was no exam for Art or Drama, just continual assessment over the year. Home Economics was similar, and I hoped that someone had choked on *my* teacakes.

The Geography exam seemed to flow quite well. I knew some of the answers, but not all, and I got in a bit of a state as I ran out of time.

History was a nightmare. I couldn't remember anything, apart from the flying shuttle, 1733, and Newcomen's steam engine, but they never even featured. I did remember a couple of facts about the Second World War which Grandad had told me about. He'd been an engineer attached to the Canadian forces on D-Day and later was part of the liberation of Bergen-Belsen concentration camp.

The Maths exam just didn't resemble anything we'd done in class. I tried my best, but beyond the basics I was lost. It was the toughest so far, and I left the exam room with my head low, knowing I hadn't done well.

Biology wasn't much different. I hadn't paid enough attention to my lessons, and there were a lot of long technical terms which I had no idea how to spell. I could, however, almost completely label the cross-section of a leaf, the cuticle, stoma, epidermis, etc., which surprised me.

Then there was English, my worst subject by far. I wasn't looking forward to it at all. There were two papers – a language and grammar paper in the morning and a comprehension paper in the afternoon.

I printed my name at the top of the first paper and set about reading the first question. I understood the difference between their and there and now and know…, Mr Sharp-Shooting Hooray had put us right on that, thankfully. But as I worked my way down the paper, I became more and more confused. I missed out huge sections and just had a stab at others. In the final section you had to write about something you were passionate about. Memories of Conly Cassle came flooding back. I could write about that, but then I remembered the humiliating episode in class afterwards, and so after a bit of thought, I decided to write about my tree. I was passionate about her. I wrote about the feelings I had when I was nestled in her branches and the energy she gave me when we were swaying to and fro. I described the texture of her bark and how strong she felt, and how she gave me a bird's eye view of all the other wildlife busying around.

At dinner I had some cheese slop and tapioca for pud and then entered the exam room for the comprehension paper, which was in the sports hall, with its array of brightly marked pitches on the floor. Hardly the most inspiring location for an exam, especially as I was sitting directly on the halfway line.

I printed my name and stared at the paper. I broke out into a hot sweat and contemplated running out and faking an illness, but two others had done just that, which didn't leave much chance of making my own stab at it look convincing. So I turned to the first page. My heart nearly stopped as my eyes scanned the question, and my hand, which was holding the pen, started to shake. Even good old anxious leg brought in an appearance. I stared at the page and felt the all-too-familiar haze descend. I was going under. I started to look in between the words, my eyes glazed over, and the patterns of white spaces started to draw me in. This was it, the beginning of the end. The void between the words seemed more powerful than I'd ever encountered it before. It was opening wide, offering me the perfect escape, and I was being dragged in. Why not finish my last academic failure in style and go for total wipeout? I thought.

It was then I had a fleeting thought of Mr Hooray, with his empowering eyes looking straight at me. Without him opening his mouth, I heard him say, 'You can do this, Crawshaw.'

I took a deep breath and scrunched my eyes up to gain some sort of normality. 'Mr Blue Sky' started running through my mind, and Mr Hooray was pointing at the sun. It was a very strange feeling, unnerving for sure, but it gave me the opportunity to gain some focus.

I brought my eyes in, to see the black letters. I had to fight it, but I made out the title. 'Comprehension'.

I took another deep breath and read the question.

1. Read through the passage below and comment on who are the main characters, what they are doing and what significance their words have on the story, and why? Feel free to expand your thoughts to where the story is leading, and what could make it different.

Romeo and Juliet by William Shakespeare.

Holy Mother of God!

12

RESULTS

I had to wait what seemed an inordinate amount of time for my results. In the meantime, I met with the careers advisor to discuss where I was going next. My predicted results didn't give much room for manoeuvre, but I definitely knew further education was not for me.

The advisor peered over the top of her glasses. 'So... John, what are you considering doing when you leave school?'

'I'm not sure, miss. I know I don't want to go to college or do 'A' levels.'

'Hmm. I have a few office places available, filing and note-taking, etc.?'

The thought filled me with dread. 'I don't think that's for me. I'm not very good at writing, and the thought of being stuck inside an office seems too much like school.'

'Beggars cannot be choosers, James... How about plumbing or welding?' she said optimistically.

I shook my head. 'It's John.'

'Sure. There's a new supermarket opening up over the road, and they're looking for shelf-stackers with possible promotion to the freezer department.'

I shook my head again.

She became restless in her seat, and her optimistic face started to look a bit cross. 'They're looking for engineers at the local pipe-making factory. You'd have to undergo some maths testing. How does that sound?'

'I'm not good at maths either, miss.'

She looked down at my expected grades. 'Oh, yes, I can see that.'

She sighed and complained about how normally there were always positions at the coal mine, but how things were looking very unsettled there at the moment, and that it was threatened with closure. I remembered the rioting miners I'd encountered going to Dad's and shook my head again.

'So… erm…' She looked at the paper in front of her. 'John! You're not giving me much to go on here. What things are you interested in?'

I shrugged. 'Dunno, miss.'

'Well, what do you enjoy doing?' she went on, with a hint of despair.

'I like sitting in my tree and watching the birds and squirrels,' I told her, trying to be honest.

She raised an eyebrow. 'That's all very well, but it's not going to help you get work, is it? You need to give me a hint of what you're interested in. What did you do last night when you got home from school?'

'Oh, that's easy, miss, I made some cheese on toast with spring onion sprinkled on top. My mum's not the best cook in the world, so it's a necessity in our house.'

'That's it!' she said, slamming her hand on the desk.

'What, miss?

'A chef. I can get you an interview on a catering Youth Training Scheme. How about being a chef? The pay is £27.50 per week. How does that sound?'

It was more than I was getting on the milk and the shop, so I thought about it for a second, nodded my head and agreed.

Well, that was it. Simple. The following week I donned my best trousers and one of my school shirts and Mum dropped me at the little office in town. I still had my lolloping walk, and both legs were shaking with fear. I could feel my throat swelling up. I tried coughing to clear my throat, so I could talk. As I approached the door, I summoned Jonny. He would be okay in there, and I needed to look confident.

A relaxed-looking lady met me at the door and I followed her to an office. She explained about the placement, and before I could say 'Yes, Chef' I was enrolled, on the proviso I attained three 'O' level passes. That meant grade C or above. My heart sank. I wish I'd known that earlier. I would have bucked my ideas up, or at least done a bit of revision. I would have been happy with two 'O' levels, but now the heat was on, and I needed three.

I still had to wait a couple more weeks for the results. Meanwhile, I decided to do a refurb job on the Silver Dream Machine and turn her into the Red Devil. I completely stripped her down and, with bright red car spray, transformed her and gave her a new lease of life. I polished all the chrome and Grandad helped me renew the brakes, seat and tyres. She was almost like new when we'd finished and had a brand-new personality, one of fiery optimism and determination. And she might well be my only way of getting to work and back.

The following day, the lady from the YTS called. She reiterated the importance of three grade Cs, and on that basis offered me a placement at a local family-run hotel as their YTS chef. My heart skipped a beat. Wow. YTS chef sounded so official. She said as soon as I had my results, I should call her, and she would get the ball rolling to organise my uniform and book a place at the training centre, where I would regularly attend for extra training.

I ran into the kitchen, where Mum was vigorously scrubbing the bottom of a burnt pan. 'Mum, I've just had news about my new job.'

'I thought it sounded positive. I'm really pleased for you, love. Is my cooking that bad?'

I laughed. 'No. I love you, Mum. Thanks for taking me to the interview and, well, just being a great mum.' We hugged, and we squeezed. It was one of those hugs which had great meaning. She knew I was growing up, but she knew that I loved her.

'Let's hope you get some good results then.' She crossed her fingers and smiled. I crossed my fingers too, ran out of the house and took the Red Devil for a long ride. I felt free, speeding along the back lanes, the wind wildly blowing my hair. I rode no-handed and punched the air with excitement as I wondered what a YTS chef would have to do.

The bright early morning sun woke me before my alarm. It was results day! I stretched my entire body under my duvet and took a deep breath. I'd been on a high since the job news, but now a wave of nervous anxiety hit me as I thought about the dismal reality of what was about to unfold. There was record unemployment. Margaret Thatcher had managed to crush the miners, and other heavy industry jobs were also affected, so I was lucky to have such an opportunity. I'd finished on the milk round. I was sad to leave on the last day, but a younger replacement had already started, and it felt like a natural progression.

I lay in bed, thinking about the possible results. A definite B in Art, that was in the bag. Drama, probably a D, which was a fail. I was also likely to get Ds in Maths, Biology, Geography and Home Economics, and I'd be lucky to get an E in English. My heart sank. I truly wished I was capable of more. As I put on my favourite jeans with the worn-out knees, I came to the conclusion that it was what it was and what would be, would be. There was no getting away from the fact I was an underachiever and thick and destined for a life as a shelf-stacker. I couldn't go back on the milk, and the shop was only one evening a week. And who was going to employ someone who was pretty much illiterate?

I took a slug of milk from the fridge and found a note on the door from Mum. 'Good luck today, son. I'll always be proud of you, whatever the outcome. Love, Mum. PS don't drink out of the bottle xx.'

I put the note in my pocket and headed down the road towards school. Richard was just ahead of me, so I ran to catch him. We didn't talk about school or our predicted results; instead, he thrust a Don Masson into my hand.

'Here's one for old times' sake, mate,' he said, giving me a friendly punch on the arm.

Richard was predicted straight As. He had his commercial pilot's licence firmly in mind, and he deserved it. I wondered whether the plane might have rubber controls. But I didn't mention it. I was grateful that he was courteous enough not to rub it in. Our lives were about to take different directions, but we just shuffled along like we always did, kicking stones and scuffing our shoes.

On arrival at the school gate, we followed the crowd into the hall. There were tables arranged in alphabetical order and a pile of envelopes on each one. I hesitated for a few seconds and then walked up to my table.

'Crawshaw... Here we are. Well done.' She held out the brown envelope.

'Thanks, miss.'

I took the envelope over to the corner, so I could open it in private, and started to peel the seal. I stopped suddenly about halfway. I did want to see what was inside, but at the same, I didn't. I was genuinely scared of what I might find. I looked around. There were lots of people jumping up and down and hugging each other. I turned my back and secretively and tentatively repositioned my thumb under the sealed flap and finished it off.

Biology – D. It was to be expected.

Geography – C. Wow, better than I thought.

Drama – D. Disappointing.

Home Economics – D. I should have gone to more lessons. And someone switched my bread buns.

Art – B. *Yesss.*

Maths – E. Hell, that's bad.

History – E. Oh, no!

Well, that only left my worst subject, and the result lay over the crease of paper. I didn't really need to turn the paper over, I knew what it would be. My vision of becoming a chef faded dramatically. I looked again at everyone hugging and huddling into groups to share their results and I just stood there, frozen to the spot, not daring to move. Three passes were all I'd needed, and I wasn't good enough. Ds and Es were shameful. I fell short, just like in everything else in my life. Jackass John, the idiot thickie.

I turned the page and immediately flipped it back again. My mouth and throat went very dry, and my hand started to shake. I turned the page again.

English – C.

My dry throat turned into a lump. I tried to swallow as I scrutinised the letter again. Grade C. A flipping-well grade C. I tried to hold it in but was actually blubbing. There were tears streaming down my cheeks. How the hell did I manage to get that?

In a complete daze, I continued to stare at the results, my tears dropping onto the sheet.

'Are you alright, Crawshaw?' a teacher said as she passed. 'That bad, eh?'

I looked up at her and with blurred vision. 'No, miss, I got three passes. I'm going to be a chef.'

There was only one thing to do. I scoured the hall for the man that made all this possible, the Lone Ranger. I scanned and scanned, but there was no sign. I walked around the hall and out into the corridor and then back in again, frantically searching. He was nowhere to be seen, and I never saw him again. He'll be an old man now if he's still with us, but I will always be eternally grateful to him. Thank you, sir.

PART II

DISCOVERY YEARS

13

INCARCERATED

So, there I was, in a tall white hat, white double-breasted chef's coat and blue checked trousers, making a prawn cocktail. It was a small hotel, about twenty rooms, a bar and restaurant. The sort of place travelling businessmen stayed in during the week and couples at the weekend. The people who owned it had won a million pounds on the Football Pools and bought it. There was the head chef and me in the kitchen, a handful of part-time waitresses, and the owners themselves, who ran the bar and hotel. I felt grown up and proud to be part of the team. One thing I'd learned from doing the milk round was that showing willingness and enthusiasm always went a long way, and that was my new plan. I was relying on Jonny more and more, though, as I tried to adapt to my new surroundings and new responsibilities.

Mine and Richard's paths never crossed again. We moved house yet again not long after I left school, and to the other side of town, so it was unlikely we'd ever see each other. Dave and the rest of the gang were also working men now – Dave as a trainee manager at the new supermarket, Smiler in Topman in town, Robbo working with his dad on a building site and Spider at the pipe factory. Karen and I had drifted apart. It was good while it lasted, but I never really felt she was the girl for me. I did learn a lot, though.

At the hotel, I worked split shifts, 7am till 11am and then 6pm till... late, for £27.50 per week.

Part of the job description was I had to go front-of-house, too, but I didn't want to be a waiter. I was happy buried away in the kitchen and not having to deal with the public. I tried it under duress and dropped a fork and onion gravy down a guy's shirt as I was clearing the plates. That confirmed it wasn't for me. Equally, I could never remember what people had ordered and made a complete mess of it all.

After my first week I received my eagerly awaited wage packet. I rushed home and couldn't wait to tell Mum.

'I'm a working man now,' I proclaimed, tipping the cash contents of the little brown envelope onto the table.

'Feels good, doesn't it?'

'It really does.'

'Your first step to independence.'

'I guess so.'

'I'll be charging you £10 per week board and lodging from now on, then.'

I laughed. 'Yeah, sure.'

'No, I mean it.'

'You're taking a third of my wage to live in my own house?'

'*My* house. And you've lived here for free up to now, so not a bad deal.'

'You're kidding. Do you know how hard I had to work for that?

'Yes.'

We just looked at each other, me resenting everything she said and Mum standing her ground.

'Yes, I do know how hard you had to work. Every day, I do

the same. I tell you what. You can have the first month and after that it starts.'

I couldn't believe how totally unfair it was, taking such a large amount off me, especially when I hardly ever ate at home now.

'Anyway,' I said, 'I've decided I'm going to take everyone out for a celebration meal. You, me, Amber and Gran and Grandad. All on me, at the Italian in town.'

'What about Derek?'

'What about him?' I said, the taste of bitterness in my mouth.

Mum had entered into a new relationship. Derek was a tall man and thickset, older than her by at least ten years. He worked with her, and Mum even told me she didn't like him at first, but a war of attrition had worn her down, and they had started dating. The minute I met Derek, I knew he didn't like me, and I didn't like him. My gut was telling me something, but I didn't know what.

So, my joy was kind of short-lived. I now had to fork out to live in my own house and Mum's new partner was moving in on my patch.

At work I learned how to make most of the starters: pâté on toast; melon balls formed from a special scoop; soup, which was easy, and of course, prawn cocktail. A handful of frozen prawns run under a hot tap until defrosted – and I mean still in your hand. Then straight into a wine glass on top of shredded lettuce, and Marie Rose sauce to finish. (Never try this method.)

The head chef was a thin man, with a very pale face and patchy beard, like large lumps had completely fallen off and probably into the soup. I found his banter took some getting used to.

'Being a chef, is all about teamwork,' he proclaimed one day, while I was washing up at the sink and he was basting chickens behind me. 'Working in such close confines, can be frustrating, don't you agree?'

'I'm not sure,' I said, thinking it was a strange thing to say.

'You have to take one for the team now and again, especially when things get hot and sticky in here. Do you know what I mean?'

I shook my head. 'It does get hot in here, though. We could try opening this window. Looks like it's never been opened.' I looked at the thick layer of grease on the hinges.

'Making sure you please your boss is essential too. Don't you think?'

I felt him come close behind me and then something hard touched the inside of my leg, just below my buttock. I moved away quickly to reach for the tea towel and saw him handling a large cucumber with both hands. I laughed a fake laugh and flicked it with the towel.

'Ooh, naughty boy,' he said looking me up and down.

'Shall I sharpen the knives?' I asked nervously.

His banter reached an even more uncomfortable level when he invited me to his room to look at some 'boys' magazines'. This made me feel very awkward. I told him I wasn't interested in the *Beano* and *Whizzer and Chips* any more, and I declined.

The thing which made me most uncomfortable was the showing of hardcore pornography in the bar on a projector screen when we were closed during the day. At sixteen, I had never come across anything like it, and it made me feel sick. Actually, it was shocking, and I made up my mind to ask my supervisor for a different placement. I didn't want to tell her specifically what had happened. I was embarrassed and didn't want to get anyone into trouble, so I told her the split shifts were the issue. She didn't look pleased but did say she had a new placement coming up and she would let me know when it was confirmed.

· · ·

So, there I was again. In my tall white hat, white chef's coat and blue checked trousers, making shepherd's pie and Manchester tart for category A prisoners. Gone were the split shifts. Instead, 7am till 3pm, with half an hour for breakfast. I was a chef in a maximum-security prison. I was security-checked in every way possible. They even wanted to know what my dad and grandad did for a living. And every day I watched cameras follow me into and out of work, and had my bag checked regularly.

So, when I say Category A, I mean seriously bad people. Murderers, rapists and violent offenders formed the majority, but at that time the prison also housed many convicted IRA activists. Often on my way in and out of the gate there would be a protest march, with banners and ringleaders shouting messages of encouragement on loudhailers, so that they could be heard over the wall. Sometimes I just couldn't get through and had to wait it out in security.

The walls were thick and high and on top of them was what the officers called 'the beak'. This was a smooth, beak-shaped coping designed to withstand grappling hooks slung from the outside. 'The beak' made it impossible to climb over from the inside, too. I would often go over to the wall and place my hands on it, and feel how cold it was. I'd tilt my head back to see if I could make out the top, but it was too high. It was working within those walls that I began to understand true freedom. There was no way out of that place, no door you could just open to let yourself out, and usually the inmates only saw the light of day for an hour or so, before the impenetrable metal doors were once again slammed in triplicate behind them. For the other twenty-three hours they were incarcerated in their inner sanctum. The whole place was extremely repressive.

The guards usually kept disruption to a minimum, helped by the presence of the dog patrols. Those dogs looked like they wanted trouble, you could see it in their eyes. Most commonly stocky German Shepherds, they looked at you as if you were a piece of meat, prisoner on not. I gave them a wide birth. That was another thing, we never called the prisoners 'prisoners'. Inmates was the official term, more commonly 'cons', short for convicts, but within the kitchen, we referred to them as 'the baddies'. I never gave it any thought at the time, but now it seems more than a little weird to call another human being that. Or maybe I've forgotten the horrific crimes those people had committed against other humans.

I was posted to the kitchen within the training wing. It was more open there and slightly less repressive. This was where prison employees from all over the country came to do courses, officers, psychologists, chaplains and governors undertaking various training, from hostage-taking, riot control, one-to-one counselling and pre-retirement. We usually catered for around 300 people per sitting per day – that's breakfast, lunch and dinner.

The catering industry generally has a similar hierarchy to the army, from the general manager, head chef, second chef, sous chefs, porters, pot washers and trainee chefs to the YTS chef right at the bottom. I was one of twenty plus within the brigade and the lowest of the low in the pecking order. Our head chef was an ex-sergeant major in the army, and boy did we know it. He would bark his orders, and we jumped to it, and at double-quick time. We scrubbed the numerous stainless steel table legs with toothbrushes, and just so we knew we were at the bottom of the pile, we did it over and over again, even though they were immaculate. When we chopped the parsley, it had to be like 'prairie dust', and we made it so.

Of course, that was never good enough either, and so then you would be on some kind of punishment, like cleaning out the chest freezers or hand-cleaning the deep-fat fryer. And then that was never good enough, so you were confined to the damp veg prep room and faced with peeling carrots and potatoes for 300 people.

We prepped everything from fresh. All the vegetables were peeled, washed and chopped into juliennes and brunoises. We butchered our own meat, and boned and rolled our own meat roasts, and the turkeys for Christmas.

I learned how to make soups, stocks and sauces, béchamel, velouté, consommé béarnaise, gazpacho, fondant potatoes and suet and sponge puddings, all with homemade custard. Nothing came out of a packet in that place.

In terms of being out of the sleazy hotel, I was glad, but it seemed like out of the frying pan and into the fire.

'Crawshaw!' the head chef shouted at the top of his voice.

'Yes, Chef?'

'You ever made custard before?'

'No, Chef.' I had a picture in my mind of the rusty blue, yellow and red tin of Bird's custard in the cupboard at home. Mum used to pour it over tinned peaches. It always tasted metallic and had lumps in it.

'Well, you're going to learn. How do you think we make it?'

'Dunno, Chef. From a tin?'

He closed his eyes and shook his head. 'You call yourself a chef, boy? Anything out of a tin or a packet is for lazy people. People who don't know how to cook, not chefs.' He slammed his hand down on the table, revealing what he'd been grasping in his clenched fist. 'Vanilla pods. Cut them down the middle and scrape out the seeds. That's the flavour. Got it, Crawshaw?'

'Yes, Chef.' I picked up my knife and got to work.

'Not now, Crawshaw. You're not listening to me, are you?'

'Yes, Chef... I mean, no, Chef.' I started to get in a muddle and could feel my anxious leg begin to knock the stainless-steel table leg.

'Come over here.' He beckoned me over to a large metal saucepan the size of a water butt – well, almost. Within it was another pan.

'This is a bain-marie. What is it?'

'A bain-marie, Chef.' Both legs were starting to shake now.

'Milk, in there, three-quarters full and starting to warm up. Then get your arse back on the vanilla and get the pods in the milk. Don't let it boil, you understand? Let it boil, and I'll have you on carrot peeling for the rest of the month. Okay?'

'Yes, Chef.'

I got to work, with him breathing down my neck and my legs rattling around in my blue checked and rather large trousers. I scraped out the contents of the vanilla pods and put them carefully into the milk. I learned the bain-marie was a pan within a water bath. It effectively allowed the liquid to warm, without a concentrated heat at the base, which would burn the milk and cause it to stick to the bottom.

'Okay, good. Next, eggs. All of them into this bowl and mix in the sugar and corn flour. Yes?'

'Yes, Chef.' I started cracking what looked like a skyscraper of eggs, on trays stacked one on top of each other to the ceiling.

'What are you doing over there?' he boomed.

'Just making sure it's not boiling, Chef,' I nervously replied, not really knowing whether it was boiling or not.

'Eggs, boy, eggs! Stop messing about. Eggs, come on!'

I definitely didn't want to be on carrot duty. I'd done many stints in the tiny, wet and cold veg prep room and the thought of another month with wrinkled and bleeding sore hands wasn't appealing. I wanted to make sure the milk wasn't going to boil and the pressure started to get to me. I didn't dare ask for help on the eggs and so I kept my head down, cracking and mixing like my life depended on it.

It was then Chef completely blew his top. 'Crawshaw! Get here now. What's happening to this milk?'

I rushed over to see the milk starting to bubble.

'What did I say about it boiling?'

'But Chef –'

'Don't 'but Chef' me, lad. Do you want to be a professional like me?'

'Yes, Chef.'

He jabbed me in the chest with a ladle. 'Then you make sure you don't piss me off, ever. You got that?'

'Yes, Chef.'

After food service, I was shattered. The custard was a great hit, thankfully, but I went for a five-minute break in the cigarette-smoke-filled staffroom to recuperate. No sooner had I sat in the seat, than I heard Chef booming again.

'CRAWSHAW!'

I took to my feet in fear and tentatively approached the kitchen door. 'Crawshaw, in here, on the double.'

He and a couple of the other chefs were in the cold room. This housed most of the perishable foods and the gigantic walk-in fridge. He called me in, gesturing quickly with his hand. As I approached, he opened the momentously thick fridge door, which looked like something from a bank vault – heavy steel with gigantic hinges, and a heavy-duty clasp-locking mechanism.

'Can you help me with a beef carcass?' he asked with a smile. There were usually two or three different animal carcasses hanging in there, ready for processing. I eagerly entered the fridge and suddenly it went dark. Pitch black dark. The bank of industrial fans switched on and I heard and felt the full weight of the door close on me even as I tried with great force, to prevent it trapping me in.

I banged on the door and shouted to be let out, but nothing happened. It began to get colder. I stumbled over something on the floor and my face brushed against the bloody carcass. I was scared, so I tried kicking the door, but it was solid. I immediately searched for the alarm bell, which was one of the security devices in case someone did get trapped in there. It took me a while to locate the button in the dark and I pressed it. I listened to whether I could hear it ringing outside, but all I could hear was very faint muffled laughing. They'd removed the battery, I knew it. I'd witnessed it before, when the kitchen porter had suffered the same fate. What worried me most was, he'd been left in there for an hour. I kicked the door repeatedly and banged with my fist. I could feel a panic attack brewing, my heart was racing, and I was severely agitated. I was frightened I was going to suffocate and felt faint. I remembered the metal rod which protruded through the door. This was the second safety system, and if you pushed hard, it acted against the door clasp and released it from the inside. In the pitch black, I anxiously grasped it and with all my force pushed it. The whole thing shot straight through the door and I heard it hitting the tiled floor with a heavy clink, clink, *clink*! They'd removed the locking-pin, rendering the whole mechanism useless.

I was well and truly trapped in there and I was shivering. In a fit of panic, I kicked the door and bashed it with my fists and shouted at the top of my voice, before collapsing onto a milk crate. I tried to banish any idea of total panic setting in by controlling my breathing. I tried to think positively that they would let me out before they all went home, and not think about how they could potentially leave me in there all night.

Twenty minutes is a long time to be detained beyond your control. I was eventually released, and as I heard the door open and my eyes adjusted to the light, the two chefs stood laughing and pretending to shiver, with their arms wrapped around their torsos. I looked at both of them. Head chef was nowhere to be seen. His henchmen had been instructed to release me and test my resilience to the bullying which was an everyday occurrence.

I knew if I showed any kind of anger towards them, or even showed I was remotely flustered by the escapade, it would be the green light for more, and I would become a victim again. The weak in there didn't survive long.

'Was it dark in there?' one of them mocked.

'I quite liked it,' I said calmly, brushing past them. 'Helped myself to a cheese sandwich and a trifle. What's not to like?'

The following week, I proudly led the family into Piccalino's Restaurant.

'Shall we have starters?' I asked everyone. 'Garlic bread?'

'I'll have bread, but not with garlic,' Grandad said, and Gran nodded.

'I'd like garlic bread,' Amber replied enthusiastically.

Mum nodded, 'Me too.'

I took control and decided we would have garlic bread to share. The garlic bread was great there, a round, pizza-style bread oozing with garlic butter.

'Just try it Grandad,' I said with an encouraging pat on the back.

'I'll have melon,' said Derek.

I didn't even waste any energy looking at him and placed our order with the waiter, for whom I now had a great deal of respect.

Gran was telling us about her dreadful experience at church, when she completely ruined the Easter service. She'd watered all the flowers with what she thought was Baby Bio, but it turned out to be vinegar.

Then the starters arrived.

'Try some, Grandad,' I said offering him a piece.

'Should have gone for the melon.' Derek smirked.

'I'm not good with foreign food, especially garlic,' said Grandad, turning his nose up.

'Go on, try it,' I said, giving him a smile.

'Well, just for you, then.'

We ended up ordering another, as both Gran and Grandad decided it wasn't so bad, after all. I couldn't have been happier, seeing them tucking into it and knowing the treat was on me.

Derek made some excuse about leaving the iron on at home and left to sort it out. We didn't say anything, but the air cleared, and we munched and laughed our way through the meal. Mum, Gran and Amber ordered mocktails, and we all had Italian ice cream while listening to Gran once again telling us the walrus tusk teeth story, during which we were all in hysterics.

The biggest shock of the night was not the fact we didn't see Derek again, but when the bill was deposited at my place. It felt so good receiving the cheque. It made me feel like a man and that my hard work was worth something. I then opened it and nearly collapsed under the table. It was more than two weeks' wages! Luckily I'd brought some of my birthday money, too, as a backup, and I handed the waiter the cash, with only a slight hesitation. It was worth it, though.

14

DIFFICULT DECISIONS

B ack at the prison, my shyness had to take a back seat. I was thrust into a busy and demanding kitchen, and there was no time for being anxious or showing weakness. I also started to learn from Jonny. Instead of letting my adopted persona take control, I started to use some of his tricks myself, like putting myself forward for overtime and chatting and getting to know my colleagues.

My favourite ploy, though, was to keep my head down and graft hard. I didn't mind working, I found that out quickly enough. It meant I was away from school and that was the main thing, and in some ways being a chef was the perfect job, because I didn't have to write a thing. I could read the menus fine, and I was a YTS, so I just did as I was told and never questioned anything. The head and second chefs were in charge of writing the menus and sorting the ordering, etc., so writing was no concern of mine, and nobody was any the wiser about my disability. I also learned that by showing willing and being trustworthy and reliable, people never questioned my qualifications or ability to write. Punctuality, stamina and a 'Yes, Chef' attitude, regardless of the daily abuse, were what counted.

Within two months, I was called in to see the head chef.

'Crawshaw, come in and stand at ease.'

I didn't know what that meant, so I just dropped a shoulder and tried to look relaxed, despite being frightened to death. I thought I was in for the sack.

'There's been a lot of discussions, and despite you being a f**king arsehole, we'd like to offer you the position of trainee chef on a full-time contract, with a wage rise to £35 per week.'

He had the army-style sense of humour, which tended to destroy you first and then bring you back up so that you were eternally grateful. I didn't get the humour at all, but was both shocked and extremely grateful, and I thanked him many, many times.

'Stop grovelling now. You start on Monday, and I'll inform the YTS lady you're off the scheme. Oh yes, and college starts the week after, day release. Right, piss off.'

I ran out of the door and past one of the other YTS chefs, who was having his head dunked in a huge sink of cold water and food waste. I stopped momentarily.

'Enough is enough, eh, lads?' I shouted.

The two-finger solute I received back said it all, and I ran to hide outside by the bins.

Then it hit me. College, next week. *No.* I couldn't do that. No, way. I'd come there to get away from college. I landed a punch on the side of the steel bin and cracked my knuckles.

'Ouch!'

At the end of my shift, I rode home on the Red Devil as usual, mulling over the whole thing. If I said no to college, it could jeopardise my entire career, and it was a mighty fine offer. But I didn't want to be found out as a fraud. I'd gone from being a stupid dunce to having respect and prospects, and this could easily wreck it all. I had some serious thinking to do that night.

I tossed and turned in bed for hours. I knew how to make light and fluffy puff pastry, how to skillfully butcher an animal carcass and could delicately spin sugar into little decorative cages. Yet if I took up the offer, in effect I would be sentencing myself to a spell in an almost lawless environment, where it wasn't unusual to find eggs broken into your shoes or margarine smothered thickly into the crotch of your trousers, or even to find your entire civilian clothing burnt to cinders on the floor of your locker. There was clingfilm over the toilet bowl on a regular basis. That was normal. You could also find your bike dismantled into individual pieces, or voodoo dolls in your locker, or be locked in chest freezers and fridges, or have knives thrown at you at point-blank range, or have huge weights lobbed at you.

But my biggest fear of all was college. I couldn't wait to leave school, and now I'd be heading straight back to the hell of the classroom again, where they would surely suss out my hidden secret. I contemplated the alternatives many, many times, like stacking shelves at the supermarket or working in a shop, but after a restless night and hardly any sleep, I decided I was extremely thankful to be offered a full-time position, because there was nowhere else I could go. Based on that fact alone, I cautiously accepted the job, and it was confirmed.

Contact with Dad was on the wane. It had been for a while, but one thing he did do was buy me a blue and red Kawasaki 125cc motorbike to get me to work a little swifter, and wow, it was quick. I could ride it with L plates with no training or test, which was perfect, and I was grateful for an extra thirty minutes lie-in every morning. The bike was my first taste of motoring freedom, and I was quite simply a total idiot on it, pretending to be Steve McQueen and racing other road users. Sometimes if I went to the shop or to see a friend, I wouldn't even wear my helmet, but I loved the exhilaration and power at my fingertips.

I could park the bike in the officers' parking at work and, better still, I could park it and lock it up right outside the door of college. On my first day, though, I took the bus, as I didn't yet know if I could secure the bike somewhere safe.

I approached the four-storey building with the same trepidation I'd felt back when I went to a new school. I didn't know where to go, what time dinner was, or what I had to wear. There was only one man who could deal with all this. Jonny.

I hid just around the corner from the steps up to reception. I faced the black wrought-iron railings, gripped them tight and closed my eyes, took a very deep breath and tried to control my breathing so I could at least focus. I took the sheet of paper out of my pocket. Catering block F23, it read. A couple more deep breaths and my head started to lift. I wasn't going to be beaten. Jonny was here and we were going to find F23.

The catering block was around the back. On entering, I saw it had its own restaurant, and there were many people in their chefs' whites, and some in black and white front of house uniforms too. In many respects, it wasn't unlike work.

Up the stairs and along the corridor, I followed the numbers – F19, F20, F21, then a storeroom with its door ajar and trolleys laden with fruit and vegetables, F22 and then F24. Where the hell was F23? I instantly went into panic mode and my heart thumped so hard in my chest I could not only feel it, I could hear it. I ran back down the corridor and started counting again, scanning each door one by one.

A man with a white beard appeared from F22. 'It's not John is it?' he said.

'Yes, John Crawshaw.'

'Ah, great, hello John, please come through. F23 is a little hard to find. It's out the back of F22, with it being a kitchen.'

I nodded and followed him to a large kitchen with stainless steel tables, just like we had at work, and little wooden tripod stools, which were already filled with the other students.

I took my seat and listened intently. I scanned the other people, who were also paying attention. There was a mixture of men and women, and of all ages. I was one of the youngest. Half the class were mature students and as we rotated around the group, introducing ourselves, I learned there were chefs from schools, hospitals and restaurants, and some completely mad people, just doing it for fun.

'We have just a few formalities to run through and a tour of the college, so you can get your bearings, and then this afternoon please be in your whites and back in this room at 1.30pm for our first practical session, making custard.'

I smiled. It wasn't like school at all.

Typically, the days were split between theory sessions on food hygiene, food poisoning bacteria, and the science and history of cooking, then solid practical in the afternoon. This last was all in French, as traditionally most of the culinary tools, equipment and techniques are French. Things are very different now, of course, with Asian and cultural influences, but back then that was the way.

I heard a French family talking on a campsite we were holi-daying at recently, and I heard someone say the phrase, '*mise en place*'. It instantly took me straight back there. *Oui, Chef*!

One thing which became apparent was that my college pals were all on a release day from work, but not me. I had to work an extra day, so I could have my college day off. It seemed unfair, but I was too shy to bring it up at work, so I left it. Apart from that, I felt things were finally on the up. I finally had a sense of real purpose. I did use Jonny a lot, especially when walking into the kitchen and classroom for the first time. Maybe moving schools when I was younger did teach me something, after all. I still felt it was Jonny who was able to do it, though. I was basically just the same as I'd always been, but with a few more tools in my toolkit.

One morning I slept past my alarm and was rushing to get to work on time. We had to be changed into our chef's whites and in the kitchen for 7am. That morning I had four minutes to get to work, and it was a fifteen-minute ride on the Kawasaki. Most of the route was a 30mph limit, but at that time in the morning I thought it would be unlikely for me to get caught speeding, so I overtook a car on a bend doing 80mph. The force pulled me out so much, I hit a bollard within a raised island and *bang*! The bike threw me off, and I slid thirty yards down the opposite side of the road on the face of my helmet. Thankfully I was wearing it. Apparently, I narrowly avoided a car coming the other way, or I'd have been dead, and the car occupants seriously injured. The next thing I knew was waking up in a hospital with a suspected ruptured spleen and internal bleeding and bruising.

The helmet and a whole lot of luck saved my face and my life that morning.

Mum was brilliant. She was there at my bedside when I came around, and although I could tell I'd scared her, she was there for me, with unconditional love and support as always.

The bike was a mangled write-off. The handlebars were wrapped around the rear wheel and the petrol tank beyond recognition. Apparently it wasn't worth the repairs, so that was the end of my motorbiking career.

The doctor briskly walked towards my bed and smiled as he approached. 'How are you feeling?' He picked up my notes from the end of the bed and cast his eye over them.

'I'm sore, and my left leg seems a bit weak,' I said, not really knowing what to say, as my whole body was in pain.

'It looks like you'll be fine. Your spleen is intact, you were lucky there, and there's some internal bruising, which will feel sore for a while, but otherwise, it seems someone was looking out for you.'

I nodded. I knew Gran had been up to the church and had the whole congregation praying for me, and strangely it did seem to help.

'I'm signing you off work for one month.'

Thankfully my spleen held out, and I was lucky to get away without breaking anything. It took a while to get walking properly again, and to a point where I could stand for long periods.

Dad took me to see the bike, and the sight of the crumpled-up machine made me think I would never get on a motorbike again. My confidence had taken a serious blow.

After a week my big boss, Mr Lewis, the General Manager, summoned me to his office for an update. He suggested that if I didn't return within the following week, he'd be forced to get someone else. He also told me that the kitchen was being contracted out to a big catering company. We would more than likely all keep our jobs, but we would have a different employer. He would have to justify my position to the new people, so he had to know.

I left his office, dragging my leg. Mum was waiting outside in the car, and everything ached inside me as I struggled to get into the seat.

'How'd it go?' she asked.

I sighed and tried to get comfortable. 'I don't want to talk about it.'

Mum nodded, and we drove in complete silence until we were pulling up outside the house. 'Don't worry, the main thing is, you just have to get well. Work can wait. You're no good to them if you can barely stand up. Let's get in, and I'll make some soup.'

Mum, of course, was right, but I just couldn't risk losing my job and entire career. She helped me in, and I sat on the sofa, contemplating what to do. The agonising thoughts in my head were interrupted with a bowl of hot minestrone soup with strange black croutons and an earthy, carbony aftertaste. A thick slice of bread and butter made it all good, though. I sipped the soup from the spoon slowly, as I focused again on what my decision should be. I could barely walk, let alone stand on my feet for eight hours. I would have to tell him I couldn't go back the following week and that he should look for someone else.

I didn't sleep that night. To be honest, I was feeling sorry for myself. Why did I have to take that corner at 80mph? Why was I such an idiot? Why was life so unfair? The following day I snoozed in bed until dinner time. Mum was at work, so I got up and found she'd made some sandwiches and there was a can of Coke. I smiled and felt loved.

I tried standing on the hard kitchen floor in my bare feet to see how long I could manage. It was okay on my good leg, but the pain inside me was a strain and I only lasted about four minutes. I collapsed on the sofa and tucked into my sandwiches, but all the while I knew I had to make that call.

I wasn't fit to go back to work and I'd have to give him the bad news. I had mates at college who were working in the industry, and there might be opportunities for chefs if I asked them.

The phone started to ring in the hall, so I ignored it. Whoever it was rang off but then rang again a minute later. Maybe it was Mum checking on me.

Again it went quiet, and then five minutes later it rang again. I dragged myself to it and picked up the receiver.

'John?'

'Yes.'

'Mr Lewis here. What news do you have? I can't keep waiting, I have someone interested in your job if you're not able to get in next week.'

'Oh! Mr Lewis. Erm… Erm… I'm feeling much better today and yes, all good for next week.' A shudder went through my body and I couldn't quite believe what I'd said.

'Good. That makes things easier for me. See you Monday, 7am sharp.'

The line went dead before I had a chance to reply. I slowly put the receiver back onto the base and sat on the bottom step of the stairs, gazing blankly through the frosted window by the door.

So, I went back to work, and a week later, college. My leg had taken a battering. It wasn't broken, but some damage had occurred and had been overseen by the doctors as they concentrated on the internal injuries. For the first month or two, I had to drag it around, because it was painful to put my heel down and fully straighten it. I had no physio, and I didn't have the gumption to ask for any. I painfully and gradually trained my body again to do the hours, which were entirely spent on my feet. I took painkillers every day, and in the evenings I was dead to the world. Sometimes I collapsed on my bed fully clothed and then the following morning just got up, brushed my teeth and then caught the bus into work again. What doesn't kill you makes you stronger, Mum would say. Well, it definitely does. When you're hurting inside but have no choice, it takes something away from you, which I think you can reclaim later, but tenfold. Easy to say now, but at the time it was excruciating.

The good news was, I kept my job, and not only that, I passed my first year at college, despite the unexpected gap in learning. I was halfway to becoming a qualified chef. What surprised me about college was, I actually enjoyed it. Maybe that was partly because I had a goal and was interested in the subject matter, but it was also because a great deal of it was practical, and the exam was multiple choice, so no major writing was required, just ticking boxes.

Amber left school that summer and got a job in a local travel agents. She was great with people, always had a smile and a get-up-and-go energy about her. She was a natural salesperson. Her snipping washing lines days were long gone and she was now a young woman. I called in to the shop to see her. She looked professional in her uniform and blue and gold cravat.

Towards the end of the summer, Amber rang me at work. Mr Lewis scowled as he told me she was on the phone in his office. I wondered what was going on and dashed in to hear what the problem was.

'Can you get ten days off work? We went in early this morning because the big travel companies were releasing all the cheap deals for us to put in the window, and I've managed to get one myself. It's ten days in Greece. Crete, to be exact. We don't know where we'll be staying until we get there, but it's cheap.'

I looked at Mr Lewis. 'Erm, I'm not sure. Ten days you say?'

She jumped straight back at me. 'I have it on hold right now. If I leave it any longer, it will be gone. It's £20 each including flights and insurance. You deserve it, bro.'

I held the receiver to my chest and asked Mr Lewis if I could have time off. He scrunched up his mouth and shook his head and then told me I still had annual leave to take before the end of the year, so yes.

'Book it.'

'We don't know where we're staying.'

'Book it.'

'Will do. I'll tell you all about it later.'

I put the phone down and smiled at Mr Lewis, who didn't smile back. Instead, he quickly ushered me out of the door and slammed it behind me.

So there we were, the two of us, jetting off to Crete, and by complete chance it was the first ever Air2000 flight. We were given free bucks fizz, and Amber chatted with the flight attendant and managed to get us up in the cockpit with the pilot and co-pilot, who, disturbingly, both had their backs turned on the business end of the plane. One of them was eating his meal. Who the hell was flying this thing? I thought nervously, looking out into acres of nothingness.

It didn't take me long to realise I didn't like flying. I didn't like the feeling of being out of control. Back in my seat, I gripped the armrest for the rest of the flight, and nearly went into a panic attack at the hint of any turbulence. Coming into land was by far the worst. The plane bucked and wove in the air as it descended. By the time we were finally on the ground, I was a nervous wreck.

We ended up in a four-star hotel, half-board. We never saw a cloud while we were there. Amber was worried I was cramping her style with the local boys, but I felt she was kind of glad I was there, too.

We did a really stupid thing and hired a motorbike for a week. My biking history was obviously not impressive or safe, so a big trials bike, capable of off-roading with lots of grunt, coupled with no helmets, was risky to say the least. We explored the island, found deserted beaches and felt the wind in our hair. We loved it, and we laughed and laughed at our newfound holiday freedom. One day we actually ran over a snake, which was crossing the road. It was unavoidable as it just came out of the grass right in front of us. We both saw it and raised our legs simultaneously in fear of it biting us as it folded in half. I'd like to say no snakes were harmed in the writing of this book, but unfortunately we almost certainly killed it.

After a few days we purchased some coconut oil tanning lotion. It had zero protection, but it was good at frying your skin. We were in the knowledge that you had to burn first to get a good tan, and that was easy for me, being as white as a sheet and blue-eyed.

By day two, my whole body was on fire, but the worst affected part of my body was my ears. I burned them really badly and had to wear toilet paper over them for the rest of the holiday. The photographs looked hideous, but it turned out to be just the break I needed, and although sore from ears to toes, we relaxed, recuperated and came home feeling invigorated.

15

GIRLS

In 1987 I turned eighteen. Dave, Smiler and I, and a few other hangers-on, became fully ensconced in the night-club scene. The dance floors were buzzing with Kim Wilde, Depeche Mode, Whitney, Rick Astley, Johnny Hates Jazz, Michael Jackson and Bananarama. To mention a few.

We'd meet early evening at the bus station and crawl around a few city-centre pubs, before heading to one of the many clubs in town. The guys liked to drink, and they could handle it. Eight or ten pints of lager were easy for them, but for me, two was my limit. Well, when I say two, it was actually one. I got drunk very quickly. I tried to do eight pints one night and woke up in a bus shelter at 4am with fag ends and crisp packets stuck in my hair after being thrown off the bus for being sick. It felt like I'd been poisoned.

Most people are able to overcome shyness with alcohol, but for me, it made it worse. And it literally made me go to sleep. I preferred to be dancing, and clubbing was a great opportunity to dance with girls. I was, of course, too frightened to make the first move, and many opportunities to strike up a conversation were sadly missed. My work at the prison had brought me out of my shell to some extent, but there was no changing what was inside. It was still me, and that thing, whatever it was inside me, was still there. I guess it was a fear of making a mistake and looking foolish, or that people might think I was uninteresting. Dancing on the loud dance floors was fine though. There was no talking to do, just moving to the music, and that was a language all on its own. My stutter was always lurking in the back of my throat and ready to be triggered, and so dancing became a whole new way to communicate.

One night I was dancing on the central dance floor in Casablanca's. Smiler was my wingman, and we were aiming our attention at two gorgeous, tanned brunette girls. Smiler was doing some chat with one of them in her ear. Suddenly he waved me over, and the girls followed. He'd only gone and pulled. He shouted in my ear that he was going to the bar for drinks for the four of us and that I sit with them and keep them company.

'Oh, and by the way, they're French,' he said, as he dashed to the bar.

Oh, great. I sat down and twiddled my thumbs, trying to think what to say. My anxious leg kicked in, but I disguised it as tapping to the beat and I smiled. My stutter was now on the tip of my tongue and every time I began to talk, nothing came out. Taking deep breaths was a good way around it, because I could release the word on the out breath, which for some reason seemed much easier. But this did make me look like a creepy heavy breather.

I turned to the girl Smiler hadn't been talking to and tried to speak.

'*Je – Je – Je –*' I tried again, and she looked at me as if I were some kind of freak. '*Je – Je suis un chef*,' I blurted out, in my best French accent.

The girl looked puzzled. She gave a shrug and immediately turned to chat with her friend beside her.

Smiler appeared at that point, holding two piña coladas. As

he sat down, he whispered in my ear. 'Spanish, mate. Sorry, they're Spanish.' The girls got up and walked off while Smiler looked at me in complete disgust.

My luck with girls was not going well and they always seemed drawn to confident guys.

Later that week I bumped into Tom, a friend from the milk round. He was now attending a teacher training college. The campus was only a couple of miles up the road from home and situated in the vast, mature grounds of an old stately home. (The campus is now the Yorkshire Sculpture Park. It exhibits Henry Moore and Barbara Hepworth sculptures, as well as many others, in permanent and temporary displays. The college no longer exists, but some of the old buildings are still to be seen, derelict and being taken over once again by brambles, buddleia and small trees.)

Tom invited me to an event at college one Saturday evening. He said it should to be a good night, as there was a stage hypnotist performing at the student union bar. It was all supposed to be a great deal of fun, with the usual suspects guaranteed to get the limelight and make a fool of themselves. We met at the halls of residence, and I was introduced to the rest of the group. They were chatting and laughing about the hypnotist, but one of the girls appeared to be taking it very seriously.

'It's not real, you know,' I said.

She looked at me with complete disdain. 'What do you know? Anyway, who are you?'

I tried to look unflustered. 'I'm a friend of Tom's. He invited me. Who are you?'

'Melanie. It's just my mum had a few issues some years ago and went to see a hypnotist, and it helped her hugely.'

I was dying to ask 'What issues?' but thought it might get me into a deeper hole. So I just replied with, 'Nice to meet you, anyway, Melanie. I'm John. Sorry if I offended you, it's just I've seen hypnotists on TV, and it all looks fake to me. The people they choose seem to be the ones with egos and a taste for fame.'

She looked me straight in the eye. 'Sounds just like you, Mr John.'

My next line was stolen from me with the sound of Tom ushering everyone to the door, suggesting we were going to be late. I left it there, but I'd admired the way her eyes had shimmered in the light of the hallway and felt how appealing her dimples were – even though she was scowling at me.

We all sat on the floor in front of the stage in the union bar, in anticipation. My scepticism hadn't waned, despite my chat with cute Melanie.

Volunteers were asked to show their willingness to be humiliated, and there was a flurry of hands in the air. Not mine. Tom put his hand up, but wasn't chosen, and Melanie chose to keep her hand down, too, which I acknowledged with a glance. She reciprocated with a raised eyebrow and some more disapproval.

Surprisingly, the usual suspects were not chosen. Well, a few were, but they were promptly sent back to their seats as 'not suitable'.

The hypnotist had all the chosen ones sitting on chairs in a line on the stage. He went steadily along the line, tapping each one individually on the shoulder, and 'putting them into a trance'. Yeah, right.

The eight people chosen were, according to Tom, not the ones you would expect, and a 'strange choice', but my confidence that the whole thing was a charade was bolstered when one of the chosen ones started thinking she was an alien and had to speak in an alien tongue.

The next 'victim' was a tall, well-built rugby type. Six foot three and the size of a house. The hypnotist was only around five foot eight. He squared up to him and looked straight into his chest, lifting his chin while the lad looked down. They stared at each other for an uncomfortable two or three minutes. The audience didn't know whether to laugh or not. Then suddenly the hypnotist tapped the lad on the shoulder, and promptly sent him back to his seat within the audience.

We all glanced at each other in bewildered interest, and the show continued. I looked on with indignant disbelief as people thought they were ballet dancers and ate onions as if enjoying juicy apples. Gradually, one by one, the victims were 'brought out of their hypnotic state' and sent back to the crowd.

The hypnotist walked to the front of the stage with his arms open wide, bowing his head while everyone applauded. Just when we thought it was all over, he pointed into the crowd with a straight and certain arm. The place went uncomfortably silent, and everyone peered to see what he was pointing at. The big guy from before, the rugby lad, stood straight up and began walking to the stage.

The silence turned to muttering as rugby lad stepped on up, and an eeriness filled the air. He reached the stage and eyeballed the hypnotist. Once again, the staring went on for what seemed like forever – and then the hypnotist announced he was going to give rugby lad a chance to hypnotise him. No one entirely understood, but he explained he was going to count the lad in, and he instructed him to click his fingers on three.

Rugby lad nodded, and the audience fell silent.

One. The big lad looked at the audience and smiled.

Two. The hypnotist relaxed his shoulders.

Three. Rugby lad lifted up his huge fingers and '*click*'.

At that exact moment, the hypnotist stood rigid to the spot, but the big guy fell like a bag of bones crashing to the floor. There was no faking it. No falling onto one knee first or a hand to steady him as he fell. He went down as if he were dead. *Bang!* He'd clicked his own fingers and put himself under. This was completely unexpected by the audience, but equally unexpected by the big guy. There was a unanimous gasp. The hypnotist touched the guy gently on the shoulder and spoke quietly in his ear as he helped him to a seat on the stage. The weird thing was, the rugby lad seemed unaware of the whole thing. He looked confused, and in a daze. He wasn't laughing with embarrassment or gloating with bravado. He was, to all intents and purposes, hypnotised.

My eyes flicked rapidly between the two figures on stage, searching for the slightest hint this was all a set-up. I couldn't believe how hard the guy had hit the ground. It was as if he were a puppet with his strings suddenly cut, and with gravity at a thousand times the norm.

Applause filled the room. The hypnotist thanked everyone and gestured to the big guy for everyone to applaud him, and then the lights came on and muttering could again be heard as people began to stand from their positions on the floor. I was dumbfounded. It seemed so real and I began to question my scepticism.

We all slowly started walking back to the halls of residence and I came alongside Melanie. She had a tear in her eye and was holding a tissue to her nose.

I struggled to speak and cleared my throat. 'Sorry for what I said earlier. I'm an idiot, so sorry. That was a powerful experience.'

'Don't worry, John, we all say things sometimes when we don't understand.'

'Are you okay?'

'My mum passed away last year. She'd had a rough few years, with deep anxiety and a few other issues. Her hypnotism gave her peace when she really needed it. I wasn't going to go tonight, but what's the point of running scared? You have to face these things.'

I nodded. 'You're so right. We all have something that holds us back from time to time, but it's no good letting it rule us.'

I offered her my arm as it was dark and the path a little uneven. The others had quickly walked on ahead of us. She put her arm through mine, and we strolled and chatted some more. I could tell she was very intelligent. She used words like 'exhibitionism' and 'incoherent' – words I stayed well away from, in case I made a fool of myself, but I listened intently. We came out into an open grassy area, where the path negotiated a small pond. A barn owl flew in front of us and then over our heads, its white underside picked out by the various lamps that lit the way. Melanie was a little scared. She held my arm with both hands and came close in to me. I wasn't scared of an owl. I'd seen many from my treetop hideaway, and the thought that she was scared of the unknown made me feel strong and protective.

'It's a barn owl, hunting,' I said.

She continued to hold onto my arm. 'I thought it was a ghost.'

'Don't worry, it won't harm us. It's just looking for its supper.'

She looked at me. Her eyes were shining, just like they had earlier, but this time they sparkled. 'What do they eat?'

'They like mice and voles, and even young rats occasionally.'

'Wow, that's interesting. You've obviously read lots about them.'

I looked at her for a moment. Do I tell her I hadn't ever read a book? Well, other than looking at pictures of butterflies. I stumbled with my words. 'Oh! Erm, I –'

'I like reading, too,' she said. 'I'm reading *The Hobbit* at the moment. Do you like Tolkien?'

I thought for a second. Tolkien sounded like an Austrian beer, and I had no idea what the Hobbit was, so I nodded and smiled.

'I like Bilbo Baggins,' she said, with a big smile.

'Does he eat rats too?'

She laughed and held my arm tight. 'You know, when I met you earlier, I thought you were arrogant, but you made me laugh,

I like that, and the things about the barn owl made me forget about my sadness. Thank you.'

What a lovely thing to say. I stopped walking and turned to her. I put my hand gently on her face. Her skin was soft. I brushed her cheek with my thumb and then I slowly but purposefully pulled her closer, so that our lips just touched. My heart was pounding ten to the dozen, but I remained cool and composed. I pulled away slightly to give her a chance to break the embrace if she felt uncomfortable, but instead, she put her lips back on mine, and we locked together. It was a kiss I'll never forget. It was so tender. She felt vulnerable and delicate in my arms, but I was excited by her. Excited by our differences and excited by her soulfulness and compassion. I remember kissing and kissing as if it were the only thing we needed to stay alive. She was beautiful.

I walked her back to her accommodation block. It was appropriate not to overstay my welcome, so we said our good-byes and we had a last kiss, which was like nothing I'd ever known before, and somehow, I knew she felt the same.

I walked up the hill to my bus stop and kept looking back. She waved a couple of times and then after the third time she disappeared inside. I spent the whole of the journey home with a massive smile on my face. I remember the bus driver thinking I was drunk, and he told me not to be sick on the back seat. Little did he know how elated I was. This girl was special, and it wouldn't be long before I was back on the bus for another visit.

It was two weeks, to be exact. Work was demanding, and I was working sixteen-hour shifts at the prison. My sister's birthday weekend, and a couple of other engagements I couldn't get out of, prevented the quick return I craved. Of course, there were no mobile phones, and I didn't have the number for the hall of residence, so I jumped on the bus on Tuesday evening, and with great anticipation headed for Tom's room first and then, hopefully, to catch up with Melanie if she wasn't too busy.

I knocked on Tom's door, and after a few seconds he opened it. 'John, I thought the hypnotist had scared you away. How're things?'

'I've been busy,' I said impatiently. 'Look, you know Melanie, who came with us that evening. Which room is she in?'

Tom looked at me in complete surprise.

'Melanie with the stunning eyes,' I went on.

He paused. 'She's dead, mate. She suffocated herself when she went home last weekend. Why are you so interested?'

If you've ever experienced a hollowness so hollow you feel like you are depleted of every nerve and fibre and the ability to ever feel anything ever again, that was how the news hit me. I was empty. Drained of all feeling, numb, out of control and panicky. I kept touching my forehead in disbelief. I walked away without a word and went and sat up in the woods, where I could sit in solitude and pour my heart out to the trees.

I wondered what she must have been going through to take her to the end. If only I'd returned sooner, could I have helped her? I had my own things to deal with, but I could have taught her more about nature and how it seemed to help me. I became transfixed by a leaf falling effortlessly to the ground and as I focused intently on it, I suddenly felt much calmer. My eyes were fixed on the leaf and nothing else. I felt myself going under, like into the void, but this time no page full of meaningless words, just a leaf. My peripheral vision was acute, but also focused sharply on the leaf. I wasn't able to move. It was as though I were hypnotised.

16

HUMILIATION

At nearly nineteen, I felt like I'd overstayed my welcome at home. I still got on okay with Mum, despite the 'board and lodging', but Derek was now a permanent fixture, and one day she'd announced we were all moving in together into a new house. Derek was charming with Amber and she seemed to like him. I found it a bit creepy, and I could see he was trying too hard with Mum, too. There was a falseness about him I just didn't like. He tried to be matey with me at first, with gestures like helping me with repairs on my car, but things soon turned sour.

My car was a peppermint-green 1.1L Fiesta, with a black spoiler and dual fog lamps, which I'd fitted myself. They never made that colour after that, surprisingly. I loved it, though, despite the rain leaking into the footwell and the fact it had no stereo. A ghetto blaster on the backseat more than made up for it, but that's exactly why the car needed repairs. I was driving home from work one day and as I turned around to flip over my tape, the traffic in front of me stopped suddenly at a pelican crossing. Except I didn't. I was only third-party insured, so there was a fair bit of 'self-repair' work to be done.

Derek soon turned into a grumpy old man, and he didn't seem happy with anything I did. In fact, he secretly became quite mean. Not with my mum and Amber. He still had them eating out of his hand, but to me, he wasn't the 'great guy' they thought he was. Anyway, it was Mum's relationship and shouldn't have been any of my business, but there was something which made it feel very much my concern.

I'd witnessed him talking down to Mum, belittling her, and most often in front of other people. I felt he was controlling her, in a very subtle way. Nothing aggressive, just psychologically, it seemed.

We were at a friend's barbecue and Mum was instructed to bring bread and coleslaw. The organisers were obviously aware of her penchant for overcooking things and had gone for a safe bet, but on arrival she realised she'd forgotten to bring the coleslaw she'd been preparing all of the previous day. To be honest, it wasn't such a bad thing, especially since she'd used pickled onions, because we'd run out of normal ones. Anyway, there was plenty of other food which others had brought, so it wasn't an issue. Except for Derek.

'Where's the coleslaw?' he boomed, so that everyone could hear, even above the music. 'You're hopeless at remembering things. How many times did I tell you not to forget it?'

Mum looked embarrassed. 'I know, sorry. I wanted to leave it in the fridge till the last minute.'

'I'll have to go back and get it. We can't have burgers without coleslaw. You'll have to make everyone wait now until I go back and help you out of this mess.'

I couldn't help but say, 'That's crazy. It's just some coleslaw and it's an hour's drive there and back.'

'Stay out of this, lad.'

I could see everyone was uncomfortable, but especially Mum.

'I'll go, I'm so sorry, I am getting forgetful,' she said,

looking flustered and continuing to look in her bag for it, in the hope it would magically materialise and calm the situation.

'This is your fault I'm having to go back all that way. I can't be there to remind you about everything.'

There was an uneasy atmosphere and people were beyond hungry. Derek insisted on going back for it. Mum was consoled by her friend in the conservatory. Another hour went by, with no sign of the offending coleslaw.

'Does anyone want a sausage to put you on?' said one of the dads, and everyone raised a hand. I decided to load my plate and all the other kids, too, followed by everyone else. After three hours Derek returned, with some excuse about a flat tyre. I rolled my eyes and gave Mum a hug and then she laid out the bowl, still flustered. No one touched the coleslaw, other than Derek. I watched him with disdain as he munched on his burger and complained it tasted a bit vinegary.

I didn't like what I was seeing, and it made my stomach turn. What could I say, though? Nothing much. I tried to talk to Mum, but she shrugged it off as him being new into the family and me being a little touchy.

A few weeks later, Mum and Derek announced they were holding a murder mystery dinner for Mum's friend Pat and her family, who she'd just reconnected with. *Murder on the Orient Express*. We all sat around the dining room table – Mum, Derek, Amber, me and four people I'd never met before. They seemed friendly, and off we went. At various stages, certain people had to read a passage from the card they were given, and then questions would be answered, with a view to establishing who was the murderer.

Mum started by reading out her card in a very posh accent. 'I'm travelling to visit my lawyer after the death of my very wealthy sister. Escorting me is my travel companion and very good friend Eduardo.' (I was Eduardo.) 'I do hope this train journey won't be too much longer.'

'I'm sorry to hear of your news,' Pat said in a convincing Italian accent, reading from her card. 'How long will you be staying away?'

Mum dropped into character again. 'Just until the will is read and everything settled.'

Amber was next, assuming the role of the train's waitress. 'Drinks everyone. Who ordered the sparkling Champagne?'

I could see my part was approaching, and my mouth started to dry. I shuffled on my seat. Both legs felt as if they weren't in touch with the ground and they began to tremble. I knew I would inevitably stumble reading my card. In front of family that was okay, but there were strangers present.

Amber finished her piece. 'Don't leave it too long, the rumbling of the train can make it go flat very quickly.'

The next line was my cue and my anxiety started to take a stranglehold on my throat. I tried to subtly cough to clear it, and everyone thought it was part of the script, so I waved my hands and coughed again to show it wasn't.

'That Champagne looks very dark for an early vintage,' Derek boomed in his typecast role as the chief inspector.

There was a silence. A long silence, and everyone looked nervously at each other, and then all eyes were on me, I could feel them penetrating my brain and making it go to mush.

'H – H – H – Here, let me see that bottle. It's a Dom Per – Pe – Per – Peri –' I didn't understand the word and I couldn't spit it out. I felt embarrassed. I was stuttering and I was letting everyone down.

'Here we go, watch the dyslexia, lad,' Derek said with a hint of a smile. But no one else was smiling.

I froze. I wanted to be sucked up and taken straight out of the humiliation. I could see everyone looking at me. I looked at Derek, who was now laughing. I stood up and threw my card on the table and made a hasty escape to the kitchen. Mum followed me, and I told her that it was totally unacceptable, and I wasn't going to be carrying on. She tried to calm me and persuade me to go back in, but I couldn't face any more embarrassment. I slammed the back door and headed out for a walk.

How dare he say that in front of those people about dyslexia? What did he know? It wasn't as if I had a disease like that. It was outrageous. He'd made me feel small, and once again I felt worthless and inadequate.

I'd rushed out without a coat. Within minutes I was drenched to the core, but I carried on walking. The torrential water was running down my face and soaking up through my shoes. I strode along, soaking and freezing, but determined not to go back. I began contemplating an escape plan, anything to get me out of there A mate from college had just got himself a chef's job on the QEII. That was an option, I thought, sailing around the world. Or maybe just travelling, backpacking or something.

I eventually became so cold, I could barely move. I sat under a holly tree, which gave a little shelter, and sobbed.

It all came to a head one day when I hadn't shut the gates to the drive, like he always insisted upon. When I entered the house I could hear him criticising Mum about how stupid she looked doing her yoga. I went straight back out and busied myself trying to find where the water was leaking into my car. I started to prize off the rubber seal around the door with a screwdriver. Out of the corner of my eye, I spotted him coming out of the kitchen, past the other side of the car and down to the end of the drive to close the gates. He slammed them shut, making an exaggerated point about them, then, as he came back up the drive, he came up behind me.

'The gates have to be closed every time you leave and every time you enter, for security. How many times do I have to tell you? Are you stupid or something?

Well, that was it. I turned around. 'Don't tell me what to do, you controller. You can't control me like you do Mum.'

At that, he grabbed me by my shirt and pulled me up to his

face. 'Don't you ever talk to me like that you pathetic, stupid boy.'

He made me feel helpless and worthless.

I could feel the screwdriver in my hand, and I gripped it tight. 'Let go of me now, you psychopath,' I said, struggling to get free. He was much taller than me, and he pulled me up further by the collar, so it was difficult to breathe. 'I'm onto you,' I said, struggling for breath. He then lifted me up so that my feet were off the floor, pushed me up against the wall and continued to tighten his hold around my neck. I started to panic. My breathing was almost halted. It was at that point, and in sheer panic, I increased my grip on the screwdriver and brought it up, so that the tip was touching his neck and just under his jaw. I pushed it up against his skin.

'Go on, then,' he said, goading me.

I felt the urge so bad to push it in and to be released from his tightening hold. I gripped the handle tighter and pushed the long metal shaft so that it indented his skin. My breath was weak, and I was beginning to choke, but he wasn't relenting. I looked him deep in the eyes. This was for Mum, not for me, and the intention must have been clear in my expression. Suddenly, he let go and I dropped to my feet on the ground. I stood hands on knees gasping for breath as he walked away from me. I held the screwdriver tight again, still angry that someone would do that to me, and then let it drop to the floor as I fought for my breath.

17

SCAR

An enormous wave battered the boat, then another, and as I struggled to keep afloat, I lost one of the oars overboard. With the other oar, I tried to stop the boat spinning around in the vicious wind. I thrust my hand into the freezing water in the hope of recovering my only way of powering the tiny wooden craft. My hand touched something just below the surface, something hard, but the sea was dark, and every time I made my desperate grasp, the relentless waves thrust me out of my seat, and I had to use both hands to stop myself being thrown out into the vast ocean.

There was nothing I could do. I was a tiny object in a ferocious and unrelenting sea. With just one oar, I had no way to direct myself and no escape. I thrust my hand back into the water. An almighty wave came side on, drenching me to the skin and filling the boat, so I was sitting in the bitter cold. I was sinking. Frantically I attempted to bail the water with my hands, but it was futile. I could sense my impending doom. I let go of the other oar and held on tightly to the wooden seat as, once again, a powerful wave hit the boat and tried to knock me overboard.

And then another, and then finally a swell so deep, I felt almost weightless and then... *Crash*!

I opened my eyes. Gradually I made out the back end of a half-finished Lego naval submarine wedged under my bed, and an old school sock dangling from the springs. I lay on the cold floor, shaking. The sock had been there for years. I grasped tightly onto the carpet and reassured myself I was okay. I hadn't had a nightmare like that for a while.

In the dark days to follow, I often thought about Melanie. I was finding it impossible to come to terms with her death. She'd left a big hole. I didn't understand why exactly, and I kept telling myself, I was stupid feeling like that, because I'd hardly got to know her.

My mind was all over the place and I struggled to see a way forward. I was entering into a dark place and lost all motivation. I was trying to process too much at once and the enormity of everything bore down on me with overwhelming force.

Months went by in which I just drifted. Like a tiny boat cast adrift in a mighty ocean, aimlessly going nowhere.

My home life was unbearable. I felt out of control and lost in a mire of uncertainty and unhappiness.

I needed an escape, and the bright lights of the city became an obvious draw. The weekends were wild, and there was always an air of danger as brawl after brawl spilled out onto the streets. Blue lights and sirens were a regular feature, along with the crowds of revellers queuing to get into the vast array of pubs and clubs.

The bus pulled into the bus station, and Dave and Smiler were waiting as usual under the clock. I wore a white shirt and black trousers, black leather shoes and no socks. They had on their open-necked shirts and jackets, and they'd obviously spent half the day on their big hairstyles. I jelled my hair and looked like a sad Adam Ant, some said. It was a persona I liked to hide behind, another incarnation of Jonny. Jonny dressed on-trend, and he looked confident. The music of that year made him come alive. The pubs and clubs of the city were the perfect places in which to lose myself in the vibe of 1988.

Casablanca's and Skyrock Gardens were our clubs of choice. They were next to each other, and at a certain time in the night they opened a door between, so you could dance to different music and go and see what new female talent might be in the other place.

In Skyrock Gardens there were little tables, which we used to load with pints of beer. This was easy when it was 10p a pint night, and of course I usually only spent 10p, whereas the others would push the boat out and commit a whole £1. The only thing preventing a complete tableful, was the red telephone in the middle of each one. These had huge numbers on, 01, 02, etc. If you fancied the girls on 04, you could call them up and ask them for a dance. The phone would light up and everyone would scream until someone was brave enough to answer.

That's how I met my new girlfriend, Sasha. I'd spotted her at the bar earlier, and it was Dave who called their table.

'My mate thinks you're gorgeous, table 07,' he said, while I tried to look cool and nonchalant, 'and your mate's all right, too!'

Sasha was hot – and I mean *hot*. Long blonde hair, tall, curvy, she wore a white dress with power shoulders and a split that ran all the way up one leg. I remember thinking she was stunning and too good for me. Anyway, Dave had done the deed, and the next thing I knew we were all on the dance floor. I liked to lose myself dancing, and so did Sasha. We danced all night together, and we laughed as the sole of one of my shoes starting to come away at the toe. I looked like a tramp with old shoes but managed to make light of it. I bought drinks, and we made it all the way to the slow songs at the end of the evening. I'd missed my bus, and Dave and Smiler were long gone. It was just us, and as we came close together for a slow one, I put my hands on her hips, and she put hers on my shoulders. I pulled her closer and gave her a kiss on the cheek. She smiled, and we carried on dancing until the bouncers started to clear us out of the building. I waited for her dad to come and pick her up. It didn't give us much time, but I thought, what the hell? I pushed her up against the wall of the kebab shop and kissed her full on the lips. She responded and – well, it was like dynamite. I had to walk the five miles home that night as I'd run out of money, but it was worth it, and I floated on air.

I don't know how I managed to pull her, but something clicked between us and she made me feel a whole lot better about my life. We took things steady for a few weeks and started to develop a relationship. Amber had told me not to rush things with a girl, take things slowly, and always ask if she's okay with what you're doing. Great advice and I stuck to the plan.

Sasha was a year younger than me and in sixth form doing 'A' levels. She was bright and, jeeze, that made her even more attractive. After we started going out together we would do stuff at the weekend, playing tennis or badminton, walking in the woods and climbing trees, or go for coffee somewhere in the Fiesta. The car was an immense conduit to freedom for us as a couple. One Sunday I picked Sasha up and told her we were going on an adventure. She pressured me to tell her, but I managed to keep it a secret. We drove across the Pennines to Manchester Airport and parked in the multi-storey car park.

'Here we are,' I proclaimed, with great joy.

'Are we going somewhere? Are we getting on a plane? I haven't a bag, or clothes, or anything.' She looked a little nervous.

'No, silly. I thought we'd have a day at the airport, look at the planes and have some dinner. There's shops, too.'

I thought it was a genius idea, but from the sour look on Sasha's face I didn't think she was impressed.

We did have an enjoyable day in the end, and I bought here a little purse, which she loved. I enjoyed being a man and making plans and the car enabled us to grow our relationship and spend quality time together. As the weeks progressed, I used to drop in when she was babysitting for a neighbour. It was forbidden by her parents, but we risked it. The car was very noticeable so I used to park half a mile away, so as not to be rumbled, and slowly we got to know each other more and more.

Friday nights, though, were sacrosanct and were always a lads' and lasses' night. Not a night for couples – Saturday or Sunday was more for that – so what we used to do was go out with our mates, have a few beers (in Dave's case a few crates), and then I would meet up with Sasha towards the end of the evening in a club or pub for a dance and a smooch.

One place we regularly used to meet in was Bitz. It was a pub with a grubby club/disco bit right at the end and was reportedly the 'longest bar in England'. Bitz was handy because you didn't have to pay to get in and, although small, they always played great music.

One particular Friday night, the lads had consumed their bodyweights in beer and gone for a curry, but for some reason that night I hadn't drunk at all. I never really did anyway. Besides the adverse effect it had on me, I didn't actually like the taste of it. I participated in the buying of rounds and then would tip mine in a rubber plant or leave it on the bar.

I left the lads and went to meet Sasha in Bitz for the last dance and, hopefully, some full-on snogging too. It was a bit of a strange night, because I had a weird feeling inside me, a kind of apprehension. I put it down to being excited to see Sasha, but Smiler had had a Malibu and pineapple thrown all over him when he inadvertently walked past a couple having a row, Robbo had gone home early after being violently sick, and Dave had apprehended someone trying to steal his wallet out of his back pocket. All of us had dodged the usual brawls and people puking out of doorways. Fortunately, I remained unscathed.

The lads disappeared and I carried on up Westgate to the pub to fight my way in through the crowds of people at the door. It was a popular place, and it wasn't easy to get anywhere fast. Eventually I managed to negotiate myself to the disco end, and amongst the flashing lights and people dancing, I spotted Sasha in six-inch red heels and skin-tight red dress with a low-cut back. Wow, she looked incredible, and she was all mine.

The dance floor was crowded. I made my way over to her, trying to fit into the beat and flow of other people's movements, so as not to barge into anyone. I caught her eye and started dancing with her. In those days, you just danced in front of each other, and it wasn't until the smoochy songs came on that you got close and touched each other.

We were dancing to Starship's 'Nothing's Going to Stop Us Now', and she smiled at me in that way which made my legs go to jelly. At that point, a tall lad, who must have been six foot plus, started to invade our space and began dancing as if we were a threesome, and after a very short time, started to grind his pelvis very close to Sasha, trying to block me out. She ignored him, but he carried on. We were used to drunk idiots pretending they were John Travolta. Usually after a minute or two they fell over or went to pester someone else.

This guy was different. He had a purposeful look in his eye and was deliberately trying to sideline me. I wasn't going to be pushed to one side, so I danced a little closer to her, to show her he was no threat, but suddenly he tried grabbing her hand. She shrugged him off, but he came back and tried to hold her hand again. That was totally out of order. I leant over and shouted 'On your bike, mate' and gestured to the door. My heart was racing, and I was shit-scared, but I couldn't let another man take my girl.

To my complete surprise, he just walked away. I'd done it. I'd got a bit of courage from somewhere and seen him off. I knew I could do it when I needed to and I held my head high. I immediately took Sasha by the hands and started to dance closer.

'Are you okay?' I asked gallantly. She nodded and gave me a kiss on the cheek. I knew a girl couldn't resist a bit of bravery and my anticipation grew as I longed for the snogging to commence.

At this point, my whole life changed. Not just a little bit, but fundamentally, forever. I felt a tap on my shoulder. Probably Dave fancying a late-night boogie after his curry, I thought, but no. It was the tall, weedy guy, back for more. For a split second, I remember his eyes looking down at me. To this day I thought they looked red, like the Devil's, and then it happened. Out of the blue, and as quick as lightning, I felt the full-on impact of a pint glass being stabbed straight in my face.

I fell to the floor and remember being kicked in the head three or four times before it stopped. I was left feeling disorientated, brutalised and blind. I couldn't see anything as I crawled along the floor, trying to get to my feet. My head was a blur of loud thumping music, panic, and total confusion. I managed to feel my way to the top of a fire escape, and as I opened the door, I fell down the metal steps into the alleyway at the side of the club.

I lay there in a heap and my fingers automatically went onto my face. I tried to feel my eyes to open them, but all I could feel was blood gushing out. I can't remember any pain at that point, but what was to come put me into shock. I could open my right eye a little, which gave me enough sight to orientate myself as I stumbled up the trash-filled alley for help. I distinctly remember putting my fingers into my nose. It was hanging off. My fingers went into a perfect slit right across my face, and I could feel the soft flesh inside, which didn't feel right at all. I crumpled on the floor amongst the broken bottles, bricks and debris and tried to fix my partially attached nose back to my face by pushing it into place, but it didn't feel part of me anymore.

I staggered into the main road where a few people helped me to my feet. I remember them saying, 'Shit, that looks bad.' I could only see a faint blue flashing light in front of me, and then someone said, with authority, 'What's this, then? Another Friday-night brawl? You'd better get in here.'

I said nothing and clambered into the back of the ambulance.

The next thing I remember was waking up in the hospital with Mum by my side. I could see her, and that was a massive relief. But only from one eye. I had a huge bandage wrapped around my head and over my left eye.

I looked at her, and she looked at me. My heart was thumping in my chest. She was there, I needed her.

'Is my nose going to be okay?' I asked.

She hesitated a little 'Maybe your eye is of most concern. The glass sliced straight through the middle of your cornea and the surgeon had to stitch it back together. He said it has a good chance of healing, though.'

'What about my sight?'

'It's touch and go, but he seems confident you won't lose it completely. Do you want some water?'

I nodded, contemplating her words. And then I relived the event in my mind, thinking of how I could have avoided it.

The vivid memories are etched into the inside of my brain, and although now it almost seems like someone else is in the pictures playing in my mind, I have never forgotten the pain. And I've never forgotten what it feels like to be scared, scared out of my mind.

Some days later, the police came to get a statement. It turned out that the guy had previously knifed his own mother in the stomach and also Stanley-knifed another man's face, so in a way I was lucky. Just unlucky to be in the wrong place at the wrong time.

Over many weeks, I had to return to the hospital to have the stitches removed from my face. This part didn't hurt too much, and it felt like a positive move forward to recovery. But that wasn't the case with my left eye. The sharp glass had indeed sliced through my eyeball, right in the middle. It took five stitches to pull it together, and they said it would affect my vision for the rest of my life.

The removal of those stitches was horrific, and I don't use that word lightly. I was given an anaesthetic eye drop, but I felt the first stitch sliding through my eyeball and immediately ran to the sink to be sick. One down, four to go!

That was the last time I went out in my home town for thirty years.

The whole event left me shaken and nervous about going out, full stop. It took years for my nose to heal properly and many years more for my eye, although I only had to wear the eyepatch for a year. You can imagine the jovial pirate comments I got on the bus to work.

My social life kind of ended right there, and so did my relationship with Sasha. I can't remember her helping me that night. Maybe she did, I'll never know, but I still have a hint of sadness about that. She was probably in shock, too.

It was evident my eyesight would be compromised, and I would have a scar across my face for the rest of my life. I didn't want to go out, and I didn't want people to see me with a disfigured face.

The perpetrator got a prison sentence for grievous bodily harm with intent and served six months of an eighteen-month sentence. I heard later he got out on 'good behaviour'.

I had plenty of rebuilding to do. My confidence was knocked to the floor. I couldn't even muster Jonny. I felt like I had nothing to give the world, and I was trapped. Hemmed in by someone else's actions. I had the constant battle between wanting to defy him and my inherent belief that I was worthless. It was easier to stay in and hide, yet I hated that too.

18

HOPE

It was an almighty struggle maintaining any kind of normal life after the accident. Every day it was an effort to summon up the will just to get out of bed. And even when I did, Derek made me feel I was in the way. One day I mustered the energy to make a jacket potato. I was adjusting the red-hot shelf in the oven when I accidentally dropped it on the kitchen lino. It was the type of lino which instantly melted on contact with any hot metal. Derek would go berserk. I panicked and hopped around the kitchen, not knowing what to do. My one glimmer of hope was that it was a single tile and didn't affect the remainder of the floor. I decided to inform Mum, who promptly devised a distraction operation. She retrieved a new tile from the loft, while I patrolled the door like a prison guard. The problem was that the tile was clean and new and stood out from all the others. Derek was sure to notice, so we both looked at each other with fear in our eyes.

'Man the door, John, while I take it out into the garden and rub it in the potato patch.'

'Okay. And stamp all over it with your shoe.'

'Great idea,' she said knowing we were both in this together.

It had to be one of the longest waits in memory. I had to create a diversion to a loose door handle when Derek approached the danger zone. I knew he wouldn't be happy about a door handle that wasn't perfect. This held him at bay just enough for Mum to complete the 'ageing' process.

Mum managed to pull it off with great creativity, even a dusting with some flour, which instantly added to the camouflage. Mum was great, but we were scared of him. Something had to change.

The scar across my nose looked angry while it was healing. The fifteen or so stitches had left holes which bled from time to time and I had to keep applying antiseptic cream, which was thick and bulky. Again, I felt self-conscious. Walking through the park, I witnessed a mother drag her little boy to avoid me. I must have looked dangerous. How else would you judge someone with such an aggressive-looking injury?

But I had to keep going. Day after day, waking up and looking at myself in the mirror was soul-destroying. I struggled to recognise my reflection and sometimes even scared myself.

Yet again, work was on my back to see when I was coming back. I'd only been off a few weeks, but I knew they would be lining someone else up to replace me. I couldn't let them down and I had a college course to finish. I dreaded my first day back. I would be the butt of all the jokes and I was scared about being bullied, and concerned about the effect on my worsening mental state.

With clean, fresh uniform in my bag, I adjusted my eye patch and headed in through security. I had to show my pass on at least five occasions as they'd forgotten who I was, and I looked a tad different too. My first step in through the kitchen door felt heavy, as if carrying the whole weight of my anxiety. The next step, and

I would be fully in the kitchen and there would be no going back.

'Hi, John, good to have you back.' One of the pot wash girls met me with surprise as she headed from the washrooms.

'Hi,' I said nervously. I could see Chef through the glass in the double swing doors, holding one of the YTS boys by the scruff of his neck. I took a deep breath. Then another. It was showtime.

'Eh up, it's Long John Silver. Where's your parrot?' he shouted, so that everyone could hear.

I smiled a disingenuous smile. 'Hello, Chef.'

'Looks pretty bad, lad. I've seen worse. In the Falklands we jumped out at 10,000 feet and Geordie Peters caved into a corrugated iron roof, slicing his face. Nasty. Makes you look less like a puff, though. Get changed and I'll brief you.'

'Yes, Chef.'

Bizarrely, his attitude changed towards me. He was the same old slave-driving maniac – that didn't alter – but he seemed to target his energies elsewhere, which was a welcome relief. I did get my front tooth knocked out by a flying metal fish slice though, some weeks later. He'd thrown it at someone else in a rage, and I didn't duck quick enough.

I managed to complete my final year of college. I'd missed many sessions, but I was given a pack of information to help me catch up. I worked day and night, struggling with the pages of written text, menus and food science information. My reading was still extremely slow. Often my mind would glaze over, and occasionally I visited the void, because I couldn't help it. Deep, deep down in my heart, I felt I had to fight on. I remembered the elation I'd felt when I opened my Grade C English results and somehow it seemed to inspire me to try and make sure I didn't fail.

I was awarded City & Guilds 7061 and 7062 and became a fully qualified chef. To say I was ecstatic was an understatement.

The agonising nights spent going through the course were almost forgotten. I had a handful of certificates which really felt like they were worth something.

On the Monday, I returned to work and plonked my certificates on Chef's desk.

'I did it,' I said nonchalantly.

'I know. I called college. Better get your act together now and prove you're worthy. I'll put you in charge of some of the trainees, now f***k off.'

'Yes, Chef.'

I made some tea for myself at the large steel water boiler, which constantly steamed away in the corner, before heading to the washroom to change into my whites. I heard whimpering coming from the staffroom next door. I poked my head around and saw one of the trainees, sitting alone with her head in her hands, crying.

'Here, do you want some tea?' I said, taking the adjacent chair.

She nodded and wiped her tears with a small scrunched-up tissue.

'Are you okay? What's wrong?'

'It's nothing, I'm just a bit out of sorts today.'

'Is it... him?' I probed.

She looked at me. 'I don't think I can do it any more.'

'You know, you shouldn't take it to heart. He's like that with everyone. Sooner or later someone else will be in the firing line and it will get easier.' I sounded like an old pro.

She sniffed. 'This job is what I dreamt of.'

'Look, if that's the case, no matter what, keep on trying and don't give up. Don't be beaten. Sometimes when you think you can't go on, you have to dig deep and find that spark. You just have to show him you're not affected.' Now I really was sounding like a pro.

She took a sip of her tea. 'It's alright for you...'

'No. It's not! It really isn't. We're all in this together.'

She smiled and I felt strangely empowered. I wish I could talk to myself like that, I thought.

As time went by, I began to heal and eventually I felt a little more at ease with myself. I felt the perpetrator of the attack no malice whatsoever, strangely, and never felt any anger or hate towards him. My inner peace somehow gave me an inner courage, even though the years of recovery were hell. The ridicule, loss of eyesight, the impact at work and the permanent scar are a constant reminder, but within, the peace gave me strength. It was a feeling that things couldn't really get much worse and I either stagnate and internalise everything, or fight back and make something of my life.

Following my exam success, I was offered a promotion to the position of Second Chef, which I begrudgingly accepted. In the back of my mind I was still itching to escape, but felt trapped by the offer of work, while millions of people were unemployed. I also had to get fully well and strong again. As Second Chef I had to make sure all my subordinates were all up to scratch and on the ball, and also had to get involved in menu-planning and ordering. I'd obviously avoided this as much as possible previously, but now I felt I had to embrace it, too. Chef had a devious way of handing down responsibility and then suddenly taking it all completely away. It reminded me of Derek somewhat and I didn't like it.

I'd only been in my post a few months when we were scheduled a visit from the big, big boss, the area manager, Barbara. Her fierce reputation preceded her.

She walked around the kitchen with her hands behind her back, examining what was going on and asking questions, glaring down her nose when people answered. With her stern face and tightly pulled back hair, she frightened everyone, not least me.

At service, Barbara watched intently as I ran around like a

headless chicken, making sure all went well. Part way through service we ran out of pork chops, they were so popular and dinner ended up being a complete shambles. In addition, one of the chefs sliced his finger while prepping onions, and I had to undertake some swift first aid. Trust it to happen on the one day I didn't want it to.

Towards the end of service, as the commis chefs were cleaning up, I was summoned into the office. As you can imagine, I was shitting myself.

The door opened, and I was shown into a seat opposite the desk where she was standing. She shook my hand. 'Hello, I'm Barbara, please sit down.'

'Nice to meet you,' I said nervously.

'John, we've seen you progress rapidly through the ranks here, and by all accounts it hasn't been easy for you. But basically, we like what we see and we'd like to offer you a promotion.'

'I didn't know the head chef was leaving, miss,' I said, confused.

She smiled. 'This isn't the head chef's job, John. We're offering you a trainee manager's position.'

'Manager? Me? You have to be kidding.'

'There's a pay increase to £76 per week and a petrol allowance. How does that sound?'

My jaw dropped and I stared at her in disbelief.

'It's a standard forty-hour week, working at various locations, and I'd like you to attend Head Office for training on the Chef Manager programme. Would you give it some serious thought?'

I knew instantly it wasn't the job for me. It would involve doing accounts and writing, and that was all a step too far. My secret would be outed.

'I'm not too sure,' I said, shaking my head.

'We're always looking for motivated and committed

managers and your remuneration package will grow as you progress beyond the trainee period.'

'I don't think I'm up to it, miss.'

'Please call me Barbara. It may sound a little daunting, but we would like to offer you the position.'

I paused for a moment. 'You see, the thing is... I have... well, it's like this... I struggle...'

She interrupted before I could finish. 'You come highly recommended, John. Please give it some thought and let me know by the end of the week.'

I couldn't keep doing this to myself. More sleepless nights wishing I'd just come clean and got my words out. It was becoming the story of my life.

Besides the prison, the contract catering company who employed me ran various other kitchens in factories, schools and hospitals. In most of them there was a manager who was also the head chef, helped by a brigade of chefs and domestic staff. There was a great deal of variety in the position, and that element was attractive, but the responsibility of all the paperwork, banking, stock-taking, menu-planning and HR was beyond my capabilities. Not to mention more studying. I'd had enough of that and was worn out. I was barely 18yrs old and felt that those positions were meant for older, brighter people. Not a no-hoper, like me.

I called her on the Friday, during break time and told her I wasn't interested. I lied that it wasn't the job itself, but that the timing just wasn't right for me. There was a silence, and I thought I'd got my point across. Then she returned with an increased pay offer and a £1000 lump sum for a deposit on a new car, which would be essential for getting to all the establishments.

So there I was, little black briefcase in hand and a new suit and tie. Oh, yes, and a midnight-blue Ford Capri with a vinyl roof, bought at auction for £300. A further £600 went on the insurance, tax and four new tyres, and an exhaust, a clutch and a bit of welding on the sub-frame. I couldn't afford to get the heater fixed, so I just bought a big coat.

Life at home had become untenable. I was ready to be independent and, after a year, I was able to put a deposit down on a house. I was extremely glad to be moving out, and seeing the back of Derek was a fabulous thought. I was ready and it was long overdue. Mum was encouraging and helped me with curtains and bedding, and Derek, I'm sure, was pleased to have me out of his hair.

Mum surprised me with a cheque for £500.

'What's that for?'

'Well, you know all the board and lodging money you've been giving me?'

'Yes, I do,' I said, still resenting every penny I handed over.

'I saved it for you, so you can have a deposit and get yourself a little place.'

'Oh!' I said, feeling ashamed of myself.

I donned my new suit and went cap in hand with a letter of my employment to the building society, and God knows how, managed to secure a fifteen percent interest mortgage on a little one-up, one-down end terrace on the edge of town. There was no central heating and the single-glazed sash windows didn't afford much protection from the stiff northerly wind. It was a cold house and in the depth of winter my thick coat, which I wore in the car, didn't come off, even for bed. It was mine, though, and I loved it.

I was thrust in at the deep end at work. I was sent here, there and everywhere to cover absences, problem-solve and cater for hundreds of people at a moment's notice in factories, schools, hospitals, and even a monastery.

I thought I'd chosen a career where I didn't have to read and write. I could cook coq au vin, lobster thermidor, aspic-covered salmon, shepherd's pie, jam roly-poly and Manchester tart for three hundred people easily, but what I struggled with was the paperwork, and that came hand in hand with being a manager. Triplicate double-entry accounting and stock-taking was just the start of it. I had to make it work, though. It was a great opportunity, and I had a car to run and a mortgage at eighteen years old. I wasn't going to be beaten.

I worked hard, very hard. Mainly because I was conscientious, but also because I had to disguise the fact that my reading and writing were severely debilitating. I made mistakes, and my boss scheduled me for more training, but I was constantly treading on thin ice, especially when I showed a £10,000 loss just by putting the decimal point in the wrong place. I was out of my depth and I constantly felt time was running out.

Working at the monastery was a complete eye-opener. It was a Carmelite monastery set in extensive grounds, with colossal parkland trees and a mosaic of mown paths through wildflower meadows. It really was a beautiful place. The brothers and one sister were peaceful and calm and spoke softly using kind words whenever they saw you. And they actually appreciated their food, especially Brother Ben, who always wanted seconds.

One day he came into the kitchen to see if there were any leftover cold sausages (his favourite). He put his hand on my shoulder and looked at my scar and then looked me straight in the eye. 'John, God has dealt you a few blows, by the looks of things. I feel you are a good man. This is God's way of telling you that life isn't easy sometimes, but also, that you have the spirit inside you to succeed. Anyway, it is, in a way, your perfect imperfection. Let it be your inspiration, young man.'

I felt what was like a mild electric shock through my body, just before he removed his hand, a bit like when you pull off a synthetic jumper. I wasn't a believer in God. I never felt a deity was tangible enough for me to invest in, and nature seemed a much more powerful influence in my life. But there was something he had ignited in me. I would often stand at the monastery window, gazing at the land, and contemplating God. It felt okay to do it there. The view was magnificent. A rolling landscape, broken up by mature trees, and deer mooching nervously around.

I would regularly take off around the grounds, listening to the wind rustling the mighty tree canopies, and sometimes I'd stand with my back pressed hard against the trunk of the superior cedar tree, which took centre stage on the lawn. When it was very windy, I could feel her roots moving beneath me as the tree swayed to the mesmerising rhythm. It reminded me of my conker tree when I was younger. I felt the same energy I'd sensed back then. I didn't feel it was God, but there was a force for good which said positive things to me.

The problem was that one minute I felt this positivity and the next I was consumed by the pressure of my workload. I was struggling to keep my head above water with all the paperwork and having to cover up my literary ineptitude kept knocking me back.

Not long after the monastery, I was posted to a leather-tanning factory in Leeds. The smelliest, dirtiest place you could ever imagine. The raw hides came in and underwent a series of curing and treatment cycles in toxic chemicals, somehow coming out the other end as golf shoes. The people who worked there had clearly had their sense of smell removed, because despite having my smelling equipment severely altered, the odour still made me feel sick every day.

This canteen had problems. It had staff issues and was losing money, and I was sent in to pull it around and get it back to profitability.

Every day there was a problem with one or another staff member not turning up for work, and there were verbal and written warnings flying around. I lost many nights' sleep at that place. Not only was I full-scale blagging the paperwork, I also had the responsibility of getting it into some sort of order. In all honesty, it was beyond me, and for a few weeks I lived with panic on my mind twenty-four hours a day. I certainly didn't have any clue why the place was losing money.

One person who helped me out massively was Sam from the staffing recruitment consultancy. I was on the phone to her on a daily basis ordering more temporary staff, and she was brilliant.

'Sam, it's John again. Can you sort me out a commis chef and a pot washer for next week?'

'Of course, John. I know just the right people.' Her voice was smooth and soft but also efficient. In fact, she sounded sexy as hell, and she seemed to be able to calm me down in my most panicky of panicky moments.

It wasn't long before I asked her out on a blind date, and she agreed. We met at a pub just outside the city. She had a lovely face and kind eyes, and her voice was even sexier in reality. I even thought of Claire's voice for a minute, and then I reminded myself I was over her, big time.

Sam had been a manager at Pizza Land before going into recruitment. She was a southerner, too, which is why I think I found her voice so attractive.

I lifted my glass and clinked it against hers. 'You know, I asked you out on a date because your voice is just so amazing. And you've helped me so much over the last couple of weeks.'

'Don't be stupid,' she said, laughing.

'It's true. I couldn't have done it without you. The staff in that place are driving me mad. There are some serious problems there, and I'm not sure I'm the right person to be sorting it out.'

Sam took a sip of her lager. 'Don't you enjoy working there, then?'

'I hate it there. I've worked in some pretty bad places, but this one takes the biscuit.'

'I hate my job, too,' she said, to my complete surprise.

I gulped my beer and looked quizzically at her. 'What do you mean? You're brilliant at it.'

She thought for a moment. 'It's not the people. The people,

on the whole, are pretty good. It's the targets, and the pressure of reaching your targets.'

I laughed. 'Haven't I helped you with that?'

'Well, yes, ironically, but the boss always wants more, and I'm just not as ruthless a seller as he wants me to be.'

'Oh,' I said. 'I'm confused. You seem like you have everything under control.'

'I thought that about you,' she retorted.

We simultaneously took long sips of our drinks and fell silent. Then we both started to talk at the same time.

'Well, I –' she began, while I said, 'Do you ever just feel like getting out of the rat race and being free?'

'Often.'

'You know what we should do?'

She shrugged. 'What?'

'We should get a campervan, pack our jobs in and just set off.'

'You're a mad man...! Where?'

'Anywhere? Somewhere? How about... Europe?'

I could see her thinking about it. She took another drink and looked at me. 'But I don't know who you are.'

I replied quickly, 'I know, but what have we to lose? Anyway, it's only a thought. It's not as if we set off tomorrow.'

'Okay,' she said. 'Let's do it tomorrow.'

'Really?!'

'Yes.'

So that was that. We agreed, and we put the wheels in motion. Sam handed in her four-week notice, and I did mine. It felt like the most liberating and exciting thing anyone could do. We both sold our cars and headed up into Leeds to look at a VW camper for sale. A couple were selling their beloved van because their children had grown, and it was no longer big enough. It had a rock 'n' roll bed – that's a seat that pulls out into a bed – and a permanent high roof with a small bed, which we decided would be great for kit and clothes. We signed on the dotted line and drove away in our new home.

I worked on the camper in the evenings to get it ready, minor alterations and under-sealing, things like that. I wanted it to be like the old Bedford.

Sam was renting a shared house, so terminating her tenancy was easy. For me, it was a little more complicated, but Mum had a friend who was an estate agent and they agreed to manage lettings, so I could pay the mortgage and not worry about it.

At the leather-tanning factory, we operated a weekday breakfast service and dinner – that is to say, lunch. There was no service on weekends, but we did have vending machines, so the workers could get some snacks and drinks. One particular Sunday morning I called in at work to pick up a few things, and to my horror, two of the staff were running their own breakfast service and keeping the profits. I stood in the doorway and couldn't believe my eyes. They couldn't believe theirs, either.

That's why the place was operating at a loss. I hadn't been able to see it via the books. I'd inadvertently rumbled their scheme by a chance call-in.

Just before I left, I had the responsibility of sacking the employees involved, which was a very unpleasant experience. On the day it happened, a mob of angry relatives waited for me outside. I locked myself in my office and called my manager, who called the police. There was a standoff, and two people were cautioned. It wasn't an easy job to do, but all I could think about was freedom – freedom from all that mess, freedom from faking it and freedom from all my previous life.

'You're making a big mistake, you know!'

'What do you mean? What do you know about how I feel?'

'I just think you need to think carefully about what you're doing.'

'I'm a man now, Mum. I make my own decisions.'

'You've worked so hard at your career. Look at where you are now. And you have a mortgage.'

'I hate my work, stuck indoors, ten, twelve hours a day, roasting hot. I look out of the window and see the sun shining and the trees blowing in the wind. I need to go and find out what's out there, Mum. Please understand.'

She shook her head. 'You're throwing it all away.'

'Look. I'm renting the house out, that will cover the mortgage, and there will always be a job for me in catering, but...' I took a breath and looked her in the eye. 'I just need to find out who I am.'

'Two tickets to... erm... Europe, please.' Sam and I spoke simultaneously, laughing, as we booked our ferry crossing to France for the following week. It felt a bit strange. We had no plan and no final destination, just adventure ahead.

The warm May sun dazzled us as we arrived in France. We negotiated the port and then out onto the open road. It felt natural to be driving on the right, and I was amazed at how good the roads were. Open, much less busy than in England, and they all seemed to be heading south. We smiled at each other as we approached a junction.

'So, where to? Left or right,' I said, without a care.

Sam made the choice. 'Right! Right feels right!'

With a flutter in my heart, I turned the steering wheel and off we went. We drove along the coast and parked up on a quiet clifftop. We snoozed in the van with the sliding door open, feeling the warm breeze, listening to the sea crashing on the rocks beneath us, then ate baguettes with French butter and jam, drank coffee and slept some more. We both needed it. We'd suddenly let go of our stressful lives, and we were like two caged lions who'd been set free. I'd received a compensation payment for the glassing accident. Not much, but enough to fund part of the trip and to mean we didn't have to work. We were eager to explore, and with a bounding energy, but first our bodies were telling us to recuperate.

We negotiated our way along the Loire Valley, visiting many of the grand châteaux, some with numerous high fairytale towers, one which was built as a bridge over the river itself, and I particularly remembered the Château de Chambord, with its helix spiral staircase.

At the end of one warm day, we parked up at a campsite on an island in the middle of the river. I positioned the van so we could watch the dragonflies and swifts skimming the water and proceeded to make us some chicken salad and a glass of cold white wine.

Sam was sitting on the bed, with her bare feet sticking out through the side door.

'What are you doing?' I asked.

'I'm writing a diary, so we don't forget any of our adventures.'

'Wow, that seems like hard work to me. Great idea, though. Will you read it to me?'

She peered over the top of the spiral bound book. 'No.'

'Go on. I want to know what you're writing.'

'We sailed away, just on a breeze, heading to somewhere and everywhere. John has driven our home on wheels in a foreign country like a native. The castles of the magnificent Loire Valley are not a patch on our little mobile castle and our destiny is in the hands of nature.'

'Blimey! I didn't know you were a poet. It's lovely.'

She smiled. 'Thanks.'

'We're actually doing this, aren't we?'

'Yep.'

'Does it almost feel like it's someone else and not really us?'

She looked at me and paused. 'That's why I'm writing about it. Do you want to write in it, too?'

'I couldn't do that. I wouldn't know what to say and it seems like too much hassle. I'll stick to the map and plan the route.' I couldn't think of anything worse than finding my freedom and then having to write about it. Conley Cassle all over again. No, thanks.

The west coast saw us take off our shoes, feeling the sand between our toes. The blue skies and lengthening evenings loosened our ties with our jobs a little more and took me right back to my childhood holidays, as they did Sam, too. We started to relax. It took a few weeks for us to completely slow down and just breathe and enjoy, but steadily, each time we looked in the mirror, we noticed our faces changing, becoming younger and more open, more smiley, and our complexion looked healthier.

There was a fabulous campsite situated within some pine trees at the bottom of the largest sand dune in Europe. Scaling the mighty dune, 110m above sea level, enabled us to see the best sunset I'd ever seen in my entire life. The sky was filled with red, orange, pink and blue as the enormous golden orb descended slowly behind the horizon, and then suddenly, blip... it had disappeared.

Falling asleep with the smell of pine in the air and the sound of the sea tumbling onto the beach was one of my fondest memories, and I asked Sam if she would add it to the diary.

In the Pyrenees we headed up to the snow line, where we wild-camped on a mountain pass on a ledge overlooking the Spanish border. I felt like an eagle surveying the land below me. I could have taken off and swooped down across all the forest, pasture, waterfalls and isolated little wooden chalets.

High on the rocky ledge, we'd been asleep for an hour or so when I woke with a startle.

'What is it?' Sam asked.

I was in a daze and couldn't answer. 'Are you having a night-mare?' she said, putting her hand on my shoulder.

'I think so. I felt like I was pushing some of my past off a cliff edge, like I was saying goodbye to it. There were books, piles of them, and I opened the gates and was pushing with all my might.'

'It's okay now,' she said, and I lay my head back on the pillow.

My dreams continued to trouble me. Once, in the dead of night and in the pitch black, I woke again, but this time, I wasn't in bed. I was in the driver's seat of the van, with the key in the ignition, and was about to start her up. Sam sprang out of bed and, just in time, managed to stop me driving us over a 2000ft drop.

Following that, every night before bed I would throw the keys over my shoulder, so I had no idea where they were, just in case I attempted it again. The scramble to find them in the morning was always 'interesting'. Old habits die hard, and a life-time of sleep-walking wasn't something that would stop overnight. It seemed I still had issues to deal with and pent-up anxiety within me, which was going to take more than a couple of weeks to lose.

Sam was from the Catholic faith, and so a trip to Lourdes to sample the miracle waters was a must. It was the hottest day so far. We managed to squeeze the van into a huge coach park, where there were hundreds of executive buses from all corners of the globe, depositing their pilgrims. We followed the trail of people down the street which led to the cathedral and the sacred grotto where Bernadette, a young girl, had seen many apparitions of the Virgin Mary. Some hobbling with the aid of sticks, many in wheelchairs, and an enormous number laid flat out on stretch-ers. It is said that the waters have healing powers, and many come to be cured.

The streets were lined with shops selling souvenir trinkets, water bottles, figurines and candles.

We watched the throngs of people being blessed by loud-speaker and then joined the queue to the grotto. I couldn't help wondering if some of the people would have been better to go a little further into the mountains and sample the fresh air and smell the wildflowers, rather than be baked in the searing heat. Anyway, Sam took the water and seemed to have a spring in her step all the way back to the van.

In Cannes and St Tropez we felt a bit out of place amongst the jet set, and our old campervan stood out a mile against the Ferraris and Porsches. We soon moved on into the hills and enjoyed kayaking up and down the winding and dramatic Verdon gorge, and wild-camping next to the endless purple lavender fields of Provence. Lavender is still my favourite smell to this day. I will never forget snoozing in the open air as the sun dropped. We became intoxicated in the warm, heady, scented breeze, sleeping long and peacefully in the purple haze.

In the Alps, there were a few near misses with oncoming vehicles on some of the narrow roads. My eyesight was still poor in my left eye, and if the sun caught me at just the wrong angle, I was almost blind. I also had trouble gauging depth and distance sometimes, too, which I found frustrating. Sam shared the driving, though, which gave me the chance to rest it. I tried to not let it get to me, but I didn't like putting us at risk.

In Italy we parked up for lunch in the forest leading to Pisa and wondered why so many couples were going for woodland walks in totally inappropriate clothing, high heels and short leather skirts. We later discovered this was the red-light district. And I'd bared my bottom in there on my daily constitutional.

In Naples, a ridiculously busy three-lane motorway abruptly turned into a cobbled street, with washing-lines strewn across it and sheets and clothes dangling down into the road. It was like going back in time, and compared to the organised and regimented roads of the UK seemed a little chaotic.

Rome was challenging. We camped on the beach, miles out of the city centre, and there was a public transport strike the day we decided to explore. Not only that, it was the first day of the summer holidays. The roads only seemed to be open for the route out of the city, and thousands upon thousands of cars streamed out, beeping their horns with excitement. Thousands of mopeds did too, all peeping their annoying high-pitched hooters. For us, it meant walking against the manic traffic in what was starting to become a very hot and sunny day.

My tiny Kevin Keegan-style shorts prevented us from getting into the Vatican. Apparently, it was the height of disrespect, although girls were allowed shorts. Only the girls' shoulders were offensive, so we swapped my shorts for Sam's three-quarter length skin-tight white trousers, and were grudgingly granted access. Her trousers gave me a high-pitched voice and everyone around me a full view of my attributes, but we were in. I hoped the thronging masses would be too interested in the ceiling of the Sistine Chapel than in my obvious, hairy bottom, and thankfully they were. We changed back into our prospective attire in the rooftop toilets, and were then chased by the Swiss Guard back into the street, as I shouted, 'There's a guy in there with just a loincloth!'

We managed to squeeze in all of the other significant sights, too, with various clothing changes. The sun began to set. We were hot, bothered and tired, but we managed to walk the miles back to the van, trudging our feet along. The only thing keeping us going was the thought of our lovely comfortable bed. But we were in for a shock. We opened the sliding door to find the interior completely infested with black ants. They were in the food, the bed, our clothes, cupboards, crawling everywhere. In despair, we closed the door and collapsed on the sand in a heap, then fell asleep in each other's arms on the beach.

The following day we fumigated the van and stripped it bare to rid our home of the unwanted guests. I poured boiling water over the wheels and tyres and then we headed north to the mountains.

We climbed high up a mountain pass to cross into Switzerland. The roads were incredibly steep, with hairpin bends that could only be negotiated in first gear. But the van held her nerve, although Sam and I at times had our hearts in our mouths.

The real fun began on the way down. It was so steep on the descent, and the van was giving off a strange smell. I parked her on a little pull-off and crawled underneath to inspect. I knew it wasn't the clutch as my Ford Capri had a dodgy clutch, and the noxious smell from it was something I could recognise instantly. This was something different, but I didn't know what.

We carried on, keeping the van in a low gear to ease her around the bends and the sometimes seemingly vertical slopes. The smell came back, and then I lost control. I just couldn't stop her with the footbrakes and I had a terrifying few miles of hairpin bends, trying to slow down using the gears and the handbrake. Eventually I ran her off the road into one of those emergency run-off lanes that resemble a sandpit. I put the kettle on while I had a good think about what to do next, and let the van cool down. After further investigation, I came to the conclusion it was due to the brake fluid overheating and thus not being unable to force pressure through the pipes. Sounds simple now, but at the time we were petrified.

I managed to find a VW dealer in the next town to get some new fluid and get the van safe again.

Switzerland was one of our favourite places. We camped wild, swam and bathed in fresh, clear mountain rivers, ate copious amounts of chocolate and hiked through wildflower meadows with just the clanking of cowbells for company until the next impressive waterfall, and on one occasion we spent our entire weekly budget and took a cable car to the top of the mountain, to see the Roof of the World.

We met a couple from Italy who didn't speak a word of English. They were staying at the same campsite as us near Grindelwald. Their van was up on wooden blocks, with the wheels off. As we walked down to the shower block, I instantly thought about whether they were having the issue we had.

'Brakes too hot?' I asked.

The guy shrugged, so I went into the typical British mime routine, customary when trying to communicate in a foreign language. I started to frantically rotate an invisible steering wheel while pushing with an outstretched foot on the brake pedal.

He started nodding and called over his partner, who also started pushing her invisible footbrake, shaking her head, and giving the impression they were about to die by yanking on a make-believe slip knot around her neck. I understood immediately. I showed them to their brake fluid refill tank and could see that the liquid was nowhere to be seen. I gestured with my finger, that I would be back in a minute. I ran back to our van and collected our huge bottle of brake fluid, only half used, and offered it to them.

I still needed to get across the fact that they had to bleed the system. I'd done it on Grandad's old Talbot Horizon, and subsequently on our van, but how do you say that in Italian? I could barely order the bread for the morning.

I proceeded to mime the slashing of my wrists to show that I was bleeding. They looked blank, so I carried on slashing and exaggerating the performance. After a couple of minutes of what would have been worthy of a BAFTA, no one was any the wiser.

Then, Sam coolly walked up to the couple and said 'sanguinare'.

The couple started nodding and smiling and came and shook both our hands vigorously.

'Did you know that all along?' I asked.

'It took me a while to recall it, but I remembered something from church.'

'Great!'

Part of the joy of travelling was meeting people from many different countries doing exactly the same as us. At the outset we'd thought we were being radical and spontaneous, but the Europeans were already fully immersed in van life and they knew where to get the best soul food the world had to offer.

That night, we lay out in the open and marvelled at the night sky with all the billions and billions of stars. We tried to pick out the obvious constellations, but without any kind of light pollution the sky was almost literally bursting with stars, so we just let our minds absorb the enormity. We became transfixed.

'Do you ever feel small?' I said, looking straight up into the vastness.

'What do you mean?'

'I mean... like you're insignificant. I mean, look at all those stars. Some of those are a billion miles away. Driving the van constantly at 60mph, it would take us 177 years to get to the sun, and that's near in comparison. We're just a speck of dust on the pinhead of the universe.'

'Mmm,' she said, pointing with her finger and trying to count.

'What I mean is, do you ever feel small, like you don't matter?'

There was a silence for a minute, as we continued looking at the stars.

'No,' she said. 'We're all part of the universe and important in our own way. Everyone is important.'

'Are they?'

'Of course. You needed me to help you communicate earlier and I needed you to make sure we were safe and that makes us important to each other. Just because there are a billion acres of sky out there, doesn't make us worthless.'

I thought about what she said and then rolled over to look at her. 'You mean my communication was rubbish?'

'Yes.' We both laughed and roly-polyed down the bank into the bushes.

That evening we parked up on the edge of a beautiful lake. It was a popular place for other camper vans as you could park right on the shore. The sun was starting to set, and I felt the urge to juggle with some fruit we had in the van. I loved to juggle, but I also used it sometimes as a way to completely switch off and relax. It was a similar feeling to when I went into the void, a sort of loosening of my mind and a focusing from the centre of my forehead.

After a short while I heard a voice behind me. I dropped the fruit.

'Hey, you're a very good juggler. Want to try and pass between us?'

From the accent, I guessed Swedish or Norwegian perhaps. I turned and was greeted with a huge, purposeful handshake and a generous smile from a tall, blond-haired guy.

'Sure, you juggle too?'

'Of course.' He produced a similar array of apples and oranges and immediately started juggling.

I watched him and noticed he knew similar tricks to me, so I started juggling too, and then suddenly he started counting. 'One, two, three, pass.' We simultaneously threw an item on our right sides for the other to catch into their juggling pattern and then again. 'One, two, three, pass.' It felt solid and rhythmic. We continued into a steady rhythm and then I threw one from under my leg and then he from behind his back. Wow, I thought, that was impressive. We both got to the point where our arms were aching and we dropped everything to the floor.

'That was great, I've never done that before. You're a great juggler,' I said, smiling.

'You're an instinctive juggler, like me, I can tell.'

'Well,' I said. 'There's a strange thing with me. It probably sounds stupid, but I have difficulty learning somethings, especially reading and writing. I don't usually find things instinctive, but I always knew I could juggle. It's very strange.'

'Yes, you're like me. Dyslexic.'

I looked at him and shook my head. 'That's a disease isn't it? I don't have that. No, I just get things muddled up sometimes.'

'Yes. Exactly.' He threw an apple into the air. I caught it and immediately started to juggle. 'See! I bet you use both hands for other things too?'

'Well, I do. I'm right-handed at everything apart from golf, cricket and brushing my teeth.'

'See. You know juggling is linked to helping with learning difficulties like dyslexia and dyspraxia. I heard it brings both sides of the brain together, and in that fusion the magic happens. So, you can conquer the world, Englishman.'

'Please, John.'

'Viktor. Great to meet you.'

Later that night, I lay awake thinking about what Viktor had said. It was definitely the case with me. Juggling gave me a super relaxed state which I entered free from anxiety, stress and self-doubt. It gave me an inner calm. I didn't know whether it was because I simply couldn't think about anything else while all the balls or apples were in the air, or whether there was a rhythmic kind of hypnotic pattern, but it felt very similar to when I went into the void. But that didn't mean I was dyslexic.

I was changing. I could feel it. The trip had done something to me. Opened my eyes to the wider world. It had reinforced my love of maps and the information they contain. I'd experienced nature in some of its wildest and most powerful forms, dealt with brake failure, sleep-walking, relationships and self-doubt. Fundamentally, I'd relaxed. No anxious leg, no stuttering and no bluffing it.

As the winter drew nearer, we started to run out of money and we thought about either returning to the UK or finding work. Sam suggested we might find work in a ski resort. I'd never been on a pair of skis, but she'd been skiing a couple of times. She thought that both of us being catering trained might set us in good stead, so we applied for jobs.

It became obvious after a few interviews that it was a prerequisite to ski in order to work in a ski resort. The companies didn't want to waste time and resources on someone who may not take to skiing and leave. So, we had a plan for the next application.

'Hello John, hello Sam, please have a seat.' The interviewer and co-owner of the business gave us a warm smile. 'I see from your CVs you're well-qualified, and somewhat more than we would normally expect.'

Sam jumped straight in. 'We're travelling and looking for work over the winter season. We can commit to the whole six months, and yes, I'm an ex-pizza restaurant manager and John is a qualified chef.'

'Okay, that sounds good. What kind of kitchens do you have experience of, John? High-end, was it?'

I felt my leg jump straight into action and my mind jumped straight to the prison. 'Erm... yes, our diners were... demanding, sometimes! You might say.'

'Perfect, just like in a ski chalet, then?'

'Oh, yes and I'm used to big numbers too.'

She stroked her chin. 'You could be catering for up to twenty-four, does that faze you?'

Sam and I looked at each other and smiled. 'No. Twenty-four is fine.'

'Okay, well what we want you to do is come back tomorrow and cook for eight guests at our mock chalet. Five courses, including coffee, and you'll choose the menu and shop for the ingredients, and then entertain the guests, does that sound good?'

'Erm –' I began, and Sam butted in, 'Of course. What time do you want us?'

'Is 2pm okay?

'Yes, absolutely,' Sam said, glaring at me.

'Oh! Yes, there's one last thing. Do you both ski?'

'I've been a couple of times with my family, mainly in Austria and loved it,' Sam said confidently.

'John?'

'Erm... yes, I went with school some years ago, and knew it was for me.' I crossed my fingers and toes under the desk.

'Perfect. See you at 2pm.'

We must have done something right, because they offered us a ski chalet in the French Alps for twenty-four people. As we were both catering trained, we were thrust into the company's top chalet and given the responsibility of not only cooking break-fast, afternoon tea, a five-course gourmet dinner (by 'dinner' I mean tea, obviously) every day, but also making the beds and cleaning the bathrooms. Inevitably, we were invited out to the local bars in the late evening after dinner by our generous guests, and that meant usually getting about five hours' sleep before I had to walk down the mountain to get the fresh bread the following day, but I loved it. That walk became my favourite part of the day, and the job. The adrenaline surging through my body as the sun rose, lighting the white mountain tops in glorious oranges and reds, and the sound of the crisp snow crunching underfoot, made me feel alive as I made my way back with a rucksack full of the most exquisite-smelling fresh bread.

The first day on the slopes, I looked at all the colourful bodies slaloming down the snow towards me. The bright blue ski and pure white snow were blinding without my sunglasses. We walked up the slope in our clunky boots, which was exhausting, and then Sam showed me how to put the skis on. It felt ridiculous.

I took to my feet, and was off. Like a rocket, straight down and out of control. I flailed my arms around, realised I didn't know how to stop and crashed into a group of German skiers.

'Sorry, so sorry.'

'Hey, English madman, you need to learn to ski.'

I lay on my back feeling humiliated and wondering whether I was actually cut out for skiing.

Running the chalet was a skill, too. We cooked breakfast, then afternoon tea, which we left out for the return from the slopes, and then we cooked the dinner and sat down to eat with our guests. This was a feat of stamina and precision timing. I would often be thinking about my burning sole fillets while listening to someone tell me how they broke their thumb.

I learned to ski, of course, and loved it. On piste, off-piste, couloirs, through the trees, you name it. And on the white-out days, I taught myself to snowboard, too, and that became my favoured mode of travel for the duration of our time there.

Just after Christmas we received an invitation to Sam's best friend's wedding, which was planned for late May. Sam would be chief bridesmaid, so at the end of the ski season we returned to the UK

All in all, it turned out to be an amazing twelve months of freedom, twelve months of adventure, and above all, twelve months of not being judged and not having to face the grind of the rat race. We were tested, of course, but not on our ability to retain historical information or times tables, or on passing exams, but on embracing new languages, facing new challenges, living within a budget, and staying safe.

Above all, something within me had changed.

19

NATURAL ENERGY

It was great to see Mum and Amber again. Mum was still a bit frosty and it was clear she still thought I was out of my mind, leaving a respectable career and heading off into the unknown. She'd made it obvious she didn't approve, but it was my way of becoming independent and making that healthy move towards manhood.

Amber was still living with Mum and Derek. He hadn't changed. I could see the look in his eyes when I hugged Mum, so I gave him a wide berth, as much as I could, and saw Mum when he wasn't around. My dad had seemed to vanish off the face of the earth, although Amber mentioned something about him golfing in South Africa regularly. There was probably a t-shirt waiting for me somewhere.

My relationship with Sam wasn't as good as it could have been, either. We'd spent every single day of that year together and were a great team, but the romance had disappeared, and really we just became friends. Spending twenty-four hours together in close confines is a test for the strongest of relationships, and it proved to me that I wasn't ready to settle down. We were at a crossroads, and I knew once our return to the UK would be the end of our adventure together and the end of our relationship.

I wasn't sure what I was going to do or where I was going to live. My head was full of further travel ideas, but I also had to earn some money, and my house was under contract to a new tenant. The compensation I'd received after my accident had almost gone. It felt like money well spent, though, and exactly what it said on the tin. 'Compensation,' and not just financial compensation, but psychological recompense too. I felt refreshed, and I was ready for whatever was to come next.

I flitted around visiting friends, and of course popped in on Gran and Grandad, who were immensely interested in all my stories. They were my biggest fans, and I adored that. Gran mainly asked about the intricacies of going to the loo when there wasn't one, and how you could possibly manage without a fridge. Grandad wanted more detail on the brake failure and the construction details of the Leaning Tower of Pisa. We chatted tirelessly.

Later that week, and while having a coffee with Mum, she produced a piece of paper from her bag. It looked like some kind of advert. She shoved it in front of me.

'What is it?' I asked.

'Have a look. It's something you've probably never considered, but I saw it and thought it was perfect for you.'

I took the paper and started to read.

'University of Humberside. Higher National Diploma in Countryside Management. Apply on this number...'

I slid it back to her over the table and laughed. 'University? Is this some kind of joke? University is for brainy folk. People who can read and learn. I can cook food for university boffins, but I'm not one of them.'

We sat in silence for a minute or two, sipping our coffees, then she slid it back in front of me. 'It's studying trees, wildlife and countryside stuff and it's an HND, so lots of practical. Why don't you give it some thought?'

'No,' I replied. 'University is not for me. I hardly have any 'O' Levels, let alone 'A' Levels. It's not for me, Mum. I'm not going to no university.'

Mum straightened her back and raised her voice slightly. 'They welcome what are called "mature" students, people who haven't gone through the conventional system. In fact, people with a bit of work and life experience, like you. Why don't you give them a call? What have you got to lose?'

'I thought you were miffed I'd thrown away my career and wanted me to go back to catering.'

'I want what's best for you, and maybe you're ready for something new. You're not stupid, John.'

I dismissed the idea and embarked on thinking about what I realistically could do. I contemplated going back to the prison. There would be a job for me there, for sure. There was the option of going back out on the road, but my relationship with Sam was all but over, and I didn't have any money to set off singlehanded, plus the van was co-owned.

I decided to put my hiking boots on and head out for a walk in the woods to clear my mind. The wood had a luscious feel to it. The air was chilly, but the sun felt full of a new, optimistic warmth. A mass of bluebells carpeted the woodland floor, in an ocean of purple, set against vivid green. The colours and contrast, which in my mind only nature was capable of, welcomed me in, setting my mind at ease straight away. As I negotiated the intricate path network, trying my best not to trample any flowers, the trees looked like tall islands within the ocean, their buttresses hidden beneath the purple, their stems protruding like powerful eruptions of sturdy timber. I stopped to view a solitary deer, cautiously grazing on the grass in a clearing ahead. He was small and looked young. His antlers were just starting to form. I crouched amongst the bluebells, and he flinched as I inadvertently snapped a twig. He looked at me, and I looked back, but instead of darting into the undergrowth, he carried on looking and sniffing the air, raising his nose. I tried to send the message that I was a friend. He did seem to listen for a while, albeit cautiously. Ever since watching the wily fox as a child, I'd felt an equality between myself and wildlife. I realised we're all just animals sharing the same planet. Human, fox or deer, we share that huge thing in common, and that mutual respect between us is something very powerful.

Souls, spirits, or whatever it was, for a fleeting moment the deer and I were part of each other's worlds. He was wary, and I was curious, and I wanted to know more about him and his life. A fly landed on my cheek, and as I rose my arm to deflect it, he stamped his hind legs and bounded away out of sight. The brief contact with such a beautiful wild animal left me feeling humbled, and I felt privileged. I carried on peering into the depths of the dark woods to try and get another glimpse of him, but he'd gone. Somewhere alone, I thought. Somewhere where the grass was greener.

I regained my feet and walked among the trees, not on any path or trail, just arbitrarily through the undergrowth, just like the deer. I jumped over fallen rotting trees, catching my trousers on brambles which twined around my leg and sometimes tripped me up. I walked without a plan, no real purpose and no solid direction, but I felt something drawing me to the side of the wood that caught the late afternoon sun. I came out of the shadows onto a narrow path that followed the contour of the bank and occasionally leapt over a stream or two. There were various animal tracks in the mud on the path. It was obviously used by deer, and there were patches of disturbed soil, where a badger had rooted for her dinner.

The path eventually emerged fully from the wood. As I looked out across the open field in front of me, I felt I wasn't completely alone. There was a presence just out of my peripheral vision. Someone or something trying to get my attention, and I immediately turned to my left to see what it was. I scoured beneath and beyond the trees on the woodland edge, thinking it might have been that deer again, but there was nothing. I listened for movement, a footstep or a snap of a twig, but all I could hear was the gentle breeze blowing through the leaf-laden canopies. I looked up, my eyes drawn to the stout, mature trunk of an oak tree, whose canopy looked thin and in decline. I made my way towards it and examined the veteran's sturdy buttress roots anchored within the rich, leafy soil. I glanced up the fissured bark to a group of old scars, where limbs had obviously become detached, leaving a gnarly stub and slightly decaying wound. I looked closer. The scars began to resemble a face. Two eyes, one slightly lower than the other, and kind of sad-looking. A burr that looked like a crooked nose, and an oval cavity resembling an open mouth completed the vision.

I focused my eyes on the face and then stood back to regard the tree as a whole, to try and get some perspective; I felt if I looked away and then back again, I would know for sure whether I was imagining it. But no. There was definitely a face. I became transfixed and stepped up to her for a closer look. She was old, mighty old. I tried to gauge the size of her trunk by putting my arm around her. I couldn't even reach a quarter of the way around. From this, and the fact she had many decaying limbs, with some completely dead, I guessed her to be maybe three or four hundred years old. Her centre crown had sheared off at some point, years ago, leaving a huge tear down her right side which had a giant yellow fungus protruding from it. She had a scar running all the way down her trunk to the ground, which looked like she'd been struck by lightning. My immediate reaction was that her ungraceful yet gallant demise was a part of nature. She'd lost branches that were no longer required and was simply clinging on to exactly what she needed, nothing more, nothing less.

What might she have seen in all these hundreds of years? Who had walked under her? Who had climbed her, and what conditions had she endured? I'd heard a tale of a local highwayman who used to hide out in those woods, waiting for passing carriages before leaping out and relieving the occupants of their valuables and dignity. Maybe this tree was his secret hang-out?

I was trying to imagine the scene when I heard something. A voice. Well, not a voice in the conventional sense, but a presence. A feeling, a voice coming to me via the tree, through the wind in the leaves. I froze to the spot. My toes and fingers tingled as I listened intently. There were no human words, but she definitely spoke to me in what felt like a much more meaningful way, as though bypassing the usual route through ears to brain and instead, speaking directly into my soul. It seemed as though the tree directed the breeze through her canopy and then into my mouth, and then deep down inside me, filling me with immense energy. My shoulders dropped, and I felt an overwhelming calmness, too, as if all my anxieties were being released and blown far, far away. My eyesight became acute. I could see all the detail of her gnarly bark clearly. A force pulled me nearer to her, like a magnet. I shuffled my feet closer and focused on her eyes, those sad eyes. They drooped as if she were tired of life and almost ready to give up. Her physical status supported this idea. Like many oaks of such an old age, she had probably been vibrant and growing for 150 years, in full maturity for a further 150 years, and slowly in decline for the remaining years. I was fortunate enough to run into her with all of that history behind her and all her wisdom, and I could feel she wanted to give something to me.

She had just a couple of smaller limbs, and their faded green leaves convinced me she had only a few months left. My body became rigid and my heart felt like it was twisting. She was close to death. I listened closely, touching her bark and exploring the fissures and ridges with my fingertips.

The breeze gained pace and temperature, as if subtly changing direction from a cold easterly to a warm southerly. Once or twice I had trouble breathing out, as the air was forced into my mouth. I focused purely on the tree and my breathing, then suddenly the tingling in my feet ran quickly up my legs and for a split second filled my entire body. My torso felt like gravity was ten times the usual force, yet my head was floating, so light, and then… everything was calm. Quiet and still.

I slowly turned and rested my back against her trunk. It's hard to explain, but it felt like she had given me her last bit of energy before she died. The only way I could describe it was like a transfer of something powerful within her, or from nature, that filled my body, my soul, and with it came an overwhelming feeling of confidence. A feeling I'd never felt before. Other encounters with nature had brought me close, but this time it was big. I reached out behind me and put my hands on her once again, and looked out far to the horizon. My back was straight, my shoulders relaxed, and my mind clear, like a fog had lifted. I felt genuinely different. I felt liberated.

I nodded. It was the only movement I could make. I nodded again to confirm I knew what had happened, but also to show my respect to her.

It was going to be alright, she'd said. Everything was going to be alright.

I never told anyone afterwards about my encounter. I thought people would think I was mad, but I felt the tree had imparted her vast wisdom into me, and to this day, I feel I am still the custodian of her last energy.

20

A LIFE SENTENCE?

After my encounter with the oak, I began to walk differently. More upright, less slouchy. I would occasionally smile for no reason, but particularly when there was a warmth in the breeze. I would catch myself breathing in deeply and feeling the same tingling in my fingers I'd felt that day.

I thought long and hard about the university course. It sounded good, and I could learn more about trees, but it would involve reading and writing and studying. I knew I would make a fool of myself even applying and I wasn't ready for the rejection.

No. I'd give the prison a call and see if there was anything going, at least until I could find another chef's position somewhere else.

I phoned my old boss and he called me in for a chat. The place hadn't changed at all. There was still the bullet-hole in the main glass door, and the surly guards all seemed familiar. The smell was the same. It was a municipal smell, one of cleaning fluids mixed with testosterone, and as I was escorted along the corridor, all the foul memories came flooding back. I walked into his office, he shook my hand and with a wry smile offered me a seat.

'So, you're back. Fancy a life sentence this time?' He laughed, and I shuddered inside. His flabby belly and double chin that wobbled as he spoke, and the rank smell of his breath, made me feel sick.

'Yes,' I said firmly. 'I've had a year travelling, and now I'm looking for something more permanent.'

He scrunched up his lips and looked up to the ceiling. 'I do have a position. It's on the night shift, and it'll be on the same salary as when you left.'

'When can I start?' I said, holding out my hand.

He shook it with his usual limp grip. 'Tomorrow?'

That evening I met up with Sam. I told her about the job and that I thought it was over between us. She was upset, and I was too, but we agreed we'd gone where we could and that what we'd done was life changing. We hugged, and there were tears, but I knew it was time to move on. She'd taught me a great deal about relationships and about myself and I was grateful for the time we spent together. She kept her diary and we shared out the photos and said our goodbyes.

My first week back at the prison was worse than a life sentence. Working nights completely messed with my body clock, and although I was only working a ten-hour shift, it seemed to last a lifetime. The bonus was we were paid weekly, so it was good to have some cash in my pocket and a feeling of closure.

The following week, on the Wednesday, I was asked to do a double shift – sixteen hours straight through. Of course I had to say yes. If one of the other chefs didn't turn up, you had to cover, simple as that.

My evening shift ended, and instead of going home to sleep, I started the morning shift, with 300 breakfasts to cook. Physically, it nearly killed me. Mentally, I was determined it wasn't going to get to me. I kept telling myself it was only the shock of not working for so long, and that it would get easier. My eye had never regained full vision. It would become tired and it didn't like the intensely bright fluorescent lights which illuminated the kitchen and didn't like me having to concentrate for sixteen hours. I resented having the disability, but again, was determined it wasn't going to faze me. The reality was, I wasn't coping very well at all. My damaged eye gave me a skewed perspective when things were in close range, and that became worse when I was tired. While chopping carrots, late into the double shift, I sliced the end off my thumb and had to go to the hospital to have it stuck back on.

The following day was my day off, thankfully. I slept for a solid twelve hours, and when I woke, I decided to walk to the local shop and get the newspaper with the local job listings. I could hear the rain falling on the kitchen window, so I donned my raincoat and headed out. I made my way along the narrow alley that ran down the back of the houses, scuffing my shoes, head down in the driving rain. A water droplet ran down my hood and into my face. I stuck my hand in my pocket to see if I had a tissue and pulled out a folded note.

It was hard to see properly. With my left eye not able to make things out, my right eye was doing twice the work, so I opened the note and focused as best I could. It was the advert for the university course, which Mum had given me. I sheltered in a small doorway, dried my eyes, and read it again. I paused for a moment, then shoved it back in my pocket and sighed.

When I returned home, I made a brew and spread the newspaper out on the table.

Chef's job at a restaurant in town, evenings.

Catering manager's job at the rugby ground.

Washer-upper at a café on the high street.

I didn't fancy any of them. I sat back in my chair, drank down my tea and reached in the pocket of my coat to look at the advert again. I couldn't do a university course. No way. I read it again, then placed it on the table beside the newspaper. Then a few seconds later, I read it again. It was tormenting me, but I knew I wasn't worthy of university. They did lectures and walked around in mortarboards and gowns. I was thick and unintelligent. I scrunched the note up and threw it across the room, aiming for the bin, but missed.

I had to pull myself together. I was a chef, a qualified chef. I was good at my job, and it suited me – minimal writing, minimal reading and practical. It was head down time for me and time to stop thinking about something I was just not capable of.

I made a sandwich and watched a bit of TV, a crappy black-and-white war film. I kept looking over to the scrunched-up paper lying beside the bin. I couldn't turn my mind away from it, and it was annoying me that I'd missed my shot, so I got up and retrieved it, ready for another go. Just before the re-throw, I slowly opened it again. The ad had a picture of a stately tree in impressive grounds. It made me think about my encounter with the oak tree.

'Damn it!' I said out loud. What did I have to lose? I walked over to the phone on the windowsill and dialled the number. It was late in the day, and no one would be there, I thought, but at least I could get it out of my system.

'Hello, Countryside Department, Jim Vicarage speaking.'

I instantly put the phone down and went and sat back in the chair. Shit, there was someone there, and I hadn't rehearsed what I was going to say. It was a university. I had to sound posh and get it right. I gave it five minutes and then, with a few rehearsed lines in mind, I redialled.

'Hello, Countryside Department, Jim Vicarage.'

'Hello, my name is John Crawshaw, and I'm interested in the countryside management course,' I said, in my best plummy voice, which I thought sounded intelligent.

'Hello John, that's good to hear. Are you doing 'A' levels?'

'Erm... no. I've been working and travelling for the last six years since school. I trained as a chef, but I'm passionate about trees, and my travelling in Europe has given me time to think about a new career.'

I clenched my fist and scrunched my face up. I'd spoken honestly and was hoping with all my might that I hadn't blown it.

'John, we are actively encouraging mature students, with life experience, and you sound like just the kind of person we're interested in. Do you have 'O' levels?'

'Yes, including English.' I cringed at my stretching of the truth.

'That's perfect,' he said enthusiastically. 'I'd like to invite you to interview. It will give us a chance to tell you more about the course content and for you to ask questions too. And I can show you the campus.'

'Okay.'

We set a date. As I put the phone down, I couldn't move. My breathing was rapid. I grabbed my hair with both hands and tugged down, trying to jolt myself back into reality.

An interview at a university. Me. You've got to be kidding.

Two days before the interview, I had to have my wisdom teeth extracted. If the walk up to the main entrance wasn't intimidating enough, I now had a swollen and painful mouth, and I could barely speak. This only made me feel a little bit nervous. I'd expected my anxious leg to kick in, as normal, but it didn't, and it felt strange.

Jim met me in reception and took me to his office overlooking the impressive mature parkland. Luckily, he didn't ask to see any of my 'O' level certificates. I hadn't brought them, anyway. But what he did do was talk to me like an adult, and an intelligent one at that. He made me feel good about myself as I told him about how travelling had changed how I thought, and how meeting people from different countries and cultures had

opened my mind to learning new things. He too, had been travelling when he was younger and he seemed to understand.

'There will be set lectures on the various subjects outlined
here.' He pushed a piece of paper in front of me. 'In addition,
there will be self-study time, an onerous assessment schedule,
practical sessions three times a week, covering things like hedge
laying, dry-stone walling, tree planting, and stile and gate
construction. How does that sound?'

My eyes lit up. I'd always wanted to know how to build a
stile. He reached over and thrust another piece of paper in front
of me. 'This is the recommended reading list. It would be useful
if you could get stuck into your reading before you start.'

I looked closely. There must have been thirty books on there,
and the titles all sounded very academic. I just nodded, but my
heart was sinking fast. There was no way I could afford to buy
those books, and the thought of reading them petrified me.

'Okay, well, let me show you around the campus so you can
see if it's the sort of place you might be comfortable in. Let's
start in the refectory.'

What the hell was a refectory?

We passed various lecture rooms and offices, and there
were sports facilities, estate yards with tractors and piles of
timber ready to be made into 'countryside furniture', an entire
equine department (and that meant girls, so that was a bonus),
and the refectory turned out to be the canteen. As we walked
in, I spotted the kitchen staff beavering away behind the
counter, and it made me stop in my tracks for a couple of
seconds.

'Everything okay?' said Jim.

'Yes, everything is just fine,' I said, with a smile on my face
and sore gums.

'Well, what do you think? Do you need time to go away and
give it some thought? I'm sure you have other places to view,
too.'

I looked into the kitchen again at the chefs beavering away. 'No. I like it.'

'Well, in that case, we'd like to offer you a place.'

A wave of shock completely stunned me. I looked at him and then thought about the enormity of what he just said. I tried to speak, but in all honesty, it was overwhelming to hear those words. I was speechless, dumbfounded and ecstatically surprised. A tear ran down my cheek, and I started to cry.

'Are you okay, John?' Jim asked.

I nodded. The staggering magnitude of his words and what they meant to me simply paralysed me. That, combined with a huge lump in my throat and a mouth which was as sore as hell, meant I just couldn't reply. I nodded enthusiastically and shook his hand so tightly and so vigorously, I think he got the message.

So, there I was, a few weeks later, with a bulging and ridiculously heavy bag full of books and a head full of enthusiasm, heading for my first lecture. Ecology. I couldn't be more excited. I sat down and looked around at everyone else. Seventy percent were mature students, too. In fact, some of them much older than me. I sat next to a lad dressed in a checked shirt, moleskin trousers and hiking boots.

'Hi, I'm Colin.'

'Nice to meet you, I'm John.' I subconsciously touched the back of my neck to feel if my name tag was showing and looked nervously at him.

He smiled and shook my hand. 'Looks like it should be a good course.'

I nodded. 'Yes, it does. Have you read all the books?'

Colin laughed. 'No chance. They give you the list, but you won't really need half of them.' Without looking down, I kicked my bag out of sight under the desk.

On the second day I learned how to lay a hedge Yorkshire-style. I teamed up with Colin. The aim was to slice through the back of a hawthorn stem with a billhook and split it, so it would lie down and, bit by bit, produce a new living hedge, which would be thick and impenetrable to farm animals and better than an unsightly fence. Colin and I set about wielding the huge and very sharp billhook and, with one slice, I inadvertently cut all the way through. Colin was left holding the severed tree in midair. We looked at each other and then at the instructor and then just burst out laughing. It wasn't as easy as he'd shown us.

During the rest of the week we were taught how to identify ten species of tree. I already knew six – thanks, Grandad. I learned how ecology is the basis of all life, how all plants, animals, water, oxygen, etc., are all elements of our ecosystem, of which humans are only one small part. I took my mind back to when I used lie on my back in the field behind the house, contemplating the earth and nature. Everything was beginning to fit together and I began to see myself as part of a bigger picture.

My first assignment was on just that: 1500 words on Ecology. Now, I'm not pretending this was easy. It was, in fact, excruciatingly difficult. I managed to find an article about the arctic fox. It took me three weeks to research and write down 1500 words on paper. I made sure every word was right, spelled correctly and had the right meaning. It was painstaking. I didn't socialise, go out or eat much, but I was determined to break the stupid deadlock between my brain and my hand.

I wrote about how the artic fox predates upon lemmings. At certain times the lemmings have a mass suicide pact. No one really knows why this is, but it's thought it controls over-breeding and disease and opens up the genetic pool, and is there-fore better for the population long-term. Anyway, the lemmings dive off cliffs and numbers become radically reduced. The arctic fox suddenly doesn't have enough to eat and looks for different food sources, which usually means migratory birds. As a result, the bird numbers heading south to northern Europe and Africa are greatly reduced. The ecology is vastly changed, and the impact of the lemmings' deaths upon other, completely different animal species is significant. This impact could easily escalate, perhaps affecting the distribution of seeds or the increase in insect numbers, as a result of fewer birds eating and pooing.

Our essays were graded either Pass, Merit or Distinction. I got a Pass. I could possibly have chosen a slightly more detailed subject area, but for my first essay, I was delighted. All I was aiming for was a pass, nothing more. A pass was good for me. I just needed to fine-tune my writing process in order to speed things up, because I'd subsequently been dealt two other assignments, so the pressure was on.

Just to make things worse, we were instructed that the essays had to be produced on a computer and printed out before handing in. Now that was a curveball. I'd never used a computer before, other than the ZX Spectrum. We were shown the computer room. Twelve black-and-white monitors, each loaded with MS-DOS and a word-processing package, and no mouse. There was one daisy-wheel printer between everyone.

I spent days and nights in that room, slogging away. It was one thing writing 1500 words – that was one of the hardest things I'd ever done. It was another learning the computer. One-finger typing and keyboard shortcuts that weren't shortcuts, because that's just how you did it. I was frequently there till locking-up time and many times the janitors would kick me out and tell me to go home. I was determined, though, and was not going to be beaten. Of course my eye was troublesome. The blurred vision wasn't helped by the glare of the screen. I could see out of it and make out general shapes, but that was it, and concentrating at the computer sometimes made my eye feel like it was being pulled out of its socket. My other eye, thankfully, was a hundred percent, so it effectively did most of the work. As a result, I had to take breaks and rest my eyes, even if for just five minutes while I remained at the computer.

Some people seemed to waltz in, spend an hour, and waltz out again, and others took a little longer, but it was rare I shared the room late in the evening. The other students were out enjoying themselves.

I was on a mission, and I was changing and evolving, and one thing I did like was how the computer began to open up a whole new world. Sure, it was hard to learn all the nuances, and for my brain it was slow progress, but one almighty, amazing thing was becoming evident. It enabled me to make mistakes, and that was okay. I could check the spelling and make it good, which was liberating, and I started to learn. Learn about words. I experienced fear, yes, of the process, but less fear about the mistakes. It did take me forever, as I had to think about every single letter and every other word needed correction, but I knew something had changed because I laughed about it. Instead of being anxious, I was amused, and my seemingly relaxed state was enabling me to learn.

All this was pre-internet, so I still had to visit the library and read, which was literary hell, for me. I did, however, buy myself a dictionary. I couldn't believe it when I walked out of the book-shop door with the book under my arm, feeling proud. Something had happened – and it was big.

Probably my next defining moment was learning the difference between 'effect' and 'affect'. You see, I said it was big, but there was a fundamental shift that resulted in me actually *wanting* to know the difference and not only that, to remember it for when I needed it again. Something I'd never done before.

University was a scary 'proposition', but it was also 'incredibly inspiring'. I learned those words, too! It was a place of learning, and it was starting to open my mind.

The next two assignments were also tough. Again, 1500 words each – one on calcicoles and calcifuges, and the other on soil types and soil structures.

Two passes. I was happy. I had no social life, no free weekends, and not much time to come up for air, but I was getting passes.

My second home was now the computer room, but my first home, my 'digs', was an interesting place. My own house was still being rented out and was miles away from my studies, so I had to find somewhere to live, close to uni. My landlady, Mary, and her husband, Michael, were very welcoming. He was a deputy head teacher and Mary was studying for a PhD as a breastfeeding counsellor, so the whole place had a studious feel. Their home was a late nineteenth-century townhouse, where meat was murder, where musical instruments and bikes cluttered the hall, and where there were books everywhere – books on the shelves, books on the stairs and books in the loo. My room was in the attic, a single bed against the far wall and a window over-looking the street, and a small desk and chair. I was happy with my choice and I made my room like home as much as possible.

Mary would cook a huge pot of lentil casserole on Mondays, in a giant pan, which, amusingly, reminded me of the prison. As each day went on, the lentil casserole changed into different guises: lentil curry, Moroccan lentils, lentil shepherd's pie and, finally, lentil soup. I love lentils now, but back then I used to eat a bit and then sneak out for some chips or a kebab later in the evening.

The fourth assignment given to us was a big one, at 5000 words. It scared me. Just the thought of writing so many words was so far removed from anything I'd done before. I started to crumble.

At break time I bought tea for myself and Colin in the refectory. Colin had been working on nature reserves as a volunteer, and his knowledge of countryside management was already pretty extensive. He was from Wolverhampton and had a wonderful Black Country accent. The two of us talking together must have been interesting for anyone within earshot.

'Do you want any sugar in your tea?' I asked, as I brought the cups to the table.

'No thanks, John. How's it going with your assignments?'

'So far, so good. What about you?'

'Two merits and a distinction, I went over the word limit twice and was marked down.'

'Wow.' I was completely amazed that anyone would write more than they needed to. 'What about the latest one? How's that going?'

'I'm halfway through, but I'm waiting for one of the books to come back into the library, so I can finish it. Do you want it after me?'

'Erm... yes... I guess so. I haven't even started yet. To be honest, I'm feeling a bit overwhelmed at the prospect of 5000 words.

'Are you struggling?' he said, looking over the top of his glasses.

'Well, I am a bit, but I'm determined to do it.'

'You've already written 4500 words on the first three assignments, so it's not any harder than that.'

I thought about what he said and sipped my tea. He had no idea how hard it had been for me to do those 4500. I wished I was more like him. He wasn't fazed by the assignments, and he knew the books to go for, too.

'The thing is Colin, I'm different to you. I have a different brain.'

'What do you mean?'

'I don't really know how to explain, but I'm not just learning about countryside management here, I'm learning about myself, too.'

He sat back in his chair, crossing his arms. 'What do you mean?' he asked again. I don't think he'd expected me to be so frank.

'Sorry, Colin, I didn't mean to spring that on you. You're not my shrink. It's just, I'm different, and I'm no longer hiding from it.'

'I still don't know what the hell you're talking about. You can't help coming from Yorkshire!'

'Says you, Brummy boy.' We both laughed and raised cheers with our plastic tea cups.

'Do you think you're dyslexic?'

'I don't know? Maybe I am.'

'I can help, if you want. If you need a book and I have it, let me know. Saves waiting for a copy at the library.'

'I don't think that will be a problem, but thanks.'

Over the next couple of days, the sheer enormity of 5000 words, no matter what Colin had said, started to drag me down and drag my brain back to the bad old days of school. It was good, though, just talking to Colin about it. Somehow merely saying out loud that I was different made me feel I'd broken one barrier, at least.

But the more I stared at the paper, the more my negative feelings started to reappear. I hadn't felt my anxious leg for quite some time, but it was now back again, and in full flow. I sat at my little desk, took the paper in my hand and stared at the black printed words. The sinking feeling I knew all too well started to brew in my stomach, and I knew it was not a good thing. I tried to read the heading, but my eyes began to glaze over. I felt myself slowly being sucked into the void. It was a place I didn't want to go back to, but fighting it was hard, and the urge to give in and let myself be defeated was overwhelming.

I let my mind slip further and my eyes relax, then focus on the void, just as they had in my old English lessons. I was in the trap. The entrance appeared, clear and inviting, the window open to just step inside – just like the void in between these paragraphs.

'Cup of tea here for you, John.' My landlady, Mary, broke the free-fall with a knock at the door. 'Shall I bring it in?'

The sound of her voice instantly brought me back into the

real world. 'Yes please,' I said, with surprise but also relief. 'Yes, that would be perfect.'

I took the tea, and Mary asked if I was okay. I nodded and thanked her too many times, because she lingered and met my gaze inquisitively.

I sighed. 'To be honest, Mary, I'm not okay. I'm feeling a bit overwhelmed by my new assignment. It's quite a big one, and I'm not sure I can do it. I'm thinking I should just walk away from this crazy university thing and go back to what I know.'

Crikey! I'd just opened up about it again. What was happening to me?

Mary came into the room and leaned on the door-jamb.

'That sounds a little hasty. What's the subject?'

'It's about the Lake District National Park and the conflicts between recreation, cycling, walking, boating, etc., and landscape and wildlife conservation.

'How many words?'

'Five thousand. I've never written anything that long before.'

She nodded as if she understood. 'My thesis is currently 50,000 words and nowhere near finished. I just take it a small chunk at a time, and it's amazing how soon it builds. Get the first line down, and the rest will follow. And don't panic. Looking at a blank sheet is the worst thing you can do. Even just one word can get the ball rolling.'

I could understand what she was saying, and if she had written 50,000 words, she must know what she was talking about. I nodded, in my usual way and smiled.

'Don't give in just yet John. Do you want some lentil casserole?'

'Yes, please.'

I went down to the kitchen and had casserole with a huge wedge of bread, thickly spread with slightly salted butter, and my anxiety started to wane. I returned to my room and started to think about the assignment in a different light. Not by thinking about the requirements and the constraints, but about the subject matter. It helped that I'd been many times to the Lake District. I knew the fells well, had hiked and felt the energy of tumbling waterfalls, looked in wonder at the sheer rock faces, and seen the reflected oranges and purples of the bracken and heather in the water of the lakes. In fact, I had a foot in both camps. I'd camped and mountain biked, that was recreation, and I'd watched red squirrels on the banks of Derwentwater and observed the golden eagles in the North East Lakes, and that was conservation. I wrote on my page those simple words: golden eagles, red squirrels and mountain biking. Slowly my thoughts began to unravel, and I started to write.

So there I was, the following day, in the computer room. My fingers never stopped typing. Punch, punch, punch. I found a word-counter in one of the menus, and I gradually saw the figure increase and increase, and my brain just didn't stop feeding information to my fingers. I phoned an old family friend who lived in the Lakes, and he gave me some first-hand information about how the Park Rangers manage certain situations, and how signage, access and pathways attract people away from the most sensitive areas for wildlife. He also gave me more detail about the golden eagle nest at Eagle Crag, near Bassenthwaite.

I finished the essay a whole three days before the deadline. It then took a day to print it, both because of the queue for the printer, and also the laborious speed at which the paper slowly chugged out of the machine. Anyway, it was done, and I'd found it surprisingly okay. Not as big a shock as I thought, and the document actually looked good.

Well, the first thing I did after I was awarded a Distinction was to call Mum. I couldn't wait to divulge my incredible result. I then thanked Mary and Colin respectively.

No longer was the refectory or even the library an intimidating place, and the computer enabled me to check my spelling, giving me something special. That something changed my entire life. It changed my thinking, the way my brain worked, I started to understand how I processed information, and it gave me the ability to express my thoughts in words. Quite simply, I was no longer afraid to make mistakes. I started to feel free.

Those RED crossings out and double underlinings of school had been the kiss of death for me in the past. Now I discovered it wasn't that I was illiterate. I could read – slowly, yes, but that was just a practice thing. It wasn't that I was stupid. It wasn't that I wasn't interested in learning – my God, I was interested – and it wasn't that I was unable to get a Distinction. I just flipping well did that. It was that I needed strategies, a toolbox of different techniques to solve problems. It was a long-winded approach sometimes, but nevertheless, a way around the solid brick wall of the past. And the computer gave me hope, which was the greatest gift I could ask for, because up to then I hadn't had much.

I continued learning about our wonderfully diverse country-side and, moreover, I learned a great deal more about myself. There were highs and lows throughout my time at the place which had seemed so daunting at first, but was now very famil-iar, and almost felt like a second home. I eventually graduated with an overall Distinction, mortarboard on my head, black cape and all the pomp and ceremony. Not that I gloated. I had worked hard; it was as simple as that. Mum, Amber and Derek arrived late to the ceremony and missed all the pre-photos. Apparently, Derek had forgotten to lock the front door and they'd had to turn back. I was disappointed, of course, but I had some photos taken with Colin and his family.

I'd learned so much about a subject I was now passionate about. The time I spent there increased my energy and enthu-siasm for our environment, the natural world and our ecology. It formed a solid base for clear thinking, developing opinions about our world, and specifically, it gave me the confidence to make mistakes.

21

NATURE

Colin became a Countryside Ranger. It was the job most people coveted, and he deserved it. My own first job was for a conservation charity organising volunteer work parties. Occasionally he and I would write to each other with funny work anecdotes and top tips.

My job involved picking up volunteers from the train station in our white minibus. Anyone was welcome. I had to load the tools for the relevant task, instruct everyone on the practical aspects, supervise the work and make the tea. I basically worked outside three days a week, with the other two days spent in the office, organising the work with the various landowners and clients. For the first time, I gleefully went to work with a smile on my face and looked forward to what the day would bring.

We did everything: built bird hides at a large bird-watching centre; managed woodland at a local nature reserve; laid hedges to form wildlife corridors (without cutting through the stems!); installed boardwalks for wheelchair access to various nature trails; erected stiles on miles of public footpaths; built wooden bridges to open up forgotten routes; seeded and managed wild-flower meadows; carried out invasive species control on a site of special scientific interest; undertook butterfly conservation measures on chalk grassland; made and installed bat-boxes in the local woodland; planted reeds at a wetland bird reserve; created habitat for snakes, and planted trees by the thousands. It was my ideal job, and it felt good to be doing positive work for our environment.

Of course one of my most important jobs was to make sure the vast steel kettle was on the gas burner and keeping the brews coming for the volunteers. The tea breaks enabled me to chat with people, too, which gave me an insight into the kind of people who volunteer, but also helped to keep my shyness at bay. All the years of pretending and using Jonny, had equipped me with the skill to hide the fact I was shy.

Besides working in the week, at weekends I also volunteered at a local nature reserve. This was an old railway siding, where tons and tons of bomb waste from Hull had been dumped during the Second World War. Wildflower species and trees had clawed their way back through natural regeneration, creating a rich patchwork of different wildlife habitats. There was also a small lake, with yellow flag iris, water lilies and reedmace. The reserve was a testament to how nature eventually takes back control and what a powerful force it can be.

Every day at the conservation charity was different. It was a great place to work, and it couldn't have been further from those long and very hot days at the prison. Being within nature was becoming part and parcel of my daily life, and not only did I learn something new every day, I learned to respect the natural world, and the more I saw, the more I wanted to see.

One day, we were tasked with building a dry-stone wall aside a footpath in North Yorkshire. There must have been twenty or more volunteers that day. We'd also picked up from a day centre for young adults with learning difficulties. There were two boys with Down's Syndrome who always came on a Wednesday. They were always very enthusiastic, as were all the volunteers. They were also terrifically good fun. Their jokes and singing were infectious, and Wednesdays always seemed to be a popular day.

A dry-stone wall is a structure with no cement or straight edges. It can stay standing for many hundreds of years, sometimes within the harshest of environments. Constructing one is not only strenuous, it's also technically demanding. It's considered by many to be an art form. You need an understanding of physics, construction, and nature along with an eye for detail, a strong back, and artistic flair.

The morning of the task started wet, but later on the clouds began to clear, and the sun started to warm us as we fetched and carried stones and slowly arranged them, big ones at the bottom and tapering in slightly, with as straight a face as possible. I was moving along the line, instructing on suitable stones and helping people to locate the right piece in the mighty jigsaw.

The two boys from the residential centre were doing very well. Their attention to detail was an example to everyone, including me. I was helping to lift a sizeable stone for them into position, and the pair of them had me in stitches with their humour. They seemed so carefree and happy. I watched them chatting together as they worked. It was a joy to see their joviality mixed with such focus for the task. I thought about my hang-ups and disabilities, and my anxieties all seemed so minor and stupid.

'Where's John with that big stone? Is he having another lie-down?' I heard them shout.

'I'm here, I'm here,' I replied, lugging a giant lump of limestone up the hill.

They laughed. 'The Wolfman would have just put that on his shoulders.'

I stumbled with the rock. 'Wolf Man?'

'THE Wolfman!' they said simultaneously. 'Gladiators, are you ready?' they shouted.

'Ah! I get it.'

'How did you get the scar across your face, John? Was it from a chainsaw?'

I didn't really know how to reply. I touched it with my fingers. 'Yes... Something like that. An accident.'

'You must be tough.'

'Not really. I try and forget about it.'

They both growled like wolves and showed their claws. They gave me some more energy, and I picked up the stone, took the few steps and dropped it at their feet.

'You're doing really well, boys,' I said, as I saw how much further on they were than some of the other groups.

They giggled. 'We want to be like you, John. Tough and strong.'

They didn't say anything they didn't mean, so their words stopped me in my tracks, and I didn't know what to say. I watched them manhandling the stone I'd given them, and my heart felt like it was being squeezed.

'And I want to be like you,' I said, under my breath.

22

REHABILITATION

After a year, I was offered a permanent contract to set up a ranger team working on public rights of way at a county council in the Midlands.

I was now tasked with opening fifty footpaths and bridleways a year. This meant building bridges, stiles, gates, steps, surfacing, signposting and clearing overgrown areas so that they were legally open. The government had injected funding to enable the whole of the country to open all publicly accessible routes by the year 2000.

My fabulous assistant George and I opened up fifty paths in the first two months, and we found ourselves in every corner of the county. We were not only responsible for opening access to the countryside for walkers, horse riders and cyclists, we were privileged to observe deer, buzzards, badgers, weasels, stoats, kingfishers and herons, to name but a few, at close quarters.

Our fully capable 4x4 off-road pickups were just the tool to get us to the various sites, and we had to undergo rigorous training in order to become Local Authority recognised off-road drivers. We also had to undergo a theory exam... and an eyesight test. No one knew about my eye injury. My right eye had compensated so well, I'd learned not to let my injury hold me back, keeping it a well-hidden secret. A test was a very daunting proposition. If I wasn't able to drive the vehicles, it might mean me losing my job. I skilfully passed all the practical elements, climbing huge muddy slopes, getting out of ditches, negotiating woodland and reversing trailers, but on the morning of the eyesight test I felt sick. I was toying with the idea of phoning in and pretending to be ill, but that would just prolong the agony.

The testing guy turned up at 9am, and there were four other guys from different departments also attending. I opted to go last. I wanted to observe the format and try and work out a plan of action, i.e. find out the answers, so I could blag it. The guy set up a machine on the desk. We were all sent into a different room and then called in independently to undertake the test. I tried to busy myself, because my leg was shaking and my hands trembling, and I was going out of my mind with worry that this could be the end of a job which I loved so much. I closed my good eye and tried to concentrate on a map I had in front of me. All I could see was a grey blur. When I changed eye, I could see the finest details of the map, the tiny churches, rivers and contours.

When the first guy came out, I started to quiz him. He told me that he had to look into a machine, and various images, words and colours were shown to him. I needed to know whether it was for both eyes together or individually. Both together wouldn't be so bad, and I knew I could wing it, but if individually, I was stuffed. On further questioning, he confirmed it was for individual eyes and told me what some of the images were and the order. I tried to commit the information to memory. When I asked the next guy to come out, I hoped it would confirm the sequence and content. My only hope was to regurgitate what I'd been told and hope for the best.

The second guy came out, and I interrogated him. It started to look a little suspicious, as the guys just shrugged the whole thing off as a minor inconvenience of their time, rather than a job- and career-saving exercise.

I paced around the floor and went to the loo about seven times. I was in next. I just wanted to run away. I heard the door handle turn and out came the third guy, quickly followed by the testing man.

'I have an issue with my youngest son at school, and I have to go and collect him. John, I'll have to return to do your test some other time.'

Sheer relief hit me like a full-on body blow. I had a stay of execution and, boy, I was glad – for the moment, anyway.

'I'll be back within the next week, John.'

'Yes, that's cool,' I said, as if I didn't care.

'Oh! And I'll change the cards in the machine, so there'll be no cheating.'

I smiled and didn't show my complete disappointment inside. Oh, man! This was just drawing out the agony. Now I wished it had all happened there and then.

I spent the following week in a desperate heap, feeling sorry for myself and putting myself through hours of pointless eye-training exercises to try and get the sight back in my bad eye. On the Thursday, the testing man called to say he would be at my depot on Friday morning at 9am. I didn't eat anything that evening and didn't get much sleep either. I spent the night thinking about where I could go next and what sort of job I could get that didn't involve eye-testing.

9.15 came and went, with no sign of him. My heart started to beat faster with the thought he'd forgotten, but at 9.21 he appeared through the door, greeting me with a sigh.

'Morning, John, is the kettle on? I've had a hell of a journey. My car decided to give up the ghost, and I had to come on the bus.'

'Yes, of course. Milk and sugar?'

'Yes, please. Two sugars, I need them.'

I returned from our little depot kitchen, and we both sipped away at our tea.

'John... we need to get your eye test done, so I can tick off all your driving certification. I don't have the testing machine this morning. It was too heavy to cart on the bus, so what I thought we'd do is have a walk around the depot yard and I'll just ask you a few questions. That sound okay?'

'Sounds good to me,' I said jovially.

He then held up a piece of paper with various-sized road signs marked on it. 'Can you tell me what these are?'

'30mph, no entry, hairpin bed, national speed limit and school ahead.' My good eye could see them as sharp as a knife.

'No problems there whatsoever, John. This is obviously just a formality. Let's have a walk outside.'

He strolled around the car park and asked me to read out a couple of number plates on cars about twenty metres away, and then the colour of an airplane passing over. I said silvery-white, and he agreed.

'How many birds are there in that tree?' He pointed at a willow growing out of the chain-link fence.

'Five.' Again, my good eye gave full 20/20 vision.

'That's great, John. Sorry I had to draw this out and apologies for the other day. I'm sure you have better things to be getting on with as head ranger.'

I laughed. 'Sure do. I have a bridge to build over the river next week, and I'm just organising all the materials.'

'Well, that's it then, you've passed. I'll get the report signed off and up to admin this afternoon.'

I was in bed for 8pm and slept ten hours that night. I felt like I'd been spared.

My appetite for learning grew and grew, and the council facilitated many courses and further CPD, including chainsaw training and post-grad arboricultural qualifications. I was grateful, extremely grateful, and I was passionate about discovering all there was to know about our environment and the nature around us.

After a couple of years, I was offered the job of Tree and Conservation Officer. This was a desk job but involved getting out and about delivering various tree related projects. Of course, this was a daunting proposition. More money, more responsibility and increased learning were all attractive, but I still maintained my mental block about having to write or being trapped behind a desk.

I hid my insecurities well as usual and embarked on my new position. I was, however, thrown in at the deep end in terms of giving presentations. The new job involved working with the community on various tree-planting and environmental improvement initiatives, and that meant standing in front of large groups and talking. Was I ever going to get away from my insecurities? Conly Cassle and the pain of my frozen body as I was humiliated were never far from the forefront of my mind.

I inevitably used Jonny to face the audiences, coming up with inventive strategies to deflect my insecurity. The school assemblies were the most fun. I dressed up as a hedgehog and pretended I needed a new home. Hiding inside a furry costume allowed me to relax and perform, and if my stutter did return, it wasn't so obvious, as no one could see my face. I encouraged the kids to suggest what they could do at their school to help and provide a home for me and my other wild animal friends. Many, many schools rolled up their sleeves and got involved in tree planting, pond creation, making wildflower areas in even the smallest of places, creating bug hotels, and putting out bird feeders and monitoring visitors as part of their Biology curriculum.

By far the biggest project I was responsible for was the planting of over half a million trees to help with a huge development in the north of the county. I personally planted many thousands of trees, adding to the ones I'd planted in my previous jobs. I began to feel I was putting something back into our natural world and actually making an impact.

My passion for trees was now an intrinsic part of my psyche, and on the eve of my twenty-ninth birthday I decided to embarked on further post-grad training in arboriculture, at night school.

While studying, I met self-employed tree surgeons. I discovered they were earning three or four times more than me, and this sowed the seed for setting up my own tree surgery company. I thought about the pros and cons of working for myself. Leaving the security of a public sector job, with the pension, the financial red carpet and 'normal' working hours, against... well... the unknown. I'd changed direction before, and it had proved beneficial, and I felt ready for a new challenge. Somehow, all the tough challenges of my past gave me a feeling that it was okay to make changes and, moreover, not to waste time being anxious about the decision.

'I'm handing in my notice,' I said to my line manager, who was at his desk.

'I think you're making a mistake,' he said, not fully taking the envelope in his hand.

I had an instant flashback to my standoff with Mum before I left for Europe, and a shiver went down my spine. 'I've been testing the water, got a bit of kit together and I feel the time is right for me to take the bull by the horns and go for it.'

He looked up at me. 'Well, it's your choice, but I'd prefer you to stay on. How about you continue to work two days a week here, just to see your current projects through and ease yourself in gradually?'

I couldn't argue with that and shook his hand. It was the perfect way to begin. After four months my own work was flooding in, and I finally left the council to sail my own ship.

So there I was, securing myself into the top of an eighty-foot poplar tree with just a harness, rope and metal spikes secured to my feet. The view of the town was incredible as I swayed with the movement of the tree. I wasn't up there to look at the view, though. The tree had shed a huge limb, damaging the hotel lobby below. It had been deemed unsafe and we were given the job of removing her.

I'd hired in an eighty-ton crane to lift the heavy sections of tree over the building and into the car park, to be processed by my team below. I attached the clanking chains of the crane around the trunk section and then descended some twenty feet lower and unclipped the gigantic chainsaw and started her up. The blade and engine were taller than me. It was a beast of a machine and one to be treated with respect. It was incredibly heavy, and it took all my strength to maintain my position on the side of the tree and get the saw into position, ready to make the cuts.

The engine growled, and I knew if I made the slightest mistake, it wouldn't think twice about severing my body as well as the tree. I double-checked the equipment and signalled to the crane operator that I was ready to go. I had to have complete faith in the driver to take the cut-off section vertically away from me and not to swing it into me, crush me, or drop it through the roof of the hotel. I could feel my legs begin to shake.

I took a very deep breath, released the safety catch on the saw and brought it up to full revs. It instantly bit into the wood. Huge amounts of sawdust started hitting my safety visor, preventing me from seeing. I couldn't stop, though. Once you start the cut, you have to go for it, so that the crane can take the strain without trapping the saw. I manhandled the saw through the wood, the blade at times very close to my chest and shoulders. Then I felt the whole tree move forward. The engine on the crane became louder, and suddenly the entire top section of the tree, some three tons, rose above me, and as I looked up I could see it twisting in the wind. It is a bizarre feeling to see something of that size and weight going upwards instead of down, after you cut it.

The crane safely took the tree over the building and laid it carefully on the ground, where my team started their job of cutting it smaller before loading it onto the vehicles to take it away. I checked the tiny metal spikes that were securing me to the trunk and felt a wave of relief. It had all gone smoothly. I heard the clanking of the chains again, ready to secure and undertake the process on the remaining sections of the tree.

For the next ten years I ran the business successfully. It was challenging and both physically and mentally draining, but I was learning more and more about trees, understanding their internal make-up, strength, biomechanical characteristics, diseases and the beauty of the wood types and grains. But I was also learning more about myself, too, and my confidence began to grow.

Within that time, I also married and had two sons. Becoming a father was strange the first time. I felt underprepared and once again out of my depth, but I learned how to be a dad and I promised myself I wouldn't let them down, in the way I'd felt with my own father. In many ways, the responsibility made me grow up. When I say 'grow up' I mean actually graduate from a boy into a man. There was no time for me to be obsessed with my own issues, I had to show them that there was a big wide world out there and not to be afraid of it. Be strong and make the most of every day.

It's true to say that I again became caught up in the rat race, with a bigger house, renovations, expansion and spending beyond our limits. I did, however, try to spend as much time as possible with the boys. I loved time with them, especially holidays camping, building dens, climbing trees, and boring them about trees.

It was only after having worked seven days a week for many years, and renovating a house at the same time, when I found myself re-tiling the bathroom at one o'clock in the morning and arguing with my wife about an upside-down tile behind the U-bend, that I realised something had to change.

Tree surgery was slowly killing me. Climbing trees and humping timber around all day was taking its toll on my body, not to mention the many near misses and many friends and colleagues who'd been cut by chainsaws, fallen out of trees and broken backs. I decided to make things easier and train as a tree-climbing instructor. I'd always enjoyed passing on my skills with the volunteers and enabling others, so I set about enrolling on a technical instructors' course and becoming qualified.

I formed a close friendship with a guy I was training with. He was the owner/manager of a drug rehabilitation centre at his farm in the middle of the forest. Guys with hard-core drug habits would come to stay for nine months after a detox programme, and they would start their lives again from scratch. One-to-one counselling, care, love, numeracy, literacy and vocational training equipped the attendees with a new opportunity to become drug-free and get into work. He offered me a job and I immediately said yes.

I would be working on a freelance basis delivering a suite of tree surgery courses, including climbing, emergency rescues, complex rigging and tree dismantling.

So, there I was, black marker in hand, standing in front of five former drug addicts, about to go through the motions of scaling a seventy-foot mature oak tree.

I had to go through all the legal requirements of being a tree climber. It's not just a case of shinning up and enjoying the view. It's a serious business of legislation, insurance and procedures. Most people assume it's like rock climbing, but with trees, the techniques and equipment are totally different.

So, what was the most challenging aspect for me as a new instructor? Was it ensuring they were all safe and equipped with the right knowledge, teaching how to tie friction hitches and create back-up safety systems, or rescuing an injured body out of a tree and administering first aid?

No. It was writing on the board in front of the class.

My fear of making mistakes when writing had been given a respite with the advent of computers. I'd learned from the spell-checker, but one day I can spell a word, and the next day I haven't a clue. Letters still get muddled up and sometimes look backwards. Often I get into a double-bluffing situation, where I think of the spelling and convince myself that the way I've always written it is incorrect, and so I change it, but when I do, I'm always wrong. So, my failsafe policy of putting all the plausible letters in a word, so that at least some of them may be correct, is often my default. 'I'm playing all the right notes, but not necessarily in the right order,' as Eric Morecambe once said. That was my writing to a T. But I couldn't do that here. I had to look competent. I set out lesson plans and practised what I had to say and write. I guess this is just like any teacher, but I rehearsed and rehearsed. Practically and orally, I was proficient and a master of my craft now, but I had to write the word 'aerial' at least twenty times a day, and to this day, I still can't get it right. The words of my old Geography teacher were never forgotten though: 'A picture or diagram can speak a thousand words.'

Over the eight years I taught at the centre, I learned so much. The whole place was run with a Christian ethos, and the care and compassion that was given to the men was incredible. It was a genuine attempt to make this world a better place and take some of life's abandoned and written-off people and give them a second chance. The men were from all walks of life, race, class and education. Some of them were born into a life of drugs, and all of them had been abused or neglected in some way. Drugs took away the pain of being abandoned and not loved. It was as simple as that.

I saw and got to know some fantastic people. Men who were bright and capable, but who had just not had the encouragement or the positive direction to make a go of life. The guys learned a new craft, and we equipped them with everything they needed to be independent and no longer a burden to the state, either on benefits or in prison.

I was at the arboricultural industry trade fair some years later, watching the tree-climbing championships, when I felt a tap on my shoulder. I looked round to see a tall lad with a cracking smile.

'John. Remember me? I'm Ben. You taught me to climb, and I passed all my qualifications. I'm now working as a professional climber. I have a girlfriend and a flat and I can't thank you enough.'

'Ben. Yes, I remember. I knew you would make good. Probably all your years of climbing drainpipes and crawling through tiny windows!' We both laughed, and I gave him a slap on the back, in a tree surgeons' kind of way. I was actually welling up inside but didn't want to show it.

For me, working with those men was life-changing, not just because I overcame my fear of writing in public, or because I seemed to overcome my stutter. Fundamentally, working there made me look at my own life and compare it to the hell some of those guys had been through. I saw how positive they were as they went about making a future for themselves. It humbled me. In many respects my life had been easy compared with theirs, and although I'm not a believer in the Christian club, working there gave me faith in humanity. I came to the conclusion that being grateful for who you are and what you have is actually a very powerful thing, and essential for a happy life.

Government funding cuts ended my rehab career. It costs a lot of money to put someone through a nine-month residential rehab, compared to other 'conventional' systems – systems which, when I questioned them, the attendees told me never worked. I couldn't help wonder why governments could be so short-sighted.

My work was over there, but I remain grateful for the fantastic opportunity and the rehabilitation of my own psyche, in many ways. Working there taught me to be patient and understanding of other people's needs, reinforced my compassionate side and proved to me that no matter how low you get, and how close you are to giving up, there is hope.

PART III

FREEDOM

23

A TASTE OF FREEDOM

Tragically, my marriage ended. I'd entered into it, like most people, full of enthusiasm and love, but in reality we were heading in different directions. This was probably something to do with me feeling trapped. I always felt I needed to be able to at least see an escape route in everything I did, but that wasn't possible in a marriage. The boys were two and twelve, and it was a difficult decision to go, but I knew I wouldn't let them down.

So, home life was changing fast, and the same was true for my work. My teaching was now finished and I had to make some changes. Going into consultancy seemed like a natural progression – surveys, tree protection, safety examinations, etc. I would have to completely build my clientele again from scratch, and I had a lot to learn, too. On top of all that, the divorce was extremely wearing, and I was looking for somewhere new to live, while still paying the mortgage.

I'd been to see my solicitor, which was always stressful, and was driving home when I received a call from an established and important customer, to whom I was very loyal. A tree had been seen 'looking dangerous' next to the main road within their estate, and could I get there as soon as possible to check it out?

As it happened, I would be passing the site on my way back. It was starting to get dark, so I put my foot down. I pulled my truck up alongside the mighty chestnut. It wasn't unlike the tree from my childhood, sixty feet high or so, a huge stem and spreading canopy. The tree had suddenly started to lean over the road and I recognised that it needed to be felled as soon as possible to make it safe.

I had the skills and experience to deal with such a dangerous situation, and as luck would have it, I had a big chainsaw and a winch on board as standard in the truck. So, on my own, I set the steel cable from the winch into the canopy and locked it onto an adjacent large tree.

The light was fading, but all I had to do was put the directional cut in the face, away from the road, and then carefully take the saw in from the back, leaving a thin slice intact to form the hinge, then control the direction of fall with the winch and pull it over in one. I'd done it hundreds of times before, and although it was almost dark and the road was stuffed with rush hour traffic, I had everything under control. Or so at least I thought. In hindsight, I should have tackled a job of this scale with a team and contacted the police to close the road.

The giant saw's three foot blade chewed into the wood like a hot knife through butter. I formed the relevant cuts and manipulated the winch to the point where the tree should have come straight over – but it didn't shift. If I took the winch past its maximum tension, there was a shear-pin in the handle as a safety. If I popped that, the winch would be unusable, so I took it as far as I felt possible. The tree stayed solid and stubborn. The hinge section I'd created within the tree might have been cut too thick. That was a possibility, and the thing that commonly prevents a successful fell. However, cutting the hinge too thin can cause the tree to break off from its connection with the stump, leaving it to fall in any direction, which in this case could possibly be in the busy road.

I knew I had to go back to the tree and cut some more of the hinge thickness in order to get the tree over, and that was extremely dangerous indeed. Now, there's a golden rule in tree-felling, and it's the same with a lit firework. Never, ever, go back. It's simple, because the tree could fail with you right underneath it. Anyway, I had no choice. I couldn't leave it in a more dangerous position than when I'd found it, and there was no other way of getting it down, other than with perhaps a helicopter. I started the powerful saw and tried to gently nibble away at the hinge. My heart was pounding as I manhandled the saw to take out the thinnest slices possible, knowing at any time the whole tree could topple over. Suddenly, and without warning, I heard a loud crack, and then it hit me.

I felt an almighty blow to the top of my helmet and on my back, and I was crushed to the ground in a split second. I wasn't aware at the time, but I was out cold. The top section of the tree, about a two-ton section which had previously detached, was hung up in the canopy. In the dark, I hadn't noticed. During the disturbance of my activity, the section had dislodged, falling with full force to the ground, with me beneath it.

I came around after God knows how long, but all I could see in front of my nose was my foot. I asked myself out loud whether I was dead. It felt unreal, and I had to hear my voice asking the question to gain some sort of reality. This was the bit when you see yourself in some kind of out-of-body experience. The realisation of a dislocated leg and a bleeding gash down my back quickly brought me into the real world. Luckily I wasn't trapped under the section. The force had hit me and pushed me to one side at the same time, which was sheer good fortune, and the difference between life and death.

I managed to crawl a short distance. I could see the main tree was still standing. Thankfully it hadn't gone into the road. If it had, it would have killed people for sure.

I knew I was in shock because at first I couldn't feel much

pain, but I soon realised I had to put my knee back in the socket if I were to complete the task of making the tree safe.

Snapping my knee back into the joint, was the most horrific pain I had ever felt. My eyeball injury and severed nose was nothing compared to this. I lay on my back and, with both hands slowly moved my foot down and away from my head. It was the strangest feeling, seeing my leg almost detached from my body, and as I moved it further, the pain became worse. I couldn't look at it but managed to locate the socket with my hand and bring the bone into position, ready to slot it into place. I immediately felt the urge to be sick. I writhed around on the floor moaning out loud. I had no time to wallow in the agony, so I clawed at the ground with my bare hands and managed to turn onto my side, so I could use the ground as leverage, and, with all my force, I clenched my teeth so hard it seemed like even my hair was clenched. I took a gasp of air, closed my eyes, and *snap*! forced down and clicked it in. I vomited and then lay still in the long grass, taking rapid breaths. I was drifting in and out of consciousness, and not able to move, but all the while I knew I had to get the tree safe. It took me many minutes to get my breath back. I knew I had to move the winch to another tree, to improve the angle and make doubly sure it wouldn't go in the road. My body wouldn't shift. I had nothing left to give, and I started to shiver with cold in the dark, knowing there was a huge and very dangerous tree right above me. I lay there staring up into the canopy, watching the headlights from the busy road flicker through the branches. The pain in my leg was still excruciating. I felt like I couldn't go on. As my breathing became shallow, I closed my eyes and counted to three.

I grabbed at the soil beside me and gritted my teeth, searching inside my body for that thing. The thing which is only available when you most need it. I dug deep, summoning the energy I needed, and pushed my arms so that I could get up onto my good leg. I then tried to hop through the long grass, dragging my bad leg behind me. I bit hard into my knuckle to try and take the pain away. It didn't have any effect, but I had to do something. I could also feel my shirt sticking to the blood on my back. I knew I'd been cut, but had no idea of the severity.

I eventually arrived at the winch. Releasing the tension was potentially a disaster waiting to happen. If the tree were to sit back, it would almost definitely go into the road, but it was what it was, and now I had to finish the job. Even though there was a tremendous risk, finishing the job was the best option. I dragged the heavy steel winch to another tree, and the pain of my leg became unbearable. I set it up and began pushing and pulling on the handle until the slack cable became taut. I could barely stay conscious, I was in so much pain, but I pulled and pushed until I didn't have the strength to do anymore. Then *crack*! It was the same noise I'd heard all those years back at Grandad's. *Crack* it went again. All I could do was hold my breath. I closed my eyes and prayed to Mother Nature that the tree didn't go into the road. And then came the biggest almighty crash and a whoosh of air blew me off my feet. The tree was at last down, and safe.

I didn't want the client to know what had gone on. I would probably never work for them again, so I abandoned the gear in the dark and drove home in second gear, in agony. I crawled through the door, reached for the phone and called for an ambulance, then collapsed in a heap on the kitchen floor. The paramedics mounted me to a backboard and took me to the hospital alone.

I'm running 10k road runs now and I've recently been having snowboard lessons with my sons, but it took a long time to heal, the best part of eight or nine years. My tree surgery days were completely over. My body wasn't strong enough, and I'd been given the sign not to push it too far, because next time I might not be so lucky.

So, what was the point of me telling you about all this? It wasn't because I wanted to notch up another near-death story to add drama or to look like some kind of hero. I'd done a very stupid thing in tackling that job on my own, there was nothing heroic about it at all. But I learned a valuable lesson. That lesson was that no matter how stupid you are and no matter how low you get when you think everything is against you, and when you think you've had enough of fighting, you can dig deep and find that tiny bit of fire which still burns inside you, even though locating it can seem almost impossible. When you do find it, you grab it and kindle it, just as Grandad taught me all those years ago, and you use it to fuel your courage and get back on your feet.

So, there I was, teaching myself via YouTube how to set up a website, and my new business was born. My practical career was over, and my body was grateful. Now I had to heal and face my nemesis head-on – again! As if I hadn't spent my entire lifetime doing just that.

Consultancy was surely the natural progression. I'd been paving the way for a year or so, carrying out tree safety assessments and general advice, but if I was to make a proper go of it, I had to go into tree protection within planning and development, because that's where the bulk of work would be. This involved writing reports, and detailed ones at that. The reports would be scrutinised by the local authorities and by my peers, and they would be available to the general public for online viewing.

Professionally I was all set, physically I was in rebuild mode, and mentally I had delved deep once again, and I felt ready. But was the world ready for me?

It appeared not. This was 2009. The banks had crashed, and the UK was in recession. Spending had been cut in many areas, and the construction and development sectors were being extra cautious. But I had no choice other than to make it work. Keeping my overheads as low as possible, I called and emailed all my contacts and managed to source a few bat surveys. I'd qualified in that too. As my leg slowly healed, the work started to dribble in. What this forced me to do was get a decent computer, set out a report format with a professional look, and get the website up and running. I was constantly delving into my toolkit at this time, and I had a determination deep inside me.

During the Easter holidays, I took the boys to London for a couple of days. We visited Buckingham Palace and the Mews, where the Queen's horses and golden carriages are kept. We thoroughly enjoyed visiting the science museum. I got to see Newcomen's steam-pump engine, which I remembered from History at school, in the flesh – or rather, the iron. The boys enjoyed all the hands-on experiments, and we were all amazed at the collection of space rockets and moon landers. We had a go at threading a nut on a bolt behind glass using huge space-suit gloves. Not easy!

One adventure we'll never forget was riding the London Eye. We marvelled at the whole of London below us, picking out the famous landmarks, like St Paul's Cathedral, the newly built Shard and all of the huge parks, green spaces and trees, which fascinated me. As we scanned the whole city, I became aware of the hundreds of big red cranes with flashing lights towering above it. Everywhere you looked there was a crane, and the more I looked, the more I saw.

On the descent, there was an opportunity to stand on a specific mark and wait for a remote camera to take our photo. As the boys waited with impatient smiles, I kept thinking about all those cranes. Development never stops in London, I thought, and there were so many trees to protect. It was a revelation.

So, there I was, renting a small office space in central London, protecting trees. I feel immense pride every day knowing I'm contributing something back to society and, combined with our Midlands office, we save and protect, as well as plant, in excess of 10,000 trees per year.

Nearly thirty years on since I embarked on my university course, including my volunteer work, council projects and consultancy, I worked out I've saved and planted near to a million trees. I did fell a few as a surgeon, that's true, but they were the dangerous ones and would have fallen over anyway. I did apologise to each and every one before I started the saw. My planting is small beer in the grand scheme of things, and a drop in the ocean in terms of what the planet needs to hold back climate change, reverse the effects of it and sustain habitat for some of the planet's endangered species, including humans. So, more work to be done, for sure. I've become a tree geek, that's for sure, and trees never cease to amaze me.

I had a bit of a shock when my memory was jogged, in the most surprising way, while carrying out a tree condition survey in the Cotswolds village of Stow-on-the-Wold. While surveying the fabulous trees within the churchyard, I came across two mysterious-looking yew trees either side of the arched doorway into the church. The veteran trees were growing tight up against the stonework and the red, fissured stems came together to form a natural arch around the door. I took a photo and remember thinking it looked like an intriguing doorway to a mystical world. Professionally, I noted there was no conflict with the building, and when I commented on them to the clerk of the council, she brought back a memory I wasn't expecting.

'The trees are amazing, aren't they?' she said.

'They are incredible. I've never seen anything so mysterious, like an opening to a different world,' I replied.

'Well, Tolkien thought that too,' she said, matter-of-factly.

'Tolkien?'

'Yes, apparently the trees inspired *The Hobbit*, when he was writing here.'

My mind wandered to the soft cheek and the amazing kiss I'd shared with Melanie, and her enthusiasm for Tolkien.

'Are you okay?'

'Yes… yes, I'm fine. They really are incredible trees.'

24

TWENTY-SEVEN-THOUSAND FEET

I was surveying trees within the rear garden of a huge stately house on Warwick Avenue in London. The gardens there all back on to a large communal garden, the size of a football pitch, which you would never guess was there. Mature oak, chestnut and cedar provide shade for the croquet lawn and tennis court, as well as seating areas and a patchwork of wild flowers. While we strolled around the garden, the client requested I head out to their house in Provence to give them a safety report for the trees there and recommend any works to be done. Of course, he would pay for the flights and accommodation and I would spend two days making sure their property was safe and secure before their daughter's wedding out there a few months later.

The evening before I was due to fly out, I started my usual ritual of over-thinking the plane journey and working myself into a state of anxiety. I'd flown many times since my holiday with Amber, but the prospect always petrified me.

I lay there thinking about the flimsy metal can with wings held on by tiny bolts and I imagined the pilots out of control in dramatic turbulence. The slightest bump would have me grappling the armrest, my knuckles white, my heart almost exploding while I fended off a panic attack.

This was a fantastic opportunity. The client obviously trusted my skill, but as usual I was thinking of backing out. I knew it was ridiculous and I hated myself for letting the feeling consume me. I spent a few hours in painful thought, and it was then I made a drastic decision. I would deliberately attempt to go into the void and see if I could talk to my subconscious. Instead of being dragged in as usual, I would be in control and try somehow to convince my brain, that flying was nothing to worry about. It was a crazy notion, but I was fed up with feeling so anxious about something that always seemed completely natural to my fellow passengers.

So there I was, lying in the almost completely dark room, focusing on a bare picture hook on the wall. My eyes relaxed, just like when I entered the void between words and my middle eye began to penetrate the hook and then focus beyond. Slowly but surely I began to see the opening. At first I was trying too hard and had to look away and then go in for another try. Eventually the door opened, I pulled with my hands and started to drift in. I imagined I was sitting in the window-seat of a plane at full altitude, and that the seats were so, so comfortable. Ridiculous, isn't it? But I imagined it was warm and cosy, the comfiest armchair in the whole world in front of a log fire, relaxed, safe and protected. I was engulfed in its safe arms, looking with complete joy out of the window at the clouds way below. I also imagined the pilots confidently engaged in flying the plane, and completely in control, as if we were just trundling along a smooth road in a car.

I told myself it was safe, and I reassured myself I loved doing it. I then pushed my way back out of the void and drifted off to sleep.

∼

The taxi arrived at the drop-off point at the airport and I collected my bag from the boot and proceeded to the check-in. There was no queue, and before I knew it my bag was on its way to the plane and I was through security, dressed again, shoes, belt, watch etc., and waiting at the departure gate. It was then I realised I was looking at the plane on the tarmac through the window and wasn't apprehensive in the slightest. No anxiety at all. No sweats, no shaking and only one routine trip to the loo. I boarded the plane and, other than a mild panic when I found someone sitting in my seat, everything was fine. The seat issue was resolved, the guy had just positioned himself in the wrong row. I assumed my position in the window and watched the baggage handlers load the cases, trying to spot mine. When the captain announced we were cruising at an altitude of 27,000 feet, I kicked back into my seat, imagining the warm, safe armchair once again, and I smiled.

As my mind drifted to what I had done within the void the evening before, I wondered whether I'd hypnotised myself. It was certainly a powerful exercise. Anyway, it had worked and that was all that mattered.

25

THE VEINS OF LIFE

The bright, sunny morning of my forty-eighth birthday, I woke with a start. Eyes wide open, it took me a few seconds to understand where I was. I established everything was okay, that I was in bed and not sleep-driving down the motorway or looking for escape routes at the back of the TV. But I did have a strange feeling that I had something important to remember.

I hadn't forgotten the nightmares I used to have as a child, and how sinking into the colossal void used to scare me to death, but since then I had never remembered a dream, not one, to the point where I thought I didn't dream at all.

But this night, something was very different. I had definitely dreamt something. Not a nightmare, though, or even an event, but words. Words coming to me. Words as you would see them on a typed page. They came fast, and they were clear, clean and defined, poetic in nature and rhythmical of sorts.

I went downstairs to make a cup of tea and as the kettle was boiling, the nagging in my head of something brilliant trying to escape started to drive me mad. I tried to dredge my brain and subconscious for what those words had been, but I couldn't remember any of them. The feeling I had was that they were the words of a genius and should be recorded, but I could recall nothing. Who was I kidding, anyway?

I drank my tea and went back to sleep. The following day, when I woke, the feeling was there again, but nothing was forthcoming.

A couple of nights later it happened again. The words seemed poetic, I knew that, but I just couldn't find them again in my conscious mind when I was awake. They were lost on me. It was a very bizarre feeling.

Words never seemed friendly or beautiful to me, let alone poetic. I still had substantial and deep-set issues with brain to pen. I never really moved on in terms of writing on paper. The fear of making a mistake and the fact I had never developed a confident and relaxed writing style meant any attempt to write was still agony. Usually the finished article looked like a four-year-old had done it.

My consultancy work, on the other hand, was becoming both rewarding and interesting, and one aspect of my work really surprised me. I'd started to become proficient at producing reports. The computer had become a true friend once again, and I used it to my advantage. I now had the freedom to communicate, in a way I never thought possible.

I had, of course, educated myself, through necessity and rarely through pleasure. Learning was mainly agonising, to say the least, but significantly, I'd discovered the relevance of words. The words I encountered, though, were practical words, in practical books. Facts and information which were tangible and meant something and about a subject I was passionate about. Phloem and xylem, epicormic growth and photosynthesis, etc. But I was still scared of words in many ways. There was always something to trip you up, odd letters in odd places. I'd never read a novel or any fiction, so words as art just didn't feature in my psyche. (Psyche being a classic example of a word to trip you up.) Fiction appeared completely pointless, and I couldn't understand why anyone would waste their time on something so intangible.

So why was I dreaming about poetic words?

A week or two passed. I can't remember how long specifically, but my car had gone in to have a service, and the nearest, warmest place out of the snow was in McDonald's. I wasn't a fast-food fanatic, but it was warm, and there was a toilet, and it was just across the road from the garage. I had a breakfast wrap and some tea and knew I might have a long wait ahead. The thought of this made me slump back in my seat and go a bit sleepy, and into a daze, which is a huge surprise, as there always seems to be something beeping in a McDonald's restaurant. I mean, constant beeping. It made me wonder how the hell people work there. Someone at some point must hear that beeping and surely do something about it – but no one ever seems to.

Nevertheless, despite the hustle and bustle and the beeping, my mind started to relax, and my eyes focused on a tear in the wall art just in front of me. Just as it had many times before, my peripheral vision became prominent, and my central eye saw through the tear and beyond, as though it was my subconscious that was seeing. Gradually an image started to emerge. I could still hear the noises of the restaurant, but they were muffled now. The image was of a tree in silhouette. The tree was there, centre stage in my mind, but I could also make out black, orange and purple, which seemed to be moving around. Then, as I relaxed more, a very strange thing happened. A very strange thing indeed. Words started to flow into my mind. I didn't see them, I could feel them. They were words about a cherry tree in the snow, standing proud, with leaves in vibrant green. It was unnerving. Unnerving, yet joyful at the same time. The words had no formal construction, like a sentence. They were solo words, but they were poignant and crisp in my mind. It scared me.

I became aware of people close by chatting, and I slowly and peacefully came out of my daze. Without moving my eyes, I reached for my iPhone and opened the Notes app. I knew I had to capture those words. It felt like if I blinked or thought about something different, I would instantly forget them. They felt important enough, and I wasn't going to let them get away again, so I began to write. I could feel each word as though they were being projected onto the back of my skull, like a little movie theatre in my head. I wrote and I wrote and I couldn't stop. The words came thick and fast, like a torrential downpour of literary rain. My heart pounded, and I felt excited. *Excited*. What was wrong with me?

I was oblivious to the world around me and focused one hundred percent on processing the words, through my arm, fingers and onto the tiny digital page. They started to form a story, a rhyming story.

I imagined the tree as a woman, with all her qualities and strengths, her vulnerabilities and beauty. Not a specific woman, but my vision of a woman, maybe my mum, sister or one of my past partners. I'm not sure who, but the words had a romance and a passion in them.

I adjusted a few words and arranged them like a poem. The revelation was that it was easy. The words just came to me. I didn't have to work hard at finding them, it just happened. What was strange, throughout the whole experience I could feel my feet tingling, in exactly the same way they'd tingled during my experience with the oak tree, just before she died.

So, here it is. My first poem. *Cherry Tree*. Written in McDonald's!

Cherry Tree

Standing proud within winter's deep white carpet,
the robin's song should not wake her from her
slumber.
She awaits that shaft of light to stir her earthy
optimism,
the power and energy, erect to touch the sky.
Tender to the touch, her buds begin to swell,
the new birth concealed, but not for long.
Her beauty she will tell.
Glorious the robin's breast, perched on her
slender arbour.
He feels her love, her fragile core, but knows the
power within her,
the veins of life in vibrant green, enough to stop
the heart.
Her youth and beauty on display, but this is just
the start.
Nature's scars, and battle wounds inflicted by
deer's antler,
are not enough to stop her growth and blossom
year on after.

26

SEE YA

Not the work of a genius by any means, but the words of the poem were apt, because we'd had some serious snowfall, and for a couple of weeks, moving around and trying to work proved very difficult. But at last, the snow melted away, making way for the daffodils in all their bright and buoyant yellow glory. Spring was here, and there was suddenly a warmth and optimism in the air.

The world was looking a very different place now. I'd surprised myself with the poem. Well, to be honest, I'd shocked myself. It felt good. Really good and liberating. My fear of words had prevented me from exploring them. Maybe it was the years of pent-up frustration and anxiety suddenly bursting out, and in a way I least expected. I found myself walking around with my chin up, instead of looking at the floor. I love the warm sun on my face, and the late spring and summer are always when I feel at my best. I was single again and my health reasonably good, despite all the old knocks. I started to date again and I felt more and more confident about myself. Well, as confident as I possibly could. Jonny had become a permanent fixture in my life, doing all the things I was too scared to do. He was able to deal with so many social and demanding situations, I was always in awe of him. It took me nearly fifty years to realise how completely crazy that was. I *was* Jonny! I pulled him out whenever I needed him, but I'd never accepted that he was me and I was him. I've never entirely banished my shyness, but I now bring Jonny to the fore as me and not a separate entirety, and that has been liberating.

The evening I met up with Dave and the lads in my home city, after more than thirty years, was one to remember. Going back to all those memories wasn't going to be easy, but somehow, I felt there was unfinished business. It would be fantastic to see them, of course, so this wasn't something I was going to miss, but there was an air of trepidation.

The city centre was the most convenient place to meet, and on my way I walked past the place where I was glassed in the face. It was still there. In fact, other than a new name, it had hardly changed. I didn't go in, but as I looked through the open doorway a cold shudder went through my entire body. There was such a negative energy coming out of there.

I met the boys in a pub in the lower south side of the city. The boys were now the middle-aged boys, but they hadn't changed in many ways. I instantly remembered their incredible senses of humour and what decent blokes they were. It turned from being an evening of trepidation into an evening of fun, laughter and a re-ignition of friendship which I hold close to my heart.

We'd been for something to eat, and we were finishing off the evening back in the pub we'd started in. It was my round, and the bar was crowded, but I jostled for position and got my order in for the beers. The first pint came, and as I passed it back to Dave, among the crowd I saw something that scared the living daylights out of me. It was her! Standing right on my shoulder. It was her, I knew it. For a minute, I didn't know what to do with myself. My mind instantly went back to the school reception and the 'message from my mum' incident. She was there, right behind me, just like on that day. I could feel my heart thumping, drumming to the deepest beat, and my legs were like lead, welded to the spot. I'd never forgotten her, never. My first love. The tune to 'The Entertainer' came into my head.

Slowly, I turned to check it really was her. It was. Her lips were exactly the same, but on closer inspection she wasn't quite the vision of beauty I remembered.

'Hi… it's Claire, isn't it?' I said, as I passed another beer back to the guys.

'I recognise the face, but I'm sorry, I can't remember you,' she said, as if I were a complete stranger.

'John. John Crawshaw.'

'Oh! John. Erm… No…I'm sorry, I just can't remember at all.'

That's all she needed to say. In a way, I was disappointed, but not surprised. I chuckled to myself as I collected the rest of the beers.

'See ya,' I said, as I moved away and joined the boys.

Nothing had changed over all those years. She had just made plain that I was non-existent for her. In a way I was glad. I now had closure.

'See ya,' I said in my mind and smiled.

27

LIFE CHANGING

The summer of 2018 was one of the hottest on record, with mounting concerns over potential water shortages and global warming. The plastic polluting our seas and the need to absorb carbon were vital world issues. The importance of trees was also being recognised, and suddenly I'd gone from being a tree geek to not such a geek after all.

I'd celebrated my forty-ninth birthday in the spring and was a little daunted, to say the least. I couldn't get my head around how quickly the time had flown by.

I walked in the sunshine to the hospital, through the park. There's a giant sequoia I visit now and again, a mighty beast that I like to get my hands on. The bark is quite soft, and you can push it in to a certain degree with your fingers. On this visit, I spotted the little divot carved out by a tree-creeper, one of Britain's smallest birds. I could hear its call high up in the canopy, but couldn't see it.

It was a long time since I'd last been to a hospital, thankfully. It seemed busy. There were many ambulances parked outside and many people still inside them. I had to queue to book myself in and then I was ushered to a side area, where I waited.

I'd had a biopsy on my ear, just under two weeks previously. I had a niggly scab which never really seemed to heal properly.

'It's a carcinoma, and it looks like you've had it sometime,' the Doctor said, his face stern.

'A few years, probably,' I said. 'I just thought I'd been scratching it in my sleep or something.' I didn't want to tell him the truth, which was I'd neglected to do anything about it, like a typical bloke.

'At least ten years I'd say. It's pretty serious and from the results it seems it's spread deep into the cartilage.'

My stomach cramped. I was stunned and shocked.

'Most probably sun damage. Have you ever badly burnt your ear?'

I remembered the cheap Greek holiday with Amber. 'I did, but many, many years ago.'

'I need to have a closer look in surgery, but I'll probably have to remove the cartilage. There will be very little support left, so depending on how much we remove, we may have to amputate the entire ear. The prosthetics are very good these days and fasten on with magnets. The good thing is, we should be able to clear things up for you.'

I couldn't believe what he told me. I slowly walked back through the park. My joyful stride on the way there had turned into an aimless amble. All I could think about was having to wear a false ear.

I called my family to tell them the news and they were brilliant, as always. They tried to make light of it by telling me what a fabulous party piece it could make, and how I could listen to conversations around corners, but how I'd also be a potential nightmare in airport scanners.

I took a week off work. It was a shock. Cancer was something other people had, not me. Since seeing the doctor, I had a stream of questions, including the effect on my hearing, whether it would spread, and how realistic the prosthetics were. I started looking online for the answers. The information looked gloomy, so I called the doctor for a clearer idea.

'Don't worry Mr Crawshaw, a carcinoma won't spread to your vital organs. It's not that kind of cancer. It will carry on eating away at you, though, if we don't act with haste. I've sent a letter to you today with the appointment details.'

'Thank you, doctor. One more thing.' I paused.

'What is it?'

'You will try not to make me look different, won't you? I've spent a lifetime, being different.'

I took myself away for a couple of days, to one of my favourite places, a little campsite in the heart of the Forest of Dean. A small clearing in the trees, with the feeling of being miles from anywhere. I'd been building my own campervan – nothing fancy, a bed, kitchen, solar power, that kind of thing, and it was just about ready for a maiden voyage.

I arrived at the site, made sure the solar power was operating, put the kettle on and sat with the sliding door open, looking out at the valley of trees before me. Every shade of green was there in the undulating forest ocean, and I wanted to dive straight in. There was one place I really wanted to go to. It was a part of the forest that always had a certain gravitas to it. I'd stumbled on it some years previously and it had a definite energy.

Finishing my mint tea, I laced up my hiking boots and set off. I knew I was getting close when I caught the whiff of familiar earthiness. The smell of wild garlic, dog's mercury and wood anemone took my senses to a different level, my heart into a relaxed state and my head clear of the rat race. All these plants are indicators of ancient woodland. I strode carefully among the flowers, knowing there had been trees on this spot since the last Ice Age, some two and a half million years ago. The history and longevity of the place made it special, as did the fact it attracted an immense variety of wildlife.

I negotiated the low limbs of the oaks and alder that led

down to the babbling brook, where I perched on a mossy rock. I listened. Wren, Blue tit, Goldcrest just audible against the flowing water. I put my hand on my ear. It felt cold, like it didn't belong to me any more. I covered it with my hand and listened to the forest with just one ear. I didn't like it. It seemed one-dimensional and fake. I shuddered and began to sob, in a 'manly' way. A kind of crying without tears, cinema style.

I was once again feeling sorry for myself, disillusioned and bitter. Why did life always feel like an uphill struggle? What else was this world going to throw at me? I kicked a stone into the water and stared aimlessly into the trees.

On returning to the van, I received a message I wasn't expecting. Gran had died in the night of pneumonia and Grandad was in intensive care.

I immediately packed up the van and headed up to Yorkshire. Gran and Grandad had been married for seventy-three years and I'd always thought they would go on forever.

I approached the hospital with optimism that Grandad was going to be fine. Sadly, I hadn't managed to say goodbye to Gran, but I was hopeful that Grandad would pull through. I entered the ward and spotted him straight away, asleep in a bed and wired up to various machines and a drip. The nurse nodded her approval for me to go to the bedside. My heart sank. He looked so old and frail, bony and pale. Well, he was a hundred years old, but I'd never seen him looking so ill.

His mouth and nose were covered by an oxygen mask and he had his eyes shut. I stood for a moment, just looking at him, and then took his hand in mine. There was no cinema-style big lump in the throat and inward-style crying now. I was beside myself seeing him like that, and the tears began to flow down my face.

I had a flashback to us working together on the tree when I was a boy, and him patting me on the back and telling me what a great team we were. I felt a twitch in his hand and his eyes started to open slowly.

He looked at me blankly at first and then fumbled with his face mask to remove it.

'John.'

I couldn't speak, all I could do was nod and smile.

'It's good to see you.' His faint tones were just recognisable in his strained breath.

'And you.'

'She's gone, your grandmother. You knew?'

'Yes.'

'There's no point to life for me now she's gone.' His breathing was laboured.

'I love you, Grandad.'

He smiled and grasped my hand tight.

'You should put your mask back on.' I reached for it, but he stopped me.

'Make the most of every day, son. I've wasted a lot of time not being bold in my life.' He gasped.

'I know. You've had the same problems I had, haven't you?'

He nodded. 'Just make the most of every day.'

He didn't say he loved me, but I felt it through his hand as he squeezed it tight.

'There is one thing you can do for me?'

'Yes, what is it?'

'Scratch my foot, I have an itch.' He chuckled and I laughed.

'Which one?'

His breathing faint and his voice quiet, he said 'This one,' and wiggled his toes.

'There's nothing worse than an itch you can't reach,' I joked, as I gently scratched the top of his foot. 'How's that?'

He didn't reply. He was gone.

28

IN GRANDAD'S HONOUR

I walked out of the hospital in a daze. I'd lost a great man. Grandad was a huge influence in my life and I loved him dearly. Getting to a hundred years old was an incredible achievement, but he was right about making every day count, and I was more determined than ever to make it so.

A week later I was back in hospital. Mum took me in. I felt guilty that I'd got her to my hospital bedside yet again. I would say, though, she is probably at her best when there's a crisis to be sorted. We chatted about Gran and Grandad and shared a tear.

The appointment was at 8am, and I'd been instructed not to eat anything the evening before. We arrived at 7.30, as I didn't want to be late. There was an emergency case ahead of me, which pushed me back a couple of hours. I was starving and was even eyeing up someone else's grapes in the bed opposite.

Eventually, they took some bloods and I signed the forms and was whisked into the operating theatre and given the general anaesthetic.

I remember opening my eyes slowly. The light was bright, and I could make out I was still in hospital. It took me a moment or two to come round from the anaesthetic. I looked to my left. Mum was there, and she put her hand on my arm.

'You okay, love? Do you want some water?' she said softly. I nodded.

Those first sips of water were like the elixir of life and as I felt it on my lips, I knew my ordeal was over.

'How does it look?' I asked.

'I can't see, you have a big bandage around your head. Do you want something to eat?'

'Oh yes, I'm starving. Anything, absolutely anything.'

Mum produced a tin of home-made biscuits which looked dry and black around the edges. I held out my hand for one. I was desperate. Then a nurse plonked a tuna sandwich on the table and I pounced on it like a hungry cat. Oh my God, it tasted like heaven. Honestly, it was the tastiest thing I had ever had. Granary bread and tuna in mayonnaise. I was so glad to be eating.

The nurse brought me some tea and Mum talked to me about texts she'd had from family and friends, wishing me love and support. I lay back. I kept drifting into a daze and back out occasionally to see if Mum was still there.

I was woken by the surgeon, who spoke with a deep and reassuring voice.

'There's some good news and some bad.'

I looked at his kind eyes as he sat on the bed beside me.

'The bad news is, it had penetrated deep. I had to remove all the cartilage and go extensively into the tissue. It took several attempts to get it all out. The good news is you should be cancer-free, and I hope you don't mind, but I took a graft from your collar bone and have managed to rebuild your ear.'

I felt a rush of emotion and a lump in my throat. 'Does that mean I don't need a prosthetic one?'

'It will take a while to heal, and I have to be sure the graft will take hold, but, yes, I'm pleased with the result. I will see you in a couple of weeks.'

I didn't hear the rest of what he said about dressings and my GP. I was just glad and grateful. Extremely grateful.

The journey home was horrendous. The pain was unbearable. Excruciating, in fact. I didn't know what to do with myself. Once home, Mum fixed some fantastic painkillers. Whatever shit that was, it was good, and I managed to get some sleep.

It took about a year to completely heal. I kept touching my ear, but couldn't feel anything. It felt like it was someone else's ear for a while, because the nerves took time to mesh together. Working and meeting clients was challenging, of course. I felt self-conscious, which wasn't a new thing for me, but I hadn't felt that way for quite some time. In a way it reminded me of how I was as a boy, and the thoughts of the eye-patch came back to me like a painful electric shock. I wore a hoody to protect the ear and I explained why to clients as soon as I met them, so they didn't think I was being disrespectful or was some kind of dodgy geezer. They seemed to understand.

One evening there was a knock at the door. Aaron, my dark-haired and chisel-jawed, stilt-walking and fire-eating neighbour, who had become a good friend, handed me a beanie hat. It was large enough to get over my head and accommodate the bandaging comfortably. He'd seen me when I returned from the hospital as he was getting out of his car and he'd obviously been thinking about my predicament.

Grandad's words had been resonating in my head too, eating away at my barriers and the blockages I'd carried in there for most of my life. 'Make the most of every day.'

He was right. There was no point moping about life and the past. What he'd said, along with my recent operation, made me realise how quickly time had gone. His words suddenly filled me with optimism and a sense of wanting to do something profound, something life-changing.

I thought about the events of my life, my career, home life, relationships, my failed marriage and two sons. Did I regret any of it? No. I wished I'd had more courage and not wasted my time with shyness. I wished I'd not bumbled from one thing to another and had more of a plan. But then, that was me. No. I didn't regret any of it, but I was determined to make some changes, starting right now, and in Grandad's honour. But do what?

29

THE SWING

So, I had a history of low self-esteem. I had a terrible fear of words and language, and that had inhibited my learning. I certainly wasn't well-read, an expression I'd seen so many times on online-dating profiles. 'I'm intelligent, well-read and love to travel.' Everyone puts that, and I'd been envious. I couldn't declare how I'd only managed two pages of *Robin Hood* and preferred to look at the pictures.

Looking back through the pages of this book, I realise I achieved many things and grew into a very capable man, but I never believed I was worthy of any of it. I never really celebrated those achievements, and although many were hard-won, it all just felt like part of the battle of life.

The dawn of my fiftieth birthday was to change everything. I took myself up to the Lake District, where I could immerse myself in my favourite kind of soul food: nature, trees, cascading water, rugged rocks and wildlife.

On the first night, something very profound happened. I'd been out for a walk in the evening along the river bank and returned to the camper. I was drifting off to sleep, in that no man's land state, gradually slipping from conscious to subconscious and, typically, where I would have found myself wandering into the void. My eyes began to relax, and my peripheral vision became acute, but instead of feeling small and insignificant, I felt empowered and energised, unafraid and bold. For a second, the comfy armchair on the airplane appeared and then was replaced with a beautiful scene.

I pictured two people walking by a river in the warm, late afternoon sun. Pure, clear water and abundant wildflowers of bright yellow and purple, with dragonflies darting, and weeping willow dipping their limbs into the babbling brook. They were heading for a tiny and remote church just up the hill. They were running, holding hands and laughing. I could picture them vividly – her cream, summery dress blowing in the warm breeze and her playful straw hat flying off her head, and him in an open-necked linen shirt, with sleeves rolled up, helping her up the steep slope. They entered the church and the two of them were silent as they walked hand in hand to the altar. They didn't speak, they just looked at each other, deep into each other's eyes, thinking about their love for each other. They weren't getting married, it was early in their relationship, but they were exploring their thoughts, and they were exploring their hopes and dreams.

I woke abruptly and instantly felt energised. It wasn't the usual stretching and yawning, eyes barely open wake-up. This was a full-on, wide awake and ready for action wake-up. I sat bolt upright. It was dark, so I figured it was before 5am. I reached for my phone to check the time. It was 2.30am, but I couldn't have been more awake. I laid my head back on the pillow, and it was then it happened.

I'm still startled today about how powerful and clear it was. The memory of the story was crisp in my mind and in great detail. I could recall everything. The girl in summery dress and guy in open-necked shirt. It was as clear as day, and I felt the automatic urge to write it down. I searched around and grabbed a pen and a sheet of paper. I felt I shouldn't waste a moment, as I might forget the detail, and all would be lost. I put a blanket over me and began to write. I wrote so fast, I couldn't read what I'd written. I looked over my words and was terrified the story would slowly filter out of my brain and be lost forever. Writing with a pen was hopeless. I hadn't written this way in any earnest for thirty years and it was illegible. In my panic I reached for my laptop and fumbled the lifting of the screen. I needed to make sure the words were still in my mind.

I took a sip of water and started again, this time typing the words. It was a little like when I'd written *Cherry Tree*. I couldn't stop transferring the words from my brain, and they were abundant, like picking conkers from my tree. One after another, then another and another, each one better than the last and each one fat and ripe with meaning, and they were everywhere around me.

I wrote and I wrote, and the revelation was, I was enjoying it. Not a little bit, but seriously revelling in it. I could barely contain myself as I described my couple racing each other down the hill, laughing and trying to impede one another with playful rivalry. They were obviously in love, and they were on a journey, but a journey to where? I had no idea. Equally, I didn't even know who they were. Was it me? Was it a former lover? Was it someone I had never met? Maybe it wasn't me at all? So many questions, but I was intrigued to know more.

The bright red glow of the sunrise distracted me from outside the camper window and jolted me out of my writing. It was morning. I'd been writing throughout the night without a single break. I pinched myself on my arm to test whether I was in some kind of very bizarre dream, but I wasn't. I felt shell-shocked, not purely by the fact I had written non-stop, but the fact I had immersed myself in an ocean of words and bathed in the sheer delight of it all. No longer was I scared. I felt a huge burden lift from my shoulders.

The following week, the whole thing became freakier. The following morning I woke at 3.30am this time, and as before, sat bolt upright and wide awake. The words were clear, and it was the same couple, but this time there was an argument. A row about their differences and a break-up. Everything was there, slap bang in the forefront of my mind. I knew they were away on holiday somewhere and that their differences were causing a rift in their relationship. What relationship? Once again I grabbed my laptop and began to type. The two episodes didn't link together, so what I was writing wasn't a story, with a beginning and an end, just words, but I felt I could juggle around with them later if I wanted, and that thought made me enthusiastic for more.

Later that day, I started to think about how my couple might be linked and began formulating ideas on how they could fit into a story.

Then, nothing happened. I slept solidly for weeks. Not a murmur of what came next or who they were. Work was pretty full-on, so I didn't have much time to think about it, until I heard two ladies chatting on the train one day. They were talking about a friend who was going through difficulties with her male partner.

'Oh, he's not good enough for her, she could do so much better.' And 'She's really out of his league. He's working-class, you know, he can't even use a knife and fork properly, and he's common.'

How totally fantastic, I thought. That's what people say about their friends' relationships, albeit from a female perspective. I thought about what 'he' might be thinking. Maybe he was out of his depth, and maybe he had confidence issues? Or maybe they were right? As I continued to listen from my seat behind them, I took my laptop out of my bag and typed in some of their phrases, and started playing around with some of the things that had been said. 'Out of his league and working-class, you know.'

I wrote, and to my complete surprise, kept on writing and writing. Before long, I had the characters' names and an inkling into how they might have met and, of course, the holiday bust-up. I started to formulate a bit of a story and I typed, and I typed, and I typed for the rest of the hour-long journey, like the words were cherries, ripe and ready to be picked and used at my discretion. And as I plucked them, more became available, and although typing with just two fingers, I laid them down before me with a purpose.

I excitedly clicked on the word count. It showed 1978. Wow. Nearly 2000 words without really thinking about it. That was amazing, and I gave a little punch into the air, to celebrate.

So there I was, in Waterstones, looking shifty among the romantic fiction shelves, aimlessly looking for... something. I didn't really know what. It wasn't the first time I'd been in Waterstones. My first dictionary had come from there, and also my travel guides and maps. But this time I was in unfamiliar territory. I felt uncomfortable in the fiction department. I looked at the many different covers and read the titles and the authors' names with my head on a slant. What did a novel look like? What did they put at the beginning and the end? An index? A summary? Page numbers? Titles?

Looking nervously around, I placed my finger on the spine of a book, and then the young female store assistant walked past and smiled. I quickly removed my finger and headed straight over to the familiar map section to compose myself. I must have looked sheepish, and I had beads of sweat on my forehead. Eventually she disappeared down the stairs. I went back over for another look. I didn't know any authors or titles or what was considered to be 'good writing', so I plucked a book at random. It was in the 'Top 10 Bestsellers' section, so I figured it must be a good one. I first of all looked at how many pages it had, then counted how many words on each line and how many lines per page. I did the maths and worked out 400 pages equated to around 100,000 words. I gulped, put it back on the shelf and then selected another – 379 pages, and then another at over 600! Wow, that was a feat of skill, I thought, as I plucked another and started to look at the format. I tried to guess the font and size and how they began a new paragraph, and whether a full stop came inside or outside of the speech marks.

After much deliberation and one more dash to the map section, after the assistant asked me if there was anything specific she could help me with, I plucked up courage and bought a novel. It was one of Jane Fallon's. I asked for a bag, hid the book away quickly and then dashed out of the store.

I didn't read it, I just had it there as a kind of pro forma, a structural guide, as it were.

I decided to take the day off work to put the words I'd written on the train into some order. I felt I needed to give them some kind of justice and... well... it sounds rather bizarre, so bizarre in fact, it fills my stomach with butterflies, even now, thinking about it. But it felt like I had started writing a novel.

Hang on a minute. Writing a novel! What had happened to me? This was a ridiculous notion and it was fanciful thinking I could write one, having never read one. Could it be something that was always hiding within me? Was I meant to have fifty years of literary angst within me to be able to do this? Or was I just being a complete idiot? I knew the people around me, friends and family, would think the latter, and they would probably be right.

It did feel natural, though, and I could feel a passionate urge within me to make my words into a full story. I found myself chomping at the bit to make it happen.

I thumbed through my Jane Fallon manual and started to organise my page on my laptop, so it looked like a proper page from a proper book. And it did. This shocked me at first. I kept looking at it and counting the words and the lines.

The main characters became more lifelike. I enjoyed formulating their personalities. Over a couple of nights, as before, the juicy red cherries came to me, and I made haste with the harvest. I made the notes in the early hours, and the story began to unfold, and not in any particular order. No, in fact quite at random. I had no idea of the end of the story or indeed the beginning. I just typed the words as they came to me and, in a succession of through-the-night writing episodes, wrote my way into a whole new world.

Then, as soon as it had started, my story ground to a halt. The London office was growing at a fast pace, and tree protection within development sites, safety monitoring and tree subsidence claims were at an all-time high. All my efforts were being diverted towards my business. Months went by, and I had written nothing. I'd think about it fleetingly and stare at the computer screen, looking at the words, but for some reason, I couldn't do it. I had no real plan, no tangible idea of the plot, no proper structure. Some words, but nothing really joined together. It was all a stupid dream. Someone with my history couldn't possibly write a novel. I was deluding myself. I wasn't a writer, and I told myself to get real and stop wasting more valuable time. 'Make the most of every day,' Grandad had said, and I was just wasting every day with something I was never meant to do.

Out of curiosity, I watched a few YouTube videos on 'How to write a novel'. But they seemed to contradict each other and confused me more. It appeared everyone had their own writing style and production technique. I decided writing wasn't for me. It was a crazy idea to be taking time off from my work to try something so vastly removed from my life and knowledge base. So, I decided to abandon the idea totally. Until, that is, I was attending a highish society dinner as a plus one and found myself surrounded by people with plummy accents, talking about things which to me had no meaning or significance to life at all.

Trees, nature, compassion for our planet and my family were the things which inspired me and were important. Those elements didn't feature in the conversation around me. How much the vintage car collection had gone up in value, obscene trading results and talk of yachts moored off the Italian coast were topped only with stories of which celebrities they had mingled with recently and the next soirée they were attending. I thought about bringing 'Jonny' out of retirement and giving him a free rein to shoot from the hip, but I simply wasn't a part of this world, and neither was Jonny. I was the polar opposite, and to wade in with a 'I saved twenty trees from a money-grabbing developer today' just wasn't going to segue in very subtly. So I took a back seat, and I listened. It was excruciating at times, listening to such inane conversation, and of course, I found being talked at very wearing, but it got me thinking about my book again, and the possibility for a class-divide love affair, perhaps. The differences between rich and poor.

The following two days I was working away and had booked a hotel. I travelled up on the train. Halfway into the journey I felt compelled to get out my laptop and have a look at those words again. The train was busy, and thankfully I'd boarded early and had a seat. During the trip, business calls were audible throughout the carriage. The regular station announcements and 'See it, Say it, Sorted' bulletins every fifteen minutes hardly made for the best writing den, but I started to think about the conversations I'd heard at the party, and slowly the plot began to fall into place.

Then suddenly the butterflies in my stomach were back. The class divide idea had given me the glue to hold the whole story together and I could feel in my heart that I was going to do it. Over the course of the next month, writing became a daily event. I thought some more about the characters and plot and transferred my ideas bit by bit from my brain to the computer. I squirrelled myself away to write and discovered I preferred the hustle and bustle of trains, cafés and hotel lobbies, rather than a quiet writing den. There was something stimulating and inspiring about writing amongst the constant movement and voices of people. I'd seen a TV program about Roald Dahl and saw his private writing room, where he would write in solitude. That wasn't me.

There were many times I became frustrated that I couldn't write more due to work commitments, and I relished quality time. But I still had to earn an income.

About a week later, I met up with an old friend, Amy, who I hadn't seen for many years. I had dated her for a few months after my divorce. We'd both been in a similar position and we'd termed it 'therapy dating'. We were like chalk and cheese in many ways, in our backgrounds, outlook and academic achievements, but she wanted some advice on a tree issue in her garden and we agreed to have a catch-up over dinner. It soon became evident that since I'd last seen her, she'd written a couple of novels and had one published, and was going through another divorce.

'Shall we have wine?' I asked, perusing the menu and then peering over my reading glasses.

'Why not? We're celebrating, anyway.' She laughed.

'Celebrating? What, your freedom?'

'To life and freedom,' she said earnestly.

I took my reading glasses off with one hand and looked into her eyes. 'You know, what makes us who we are today is the result of what we've been through. You wouldn't wish what you've had to go through on anyone, but you're glad it happened to you, because you're stronger now, more resilient and grateful for... well... life.'

She nodded. 'You're right. Anyway, look at you, Socrates.

What made you so philosophical? There's something different about you. What is it, a new love interest?'

I wasn't going to tell her about my mad midnight scribblings – after all, she was a published author. 'Oh, it's nothing. Just work is particularly rewarding at the moment.'

'I know how passionate you are about your trees, John, but you're definitely hiding something.'

'I did save a five-hundred-year-old yew tree from developers last week.'

She scrunched her lips and eyebrows together. They weren't real eyebrows, but tattoos that moved in real time.

'Nice. But you've saved thousands of trees. That's nothing new. There's something else isn't there?'

I looked down at the wine list. 'Rioja or Malbec?'

'John!'

'Look, promise you won't tell anyone?'

'Yes'

'I've done something. Something I've never done before. It's all come as a bit of a shock, but I just couldn't keep it in anymore.'

'What is it?'

'I don't want anyone to know, okay? And I'm not even sure whether it's completely me or not. I mean, I don't know if it's a fad, or whether I'm just trying to defy my demons, or some such rubbish.'

She gasped and leaned back in her chair. 'Are you coming out? Oh my God, you're gay! I never would have dreamt that about you. I mean, great! That's really great.'

I looked at her, shaking my head. 'I'm not gay. You know that, you know when we were together... and everything.'

'Well, what the hell are you rambling on about, then? Spit it out.'

I paused for a moment. 'I've been waking in the early hours, and it's alright for you, you're good with words, but you know me. I've always been scared of them.'

She cut straight in. 'For heaven's sake, John, what is it?'

I leaned forward and clasped my hands together. 'I'm writing a book.'

She stayed silent.

'A love story, fictional romance.'

'It's not about me, is it?' she replied.

'No, of course not. Well, I did put in the bit about when you wanted to be handcuffed to that four-poster bed. Remember in Cambridge?'

'You haven't!'

'No. Only joking, of course not.' We both laughed. 'It's just a story of love and loss. You know, like real life, but with a twist.'

She nodded. 'Crikey, I know what you mean. I have everything I need for my next four novels.'

We both laughed again.

'Rioja, please, large ones.' The conversation paused as the wine waiter took our order.

'Do you want me to read it? Are you wasting your time here, John? I don't mean to be rude, but you've never written anything before.'

I didn't want to tell her I'd never read a novel, either. 'No. I don't want anyone to read it.'

She picked up her fork, leaned over and poked it into my chest. 'Don't be ridiculous. What's the point of writing it if no one's going to read it?'

'For me. Just for me. I'm just liking the words, and it feels, sort of... good. I'm happy with just the process, the freedom.'

The wine arrived, and we both waited, uncomfortable in the silence, while the waiter filled our glasses.

She gestured towards me with her fork again. 'I think you should let me have a look. Just to see if you're on the right track. Do you know about show, not tell?'

I shook my head.

'Do you know that less is more sometimes? And don't waffle on about things which are irrelevant?'

I shook my head again. 'No, but I'll take it all onboard.'

We looked at each other and started laughing. We laughed out loud without a care, and I raised my glass. 'Cheers!'

Over the following couple of months I managed to write around six thousand words. Amy kept pestering me to let her read it, but I was too embarrassed.

I didn't go out much and kept my head down. I thought I was being extremely secretive about my new-found passion and was managing to keep it well under the family radar. But of course the people who were closest to me – Mum, Amber and Mum's partner Richard – knew I was up to no good, and unusually quiet. I didn't want to tell them, and I guess I didn't want anyone passing judgement. Eventually they challenged me at a family meet-up. I couldn't lie, so out it came.

'I'm writing a novel.'

My family are from Yorkshire, and it's rare as hen's teeth there is ever a silence in the room, but following my declaration, there was a silence, and a long one at that. A real tumbleweed moment.

They all looked at each other, I looked at them, and while they looked at me, I looked at the floor. Then each of them looked back at me and then at each other again, and they gave it some more thought. And then, unanimously, they burst out into hysterical laughter. Doubled over hysterical laughter. Humiliating laughter.

'A novel?' Mum said.

'You can't even write a Christmas card,' Amber butted in.

Richard patted me on the back. 'You go for it son.'

He obviously hadn't been party to much of my last fifty years.

'Yes, a novel. Romantic fiction,' I said, trying to sound confident.

I waited for the tittering to subside and looked at them sincerely. Mum smiled and told me there were a tremendous amount of people who say they are writing a book, but never finish one, and that she knew at least five or six. Amber's jaw was still on the ground, and Richard scurried off to make some tea.

It wasn't something they'd expected to hear, and even saying the words was a shock to me still, so I understood their reaction. It made me sure I wouldn't tell anyone else about it, and made me damn sure of something else too: I was going to finish it.

I wrote the ending before I'd even finished the beginning and then changed it six times. During the following winter, I took myself away several times to the warmth and sunshine of the Canary Islands. Again, a bustling hotel lobby and sun terrace became my favoured production zones, and I wrote and wrote, and the whole thing started to resemble something like a work of more than just a couple of pages.

It took me months to complete 90,000 words. I was still two-finger typing, but I'd enjoyed typing each and every single one. I had one last bit to write. The bit where Peter has to... I won't ruin the story, but I wrote it with compassion and feeling, and when typing the final full stop, I felt a single tear run down my cheek. I closed my eyes and felt myself rise up out of the void, high into the sky. Free like a bird on the wing, with the supportive and joyous breeze under my wings.

It was done.

I was fortunate to discover a brilliant editor, who agreed to take my book on. I sent the manuscript to her. Yes, professional writers use that word: 'manuscript'. I didn't give any indication whether I was a man or woman, I just used my initials. I didn't want her forming an opinion about a man writing such a novel, and I certainly didn't give any hint I was dyslexic.

I waited, and I waited. I knew it would take some time, but there was only one thing I wanted to know. It wasn't whether the book was any good, whether the story had meaning or interest. It wasn't whether I'd got the grammar or punctuation correct, or whether it was the right length for a novel of that genre. It wasn't about happy or sad endings, or whether it led into a sequel. The only thing I wanted to know was whether I was an equal with my reader.

30

THE VOID BETWEEN WORDS

Orange and yellow flames danced around the pile of burning wood in front of us. Popping and crackling with intense heat, the bonfire reminded me of Grandad and the shed incident. I'd stacked some old bits of furniture and a fence panel at the bottom of the garden, and the boys and I stood looking at it, mesmerised by the colours and savouring the warmth on our faces.

'What is fire?' my youngest son asked.

I thought about it for a moment. 'It's nature's way of rebuilding.'

'That doesn't make sense. Fire is destruction.' My eldest son shook his head.

'Forest fires are nature's way of rejuvenating. The old trees are tuned to carbon and this becomes the food for new life. It's amazing how the green shoots come so quickly after a fire.' I paused. 'It's all about nature's energy and how powerful it is for life and new beginnings.'

I could see them still shaking their heads and not believing what I said. 'Anyway, there's another reason for the fire.'

'What's that, Dad?' they replied simultaneously.

'Well, you know when people die? You have a funeral.'

'He's going mad,' one said. 'I think it's old age,' said the other.

'This is a funeral for a very special friend. Someone I've known for a very long time.'

'Have we met him?'

'Yes. I mean, no. Well, not really.'

'He's definitely going mad,' said the eldest.

I looked deeply into the fire. 'It's a final goodbye, the end of an era and a new beginning.'

'Who is it?'

'Where's the body?' the youngest said.

I reached into my pocket and produced a small card with a tree I'd drawn on the front. 'A very close friend, someone who has helped me immeasurably, someone who was strong and bold, someone I will never forget. But its time for him to go. It's for the best. Nature's way of moving on.' I had a giant lump in my throat.

'What does it say?' The eldest peered at the card. 'Jonny? Who's Jonny?'

I didn't answer, just gazed into the flames.

The youngest grabbed my hand. 'Are you sure you're alright, Dad?'

I looked at him and smiled. 'Yes.'

I tossed the card into the fire. It curled at the edges, and before combusting with a vivid flame, disintegrated into the burning embers.

'I'm free now. It's been a long time, but I'm free.'

Time is a great healer, and I'll always remember the many times Jonny had helped me. I sometimes still see the void between words, but I'm not afraid. It's now a mindset. Delving into the void enabled me to connect with my subconscious and this, tied with the almighty power of nature, enabled me to change how I think and have the courage to carry on and be a success. Words aren't intimidating anymore. I see them as magical, thrilling, and an immense tool for learning and communicating, and I see them as an art form in which you can lose yourself. I've had to painstakingly learn those words, inside out, many, many times. The letters, the structure, the meaning, and the emotion each one can deliver when combined with others. I'm still learning. It's painful, but not impossible.

I'm a dyslexic. I know I'm different to a lot of people. But, equally, I'm similar to many other courageous people who suffer and have suffered from this debilitating condition.

If you're at this point in the book, as a dyslexic or not, I want to say thank you. A huge, incredible and heartfelt thank you to all of you who have taken the time to read my story and also maybe my novel, *The Swing*. Both Charlotte and Peter, within the novel, have their own voids and are constantly searching for their inner peace.

You see, this was never really about my life story. It was about you believing in me as a writer. About me being able to make mistakes without judgement, and about the words liberating us from the void between them.

By reading this, you enabled me to find my love and passion for words, to stop wallowing in the sludge of despair and climb out of the void with pride.

I have found freedom in words. I'm inspired by their meaning, energised by their power and grateful for their ability to set me free. Free from the shackles of internal turmoil and free to grow and learn.

I hope this is just the beginning of my journey to inspire anyone else, who might think they are worthless, just because they are 'different' in some way.

Be Free. Be free to be you.

THE END

ABOUT THE AUTHOR

J A Crawshaw was born in Yorkshire, England, in 1969. As a professional environmentalist and arboriculturist he enjoys a special physical and emotional affinity with trees.

The energy that he finds in trees has empowered him to overcome many of life's challenges and has influenced his writing greatly.

He is currently working on other titles, and by reading his books, hopes that you too may find yourself inspired to reach for the sky and make your dreams come true.

He enjoys spending time with his sons as well as hiking, biking, snowboarding and exploring new places in his mobile writing shack.

He would love to hear about what inspires and motivates you?

john@jacrawshaw.com

More information can be found at www.jacrawshaw.com

ALSO BY J A CRAWSHAW

If you enjoyed reading this book, please consider leaving a review.

I would be eternally grateful. Good reviews will help other readers to discover new books.

If you would like to read my romantic fiction novel *The Swing*. Please signup to my newsletter on my webpage, to access up to date information, exclusive material and release date news.

www.jacrawshaw.com

If you would like more information regarding help with dyslexia, please visit

www.bdadyslexia.org.uk

www.dyslexiaida.org

Gate Theatre presents

The Convert
By Danai Gurira

The Convert was commissioned by Center Theatre Group and originally produced by
McCarter Theatre, Goodman Theatre and Center Theatre Group, 2012.

CAST

Chilford	Stefan Adegbola
Uncle	Marcus Adolphy
Tamba	Michael Ajao
Prudence	Joan Iyiola
Jekesai/Ester	Mimi Ndiweni
Chancellor	Richard Pepple
Mai Tamba	Clare Perkins

CREATIVE TEAM

Director	Christopher Haydon
Designer	Rosie Elnile
Lighting Designer	Mark Howland
Sound Designer	George Dennis
Assistant Director	Jade Lewis
Associate Lighting Designer	George Bach
Sound Assistant	Adam Washington
Production Manager	Heather Doole
Deputy Stage Manager	Erik Perera
Assistant Stage Manager	Nicole Scott
Design Assistant	Oliver Harman
Fight Director	Terry King
Accent and Vocal Coach	Claudette Williams
Dialect Coach	Chenjerai Shire
Movement Director	Steffany George
Press	Kate Morley for Kate Morley PR
	(kate@katemorleypr.com | 07970 465648)

The Gate would also like to thank the following people for their help with the development of this production: Natasha Brown, Clare Slater, Iona Firouzabadi, Anna Coombs, Kobna Holdbrook-Smith, Kwaku Kyei, and the team at Omnibus Clapham.

CAST

STEFAN ADEGBOLA

Stefan Adegbola plays Chilford. Previous credits at the Gate Theatre include *The Christians* (Gate Theatre/Traverse Theatre).

Theatre credits include *The Merchant of Venice* (International Tour), *After Independence* (Arcola Theatre), *The Merchant of Venice, Comedy of Errors* (Shakespeare's Globe), *Widower's Houses* (Orange Tree Theatre), *The Epic Adventure of Nhamo the Manyika Warrior and His Sexy Wife Chipo* (Tiata Fahodzi Tour) *Othello* (Riverside Studios) and *Midsummer Night's Dream* (Noel Coward Theatre).

TV Credits include *Doctor Who.*

MARCUS ADOLPHY

Marcus Adolphy plays Uncle and recent theatre credits include *Macbeth* (Atrix Bromsgrove), *The Suicide, The Comedy of Errors* (National Theatre), *Backseat Drivers* (The London Theatre), *Keeler* (The Charing Cross Theatre), *Macbeth* (The Last Refuge Theatre), *The Chicago Cowboy* (Rosemary Branch Theatre), *Twelfth Night* (The Nursery Theatre), *Keeping Mum, 1867* and *A Christmas Carol* (The Brockley Jack Theatre) and *The Children of Salt* (Alma Theatre Bristol). TV credits include *Scott and Bailey, Father Figure* and *Dream Demons.*

MICHAEL AJAO

Michael Ajao plays Tamba. His theatre credits include *How to Fix a Car Crash* (Courtyard Theatre), *Play On* and *Our Town* (Almeida Theatre), *Lord of the Flies* (Regent's Park Open Air Theatre) and *Liberian Girl* (Royal Court Theatre). His work for television includes *5x5, Cuffs* and *Code of a Killer*; and for film, *Attack the Block.*

JOAN IYIOLA

Joan Iyiola plays Prudence and previous credits at the Gate Theatre include *Eclipsed, The Rise and Shine of Comrade Fiasco* (Gate Theatre).

Theatre credits include *They Drink It In The Congo* (Almeida), *Omeros* (Shakespeare's Globe & St Lucia Transfer), *A Midsummer Night's Dream* (RSC), *A Season in The Congo* (Young Vic) *The White Devil, Arden of Faversham, The Roaring Girl, The Orphan of Zhao, Boris Godunov* and *A Life of Galileo* (RSC), *Holiday* (Bush Theatre), *Toilet* (Southwark Playhouse), *24 Hour Plays – Sex Toys, His Spirits Hear Me* (Old Vic) .

TV and Film Credits include *New Blood, Younderland, Denial, The Dead Sea.*

MIMI NDIWENI

Mimi Ndiweni plays Jekesai/Ester and recent theatre credits include *Soul* (Royal & Derngate Northampton/Hackney Empire), *Wendy and Peter Pan* and *Taming of the Shrew* (RSC), *Sky Hawk* (Theatr Clwyd), *Hamlet* and *Incomplete and Random Acts of Kindness* (Richard Burton Company/RWCMD) and *This is Not an Exit* and *I Can Hear You, Revolt. She said. Revolt Again* and *The Ant and the Cicada* (RSC).

TV credits include *Yonderland, Mr Selfridge, Last of the Dragon Slayers, Doctor Who* and for film *Cinderella* and *The Legend of Tarzan*.

RICHARD PEPPLE

Richard Pepple plays Chancellor and recent theatre credits include *They Drink It In the Congo* (Almeida), *The Loneliness of the Long Distance Runner* (York Theatre Royal), *Belong* (Royal Court), *Fixer* (Oval House Theatre), *In The Blood* (Finborough Theatre), *Coriolanus* (RSC).

TV credits include *Magnum Opus, Dates, The Dumping Ground, Our Loved Boy, Run* and for film *Beast Of No Nation* and *The Vintage*.

CLARE PERKINS

Clare Perkins plays Mai Tamba and recent theatre credits include *Removal Men* (Yard Theatre), *Play On, Little Revolution* (Almeida), *The Curious Incident of the Dog in the Night-Time* (National Theatre), *The House That Will Not Stand, Fabulation* (Tricycle Theatre), and *Our Country's Good, Cyrano De Bergerac* (Nuffield Theatre Southampton).

TV credits include *Family Affairs, EastEnders,* and *Damned*.

CREATIVE TEAM

DANAI GURIRA

Danai Gurira is an award-winning playwright and actress. Her play *Eclipsed* received its UK première at the Gate Theatre in 2015, and later was produced on Broadway where it was nominated earlier this year for the Tony Award for Best Play.

Her other plays include *Familiar* which premièred at Yale Repertory Theatre in January 2015 directed by Rebecca Taichman and *In The Continuum* which she co-wrote with Nikkole Salter. As an actress, she plays Michonne in AMC's critically-acclaimed original TV series *The Walking Dead*.

Her film credits include *Mother of George, The Visitor, 3 Backyards*, and *Restless City* and the upcoming *All Eyez On Me* and *Black Panther*. She was a Hodder Fellow at Princeton University and she is also the recipient of the prestigious Whiting Writers Award (2012).

She is co-founder and President of Almasi, a Zimbabwean American Dramatic Arts Collaborative Organization.

CHRISTOPHER HAYDON

Christopher Haydon is Artistic Director at the Gate Theatre and formerly an Associate Director at the Bush Theatre. He is a 2016/17 Clore Fellow.

His credits at the Gate include *Diary of a Madman* (also Traverse Theatre), *The Iphigenia Quartet, The Christians* (also Traverse Theatre, winner: Fringe First), *Grounded* (also Traverse Theatre, Studio Theatre Washington DC, national and international tour; winner: Fringe First, Best Production – OffWestEnd Awards), *Image of an Unknown Young Woman* (winner: Best Production, OffWestEnd Awards), *The Edge of Our Bodies, Trojan Women, Purple Heart, The Prophet* and *Wittenburg*.

Other theatre credits include *Twelve Angry Men* (Birmingham Rep/West End), *Sixty-Six Books, In the Beginning* (Bush Theatre/Westminster Abbey), *A Safe Harbour for Elizabeth Bishop* (Southbank Centre), *Grace, Pressure Drop* (On Theatre), *Deep Cut* (Sherman Cymru/National Tour), *Monsters, Notes from Underground* (Arcola Theatre) and *A Number* (Salisbury Playhouse). His short films include *The Taming of the Shrew/Two Gentleman of Verona* (Shakespeare's Globe), *Devil in the Detail* (Royal Court Theatre/Guardian).

As a journalist he has written for *The Scotsman, The Financial Times, The Independent, The Guardian, The New Statesman* and *Prospect Magazine*. He is the co-editor of three books: *Conversations on Religion, Conversations on Truth* (Continuum), and *Identity and Identification* (Black Dog).

ROSIE ELNILE

Rosie Elnile studied Design for The Stage at the Royal Central School of Speech and Drama. She was the first Resident Design Assistant at The Donmar Warehouse from 2015 until 2016.

As Designer, her theatre credits include: *Macbeth* (Mountview Academy of Theatre), *Hard C*ck* (Spill Festival), *The Half Of It* (RADA Festival) and *Loaded* (Jacksons Lane Theatre).

As Assistant Designer, other theatre credits include: *Elegy* (Donmar Warehouse), *Jesus Christ Super Star* (Regents Park Open Air Theatre), *The Barber Of Seville Design* (Opera North).

This role is funded by the Jerwood Charitable Foundation, as part of the Jerwood Young Designers Programme at the Gate Theatre.

MARK HOWLAND

Mark studied briefly at Oxford University prior to training in Stage Lighting Design at RADA.

His previous credits for the Gate Theatre include: *Diary of a Madman, The Christians, Image of an Unknown Young Woman, Edge of Our Bodies, Grounded, Purple Heart, Trojan Women, The Prophet, Yerma, Wittenberg, The Kreutzer Sonata, Vanya*.

Other design credits include: *Rudolf* (West Yorkshire Playhouse); *Xerxes, La Calisto, Ulysses' Homecoming, The Tales of Hoffmann, Werther, Pelleas et Melisande* (for which he was nominated for a Knights of Illumination Award), *La Boheme, Wild Man of the West Indies, The Siege of Calais* (English Touring Opera), *Twelve Angry Men* (Birmingham Rep/West End),*The Elixir of Love & Rodelinda* (Scottish Opera), *The Glass Menagerie* (Nottingham Playhouse), *The Patriotic Traitor* (Park Theatre), *Canvas* (Chichester Festival), *The Winter's Tale, She Stoops to Conquer, An August Bank Holiday Lark, The Grand Gesture* (Northern Broadsides), *Brassed Off* (York Theatre Royal), *A Further Education, Elephants, Four Minutes Twelve Seconds, The Blackest Black, Ignorance* (Hampstead Theatre), *Pride and Prejudice – the Musical, The Man Jesus, Uncle Vanya, Dockers, The Home Place* (Lyric Theatre, Belfast), *Dancing at Lughnasa, Ghosts, Sweeney Todd* (Aarhus Theatre, Denmark), *Singin' in the Rain* (Det Ny Teater, Copenhagen), *Entertaining Mr Sloane, One Flew Over the Cuckoo's Nest, Absurd Person Singular, Molly Sweeney, Translations* (Curve Theatre, Leicester), *The Ladykillers, Hitchcock Blonde* (Hull Truck), *Measure for Measure* (Sherman Cymru), *Six Dance Lessons in Six Weeks* (Vienna's English Theatre), *Bea, Pressure Drop, On Religion* (On Theatre), *Parallel The Suit, Parallel Electra* (Young Vic*), Dick Turpin's Last Ride, Cider with Rosie, The Merchant of Venice* (Theatre Royal, Bury St Edmunds), *A Number* (Salisbury Playhouse), *The Pains of Youth* (Belgrade Theatre).

GEORGE DENNIS

George Dennis is a freelance sound designer.

His previous credits for the Gate Theatre include: *In the Night Time (Before the Sun Rises), Image of an Unknown Young Woman, Eclipsed, The Edge of our Bodies (Gate Theatre)*.

His theatre credits include: *The Homecoming* (The Jamie Lloyd Company/ Trafalgar Studios in which he received a Olivier Award nomination), *Babe* (Polka Theatre/UK Tour), *Harrogate* (also HighTide Festival), *Primetime '16, Fireworks, Liberian Girl, Primetime '15* (Royal Court), *The Mountaintop, The Island* (Young Vic), *Imogen, The Taming of the Shrew* (Shakespeare's Globe), *In Fidelity* (Traverse/HighTide Festival), *Noises Off* (Nottingham Playhouse/Northern Stage/ Nuffield Southampton), *German Skerries* (Orange Tree), *Brave New World, Regeneration* (Royal and Derngate/Touring Consortium), *Forget Me Not, Visitors* (Bush Theatre), *Eventide* (Arcola Theatre/UK Tour), *Chicken* (Eastern Angles/ Unity Theatre), *Beautiful Thing* (Arts Theatre/UK Tour), *A Breakfast of Eels, The Last Yankee* (Print Room), *peddling* (Arcola Theatre/59E59, New York/HighTide Festival), *Mametz* (National Theatre of Wales), *Minotaur* (Polka Theatre/Clwyd Theatr Cymru), *Spring Awakening* (Headlong), *Love Your Soldiers* (Sheffield Crucible Studio), *Thark* (Park Theatre), *Moth* (Bush Theatre/HighTide Festival), *Hello/Goodbye* (Hampstead Theatre), *Liar Liar* (Unicorn Theatre), *Good Grief* (Theatre Royal Bath/UK Tour), *The Seven Year Itch* (Salisbury Playhouse), *When Did You Last See My Mother?* (Trafalgar Studios 2), *Debris, The Seagull, The Only True History of Lizzie Finn* (Southwark Playhouse), *A Life, Foxfinder* (Finborough Theatre).

JADE LEWIS

Jade Lewis is a theatre director who has worked at Southwark Playhouse, The Young Vic and The Bush Theatre as a director as well as an assistant director. She has assisted on a project run by Old Vic New Voices, is currently an Emerging Artist at Ovalhouse and also Creative Associate at The Gate Theatre where she assisted Jennifer Tang, Rebecca Hill on *The Iphigenia Quartet*.

In 2015/16 Jade directed *On The Edge of Me* written by Yolanda Mercy (Rich Mix, Soho Theatre, Paines Plough Roundabout Edinburgh) which also toured across regional venues and festivals.

In 2012 she was Boris Karloff Assistant Director on the Young Vic production *Blackta* directed by David Lan and since then has worked with directors and collaborators such as Rikki Henry, Patrice Etienne, Matthew Xia and Suba Das.

GEORGE BACH

George Bach is a freelance lighting designer and production electrician. He trained on the PgDip in Stage Electrics and Lighting Design at RADA.

His previous credits for the Gate Theatre include: *Meet Your Neighbours*, *Diary of a Madman*, *The Christians,* and *Image of an Unknown Young Woman*.

Production Electrician credits include: the English Touring Opera Spring and Autumn Seasons 2015 (Hackney Empire), and Spring and Autumn Seasons 2016 as Re-Lighter, *The Kreutzer Sonata* (Arcola Theatre), *Rapunzel* (Park Theatre), *Islands and Divas* (Pleasance Theatre), *The Wind in the Willows* (UK Tour) and *Scarlet* (Southwark Playhouse).

Recent lighting design credits include: *Ugly Lovely* (Old Red Lion), *Rapunzel The Musical* (UK tour), *Baby* (Robin Howard Dance Theatre, The Place), *Storm in a Teacup* (Soho Theatre/UK Tour), *The Flannelettes* (King's Head Theatre), *The Heresy of Love, Female Transport, Table, London Wall, After Columbus* (New Diorama Theatre), *Resolution* (The Space, London) and *The Dumb Waiter* (Courtyard Theatre, London).

www.georgebach.com

ADAM WASHINGTON

Adam Washington was born and raised in Oxford and studied Theatre Design & Production at Trinity College in Wales.

Recent theatre credits include: *Rosencrantz and Guildenstern Are Dead* (Oxford Playhouse), *Wonder Season* (Shakespeare's Globe) and *1917* (MCS).

HEATHER DOOLE

Heather Doole is a freelance production manager.

Her previous credits for the Gate Theatre include: *I Call My Brothers, Diary of a Madman*, and *The Iphigenia Quartet* (Gate Theatre),

Her theatre credits include: *Carmen* (Blackheath Halls), *Kiss Me* and *Platinum* (Hampstead Theatre), *No Villain* (Trafalgar Studios and Old Red Lion), *Radiant Vermin* (59E59, New York, Soho Theatre, London, and Tobacco Factory, Bristol), *All or Nothing* (The Vaults), *Firebird* (Hampstead Theatre Downstairs & Trafalgar Studios), *Giving, The Argument, The Meeting, 36 Phone Calls, Sunspots, Deluge, Deposit, Elephants* and *State Red* (Hampstead Theatre Downstairs), *4000 Days* and *Grounded* (Park Theatre), *Four Minutes Twelve Seconds* (Trafalgar Studios), *The Session* (Soho Theatre), *Octagon* (Arcola Theatre), *And Then Came the Nightjars* (Bristol Old Vic Studio and Theatre 503), *Valhalla, Animals* & *Cinderella and the Beanstalk* (Theatre 503), *Women Centre Stage Festival* (NT Temporary space). She assisted on *Bull* (Young Vic).

NICOLE SCOTT

Nicole Scott studied at Winchester University, graduated with a (BA Hons) combined degree in Choreography and Dance and Stage Management in 2012.

As Assistant Stage Manager her credits include: *The Picture Of Dorian Gray* (Greenwich), *We Are London*, *I Am A Promise* (Ovalhouse), *Love N Stuff* (Theatre Royal Stratford East), *Press Road* (Tricycle Theatre). As Deputy Stage Manager her credits include: *Half Of Me* (Lyric Hammersmith).

Nicole has also worked in Sound Operation for *A Splotch Of Red* (Friendly Fire Productions), Backstage/Costume Assistant for *Fagin's Twist* (The Place and Avant Garde Dance Company) and Front of House for *Jersey Boys*, *The Book Of Mormon*, *Les Miserables* and *Miss Saigon*.

Her stage management work experience credits include: *A Streetcar Named Desire* (Young Vic), *TakeOver Festival 2016* (Tricycle Theatre).

ERIK PERERA

Erik Perera is a London based production manager and stage manager working across all performance disciplines from theatre to dance, including opera, circus, performance art and accapella within the UK and overseas.

In the last few years he has worked with Jasmin Vardimon, Will Adamsdale, Inua Ellams, Benji Reid, The Beatbox Collective, Uninvited Guests, Touretteshero, 1927, Gobsmacked, Acrojou, Dan Canham, Clout and Opera Erratica. He was the first production manager at The Yard Theatre between 2011 and 2013.

OLIVER HARMAN

Oliver Harman is a graduate from the Royal Welsh College of Music and Drama (2015) achieving a BA (Hons).

As Design Assistant his theatre credits include: *Sleeping Beauty* (The Torch Theatre Company), *Yuri* (Chapter), *Sand* and *St Nicolas* (The Other Room) and *Rosie's War* (Theatr na nÓg).

As well as assisting, Oliver has designed set and costume for *The Orator* (Theatre West) and realised the design for *Bordello* (Italian SALAMARZANA: Festa Medievale). He has also production designed the music video for 4th Project and their song 'Taking me over' (Pixllion).

Other credits include: workshop assistant for *Roald Dahl: City of the Unexpected* (National Theatre Wales), puppet design and construction for *Local Super Hero's* (Bombastic) and design workshop leader for *Performance* (St Davids Hall).

This role is funded by the Jerwood Charitable Foundation, as part of the Jerwood Young Designers Programme at the Gate Theatre.

TERRY KING

Terry King has worked extensively as a fight arranger at all the major theatre companies in Britain as well as many operas, musicals, West End shows and television.

His theatre credits include *His Dark Materials*, *The Murderers*, *Fool For Love*, *Edmond*, *The Duchess of Malfi*, *King Lear*, *Elminas Kitchen*, *Scenes from the Big Picture*, *The White Guard*, *Three Winters*, *Henry V* (National Theatre), *Coriolanus*, *Julius Caesar*, *Macbeth*, *Romeo and Juliet*, *As You Like It*, *Henry VI parts 1, 2 & 3*, *Henry IV parts 1 & 2*, *Hamlet*, *Pericles*, *Dunsinane*, *Cymbeline*, *Richard II*, *Richard III* (RSC).

TV credits include *The Bill*, *EastEnders*, *Casualty*, *Fell Tiger*, *A Kind of Innocence*, *Fatal Attraction*, *Broken Glass*, *Scolds Bridal*, *The Mayor of Casterbridge*, *Rock Face*, *Blue Dove*, *The Widowing of Mrs. Holroyd*.

CLAUDETTE WILLIAMS

Claudette Williams trained as an actor at Guildhall School of Music and Drama and has worked extensively within theatre and television. She now works as senior Lecturer of Voice at the Royal Central School of Speech and Drama where she gained her postgraduate diploma in Voice. She regularly works on leading theatre productions as a Voice /Dialect coach.

CHENJERAI SHIRE

Chenjerai Shire is a Senior Teaching Fellow at SOAS, University of London where he has taught both chiShona and isiZulu and African language literature. He has a particular interest in language pedagogy, masculinities and the development of the ChiShona language. He has provided individual and group tuition in the ChiShona language and freelance interpreting and translation services for over 30 years and storytelling to children and adults.

He has also worked as a researcher on a number of documentary films relating to Zimbabwe and has previously acted as a linguistic consultant to the renowned Zimbabwean musician, Chartwell Dutiro, the Royal Shakespeare Company's production of *Breakfast with Mugabe* and the Gate Theatre's production of *The Rise and Shine of Comrade Fiasco*.

STEFFANY GEORGE

Steffany George is currently the Head of Movement at East 15 Acting School Southend and taught in NYC at Stella Adler Studio of Acting from 1996 to 2006.

Recent movement direction credits include *The Master and Margarita* (Bussey Building), *Seven Jewish Children* (Arcola Theatre), *Eclipsed* (Gate Theatre), *F*ck The Polar Bears* (Bush Theatre), *Luna Park* (previewed at Soho Theatre, Edinburgh Fringe).

Gate
Theatre
Notting
Hill

About the Gate Theatre

'London's most relentlessly ambitious theatre' *Time Out*

The Gate Theatre sits above the Prince Albert pub in Notting Hill. We have been inspiring audiences and artists alike since 1979.

In our intimate, ever-transforming 75 seat venue, we produce epic theatre that tackles big ideas of global concern. We act as a loudspeaker for unheard voices from across the globe. We are a small theatre but we always think big.

We take pride in our reputation for being the home of restless creative ambition. We are a celebrated 'teaching theatre': a place where exceptional and diverse emerging theatre-makers shine, and where audiences get to see the theatre leaders of tomorrow, today.

We welcome anyone who wants to change the world.

The Gate has been inspiring audiences and artists alike for over 35 years. Thanks to our Supporters, we are able to keep telling challenging, inspirational stories, in our intimate space, on an epic scale. Our Supporters are invited behind the scenes to discover more about the performances and are given the unique chance to meet and engage with the theatre leaders of tomorrow.

Please join us as a Supporter to celebrate the most exceptional new talent whilst helping to ensure we are around for the next 35 years. Join us and change the world. www.gatetheatre.co.uk

To join as a Gate Supporter from £21 a month, please contact

Fiona English, Head of Development
fiona@gatetheatre.co.uk
020 7229 5387

JERWOOD **CHARITABLE** FOUNDATION

Jerwood Young Designers at the Gate

This year, we celebrate 15 years of Jerwood Charitable Foundation supporting the training of young designers at the Gate Theatre providing essential on-the-job training of theatrical designers at the start of their career. This partnership is an essential part of the Gate's 'teaching theatre' mission, acting as the crucial bridge into professional theatre-making for young artists, giving them time, resources and expertise to test, improve, and ultimately showcase their work.

In 2014 the Programme was extended to not only support four breakthrough Designers a year at the Gate, but also four Design Assistants right at the very start of their careers. For *The Convert* the Jerwood Young Designer is Rosie Elnile, supported by Design Assistant Oliver Harman.

By the end of the 2016/17 programme, the Jerwood Young Designers Programme will have supported 84 placements over the course of 15 years.

Our Jerwood Young Designer alumni include Soutra Gilmour, Jon Bausor, Tom Scutt, Chloe Lamford, Oliver Townsend and Fly Davis.

"Time and again the Gate Theatre and Jerwood Charitable Foundation have discovered the most visionary artists of their generation" **Christopher Haydon**

www.jerwoodcharitablefoundation.org

Danai Gurira

THE CONVERT

OBERON BOOKS
LONDON

WWW.OBERONBOOKS.COM

First published in *American Theatre* magazine, September 2013

This single edition published in 2017 by Oberon Books Ltd
521 Caledonian Road, London N7 9RH
Tel: +44 (0) 20 7607 3637 / Fax: +44 (0) 20 7607 3629
e-mail: info@oberonbooks.com
www.oberonbooks.com

A catalogue record for this book is available from the British
Library.

PB ISBN: 9781786820709
E ISBN: 9781786820716

Cover photo by Kwaku Kyei

Printed and bound by Marston Book Services, Didcot, UK.
eBook conversion by CPI Group (UK) Ltd, Croydon, CR0 4YY.

Visit www.oberonbooks.com to read more about all our books and
to buy them. You will also find features, author interviews and news
of any author events, and you can sign up for e-newsletters so that
you're always first to hear about our new releases.

Preface

The iron claw of colonization is bracing to form a fist over Mashona and Matabeleland of Southern Africa in 1896. The colony will be hard won, as the struggle between the white intruders and the African inhabitants is by no means a brief or simple one. Western cultural impositions and Ancient African traditions are making strange bedfellows, indeed, never sleeping with both eyes shut – for fear the other will strike. The White man has begun a steady and unrelenting infiltration onto this interior African nation, and he is settling for the long haul. Here is where he will experience a dominance he could only witness with envy in his native land – the weight of his lower class status bearing his back to a bend. Here, on this foreign soil vast with fertile possibility he can reinvent himself, reclaim a title and position he never had, though always felt he deserved. He comes with hopes of great wealth and luxury, armed with an inherent philosophy of his superiority over his African counterpart as his guide. He comes to prove himself an explorer, a knight, a discoverer of new and unfettered resources and exotics. He comes to declare himself a man. His strategy is a simple one: leverage his cultural practices above the natives, study them and then cheat them out of land and position, ultimately bend the African's back low to buoy his superior position, as was once done unto him. The African is caught off guard at first, sure this white storm is a passing one, that they will return to their homeland as other European traders before them. However, through sheer passage of time, the constancy of this pale man with no knees' presence, the loss of land and position by inexplicable contractual, means along with the arrival of the Christian God, there is a pulling at the very seams of an intricately woven fabric of life. There is a grappling with home, place, space and voice – on one side are the ardent keepers of culture and land and language and on the other there are those sure of the white man's superiority – glad to be free of the strictures their forefathers whom they seemed eternally unable to please and thus delighted to declare themselves the ambassadors of the new order – finally feeling significance and a purpose.

But the strictures of this new order – taxes, menial labor and Judeo-Christian morals imposed by an uninvited lord stirs the spirits of slain warriors, kings and queens who hover closely above, whispering stratagems of vengeance to their kin, urging them to bide their time and strike; to reclaim their birthright.

In 1896 the colony soon to be hailed Rhodesia was crowning, destined to an unwelcomed birth; the sons and daughters of this ancient soil were on the cusp of a battle to reclaim their freedoms, unaware that their hard fought battle led by ancestral voices spoken through brave mediums would seal their bondage for the next eighty years. After which they would regain their strength and rise again, this time to assure a differing outcome, only to repeat the cycle of oppression on their own. The clash of voice, dream, God and song is destined to be mighty, bloody and age-long.

Danai Gurira

Danai Gurira's *The Convert* was orignally produced by:

McCarter Theatre Center
Emily Mann, Artistic Director; Timothy J. Shields,
Managing Director; Mara Isaacs, Producing Director
January-February, 2012.

Goodman Theatre
Robert Falls, Artistic Director;
Roche Schulfer, Executive Director
April-May, 2012.

Center Theatre Group
Michael Ritchie, Artistic Director;
Edward L. Rada, Managing Director
April-May, 2012.

The Convert was directed by Emily Mann with set design by Daniel Ostling, costume design by Paul Tazewell, lighting design by Lap Chi Chu, sound design by Darron L West, fight direction by J. Steven White, dialect and vocal coaching by Beth McGuire, and dramaturgy by Carrie Hughes. The producing director was Mara Isaacs, the director of production was David York, the casting directors were Adam Belcuore and Erika Sellin, CSA, and the production stage manager was Alison Cote.

The cast was:

Jekesai/Ester – Pascale Armand
Mai Tamba – Cheryl Lynn Bruce
Prudence – Zainab Jah
Chancellor – Kevin Mambo
Chilford – LeRoy McClain
Tamba – Warner Joseph Miller
Uncle – Harold Surratt

The Convert was commissioned by Center Theatre Group, Los Angeles, CA; Michael Ritchie, Artistic Director.

Characters

MAI TAMBA
A woman, mother of the earth, in her mid-fifties

THE GIRL/JEKESAI/ESTER
A girl in her late teens

CHILFORD
A man in his early- to mid-thirties

TAMBA
A man in his early- to mid-twenties

CHANCELLOR
A man in his early- to mid-thirties

UNCLE
A man in his forties or fifties

PRUDENCE
A woman in her early thirties

The Lounge of Chilford Ndlovu's home, in the Boomtown of Salisbury (Present day Harare, Zimbabwe).

The home was once owned by British missionaries, now transferred to conquer native souls deeper in the interior, they left it in the hands of a budding and bright native, a stalwart for the Roman Catholic church: Chilford Ndlovu. The room is modestly furnished with great Victorian influence, though a very impoverished version. There is a threadbare chaise lounge in one corner and a simple wooden desk and chair in another, a small couch connects the two and a simple coffee table rests in the center of the room, the age of the furniture is apparent but all is impeccably placed and kept; the room is spotless. On the wall is a faded framed painting of the English countryside, and a crucifix.

TIME

The late months of 1895.

KEY

// indicates an interruption

ACT ONE

SCENE ONE

A YOUNG MAN and THE GIRL run down the street, perhaps from the back of the house, the YOUNG MAN holding THE GIRL's hand. They are moving at record speed. Both look about cautiously, THE GIRL marvels at her surroundings, at times pausing to take something in and exclaiming.

THE GIRL: *(While snapping her fingers in amazement. At those moments the young man urges her to keep moving.)* 'Eeeeeey!!!'

YOUNG MAN: 'Kasika! Kasika kani!'

They reach the house and disappear behind the back. MAI TAMBA bustles into the room, she is a stout Muzezuru woman in her late fifties, dressed in a threadbare housekeeper's uniform, complete with apron and cap, she has eyes that can never drink up too much detail. She ushers in her charge, the YOUNG MAN in tow, talking rapidly to him and to a girl of about sixteen, traditionally dressed in a nhembe (a goat skin skirt) and very modest beads only partially concealing her breasts. She is barefoot. THE GIRL has an unavoidable keenness and resolve in her eye. She looks around the room nervously.

MAI TAMBA: *(Rushing them in. In Shona.)* Kurumidza, Kurumidza! Babamn'ini varikupi? [**Come, come quickly! Where is Uncle?**]

YOUNG MAN: Vaenda kudhorobha. [**He goes towards town center.**]

MAI TAMBA: Enda ovachingamidza! Usamira mira! [**EYYY! GO and meet them as they come! Do something!**] *(The YOUNG MAN rushes back out of the house.)* Maiwee! *(To THE GIRL.)* Huuya ndikupfekedze, azviite kutiMasta vakuone wakadaro. [**I have to find some clothes for you, this Master cannot see you like this.**]

THE GIRL: Hindava? [**Why?**]

1

MAI TAMBA: Kwete Mibvunzo! Chimira panapa. **[Don't ask stupid questions! Wait here.]**

MAI TAMBA exits. THE GIRL scans the room, she marvels at every part of it, it is obvious she has never been in such an enclosure before. She touches the chaise, and pulls her hand back in shock, surprised at the soft texture of the upholstery, exclaiming, 'Eeeeey!'; she rubs the smooth cement floor with her bare feet; confused by its consistency she sinks to the floor, sitting in a manner typical of a young Muzezuru girl, legs bent to one side, feet neatly tucked under her posterior, back inexplicably straight. Slowly as if in fear that someone was watching, she leans her face towards the ground and sniffs the floor; not smelling the cow dung texture she thought all floors comprised, she verbally expresses her confusion.

THE GIRL: Eh eh?

She touches the floor almost sensually with her hand. MAI TAMBA bustles back in the room.

MAI TAMBA: Urikuitei pasi?! Simuka! Kurumidza! **[What are you doing on the floor, get up! Hurry up!]** Chipfeka hembe iyi! **[Go put this on!]**

She has a shabby dress, obviously many sizes too large for THE GIRL. THE GIRL stares at it in confusion.

THE GIRL: Eeeeeey! Chii ichocho? **[What is that?]**

MAI TAMBA: *(She shows her how to put it on, demonstrating on herself.)* Simudza maoko, pfeka wakadaiso. **[Lift your arms, put it on like this.]** Famba! Ndakugadzirisa imba – Kurumidza! **[Go! I must prepare the room – Hurry up!]**

THE GIRL exits, attempting to make sense of this strange garment. MAI TAMBA commences to sing and dance around the room with a mutsvairo (an African broom) in hand. She enters a very spiritual seeming trance, singing and sweeping over all items of the room, as though cleansing them from bad spirits. She places objects we cannot quite discern in hidden places in the room, between the couch cushions, underneath the rug and continues her dance. Every now and then she stops and sniffs a brown powder from a small pouch and gains more energy and animation. Suddenly she stops and rushes into the next room at the sound of the door. CHILFORD Ndlovu enters. CHILFORD sits immediately at his desk and pulls out a paper and pen from his worn leather satchel. He is a catechist in the Catholic Church, the only African who holds this position in the Mashonaland region. He is also an occasional assistant to the Commissioner of Native Affairs in the area of native disputes. He is a man of great deliberation and precision, never once placing anything in the wrong place, as though his calling comes with so much responsibility that it dictates his every movement. His English is that of one who has strained to sound as European as possible, though he can never fully escape his African intonations; his attempts to color his speech with as many British sayings and expressions as possible leads to several malapropisms of which he is wholly unaware. After a time he begins to write, dipping his felt tip pen in its inkwell only when absolutely necessary, writing with economic movements. He is completely focused on his letter writing, his furrow creased, his breathing heavy. He pauses and sniffs the air curiously. MAI TAMBA pushes through the door with a tray of steaming food. She approaches CHILFORD heavily.

MAI TAMBA: Good Evening Masta Ndlovu.

CHILFORD: *(Writing frantically, not looking up.)* Yes, good evening, could you just place it on the table.

MAI TAMBA: It is not good to wait. It get cold.

CHILFORD: You know I do nothing until I write my evening letter. And what is that smell?

MAI TAMBA: No smell Masta. Today you eat fast.

CHILFORD: What? No, I have –

MAI TAMBA: Today she come.

CHILFORD: *(Finally looking up.)* What? What is it Mai Tamba?

MAI TAMBA: My brotha who die – he daughter – she come to work.

CHILFORD: I never said –

3

MAI TAMBA: You say you need someone cook, someone crean rike at Fatha Hem's house.

CHILFORD: Yes, but I never said –

MAI TAMBA: So I bring ha.

CHILFORD: I never said I wanted someone right at this once, I said it would be NICE to have someone to do both like Father – I never said –

MAI TAMBA: You said it Masta. Then I say it will help us because my brotha –

CHILFORD: I know your brother passed and I am sorry about that but that did NOT mean I was going to employ your whole family// in its entirety –

Mai Tamba:// She need onry little, she smar [small] girl but she work hard – she strong, she crean the house good and you just keep ha in the back with me and she can just have sma pay to help ha motha with hut tax Masta.

CHILFORD: Mai Tamba – I cannot – I am very, very occupied// right now –

A knock at the front door. CHILFORD rushes to the door, voices are heard from outside.

UNCLE: Masta – it was him who took it Masta – prease!

CHILFORD: *(Aggressively.)* Now you WAIT! *(Abruptly shuts the door.)* Now you see what I am dealing with. These peasants have put my very patience on a trial, one of them was waiting for me AT the Commissioner's office, something about a goat and a girl, I DON'T even know what. And of course the Native Commissioner will look to ME to bring it all to a solve. Now I haven't the possible moment to sort with your niece// or whatever –

MAI TAMBA: Prease, oh prease Masta, oh, you can pay her onry what moneys you have, oh prease masta – PREASE MASTA!

CHILFORD: NO Mai Tamba and do not start –

MAI TAMBA: *(Now in a full state.)* Oh, what can I do brotha Ngoni? How do I face your spirit or that of our fathas and grandfathas fatha oh Maiwee zvangu!

CHILFORD: Enough now! What, what did I tell you about those animists ritualisms? You do NOT under any circumstances EVER speak to the dead. How many times Mai Tamba? What is it I must do? Now – GO!

Disdainfully MAI TAMBA goes to the cross on the far wall, crosses herself, all the while glimpsing over at CHILFORD like a reluctant child.

CHILFORD: Say it –

MAI TAMBA reluctantly begins to force words out of her mouth.

MAI TAMBA: Hair Mary, fur of ghosts –

CHILFORD: *GRACE* MAI TAMBA, FULL OF GRACE!!!

MAI TAMBA: Fur of GRACE. *(Trying to remember.)* Eh…ehh….

CHILFORD: …the Lord is with thee…

MAI TAMBA: The Rord is with thee…eh…Hory in heden motha.

CHILFORD: HOLY Mother in Heaven pray for our sins now and at the hour of our death.

MAI TAMBA: *(Relieved.)* Yes. *(Joyfully.)* Aaameeeen!

CHILFORD glares at her for a moment.

CHILFORD: You really are not taking your salvation very seriously; I fear that –

MAI TAMBA: Prease masta – she a good, good gir, she – want to know about God in hewen too.

CHILFORD: She wants to know about Jesus Christ?

MAI TAMBA: Yes, and the Virgin Mery.

CHILFORD: She has heard of the Holy Mother?

MAI TAMBA: Ya – her also! She want to work for you Masta so she can rearn Masta.

CHILFORD: Hmmm. *(Beat.)* Is she a clever girl?

MAI TAMBA: Yes, yes, she very creva gir.

CHILFORD: *(Thoughtfully.)* Where is she?

MAI TAMBA: Right here Masta!

MAI TAMBA runs out of the room and returns moments later, talking rapidly to THE GIRL, shabbily dressed in the oversized dress which is back to front. She takes in CHILFORD almost without looking directly at him.

MAI TAMBA: *(In Shona.)* Mastahavadi Shona. [**Now whatever you cannot say in English just don't say it – he doesn't want any Shona spoken around him okay?**]

THE GIRL: Hindava? [**Why?**]

MAI TAMBA: Iwe! Unyepere kudzidza Mwari wechirungu – [**You! Act like you want to know about the white god –**]

THE GIRL: Ndiani? [**What one?**]

MAI TAMBA: Uyo – Jesu! [**That one – Jesus!**] *(Points at cross.)*

THE GIRL: Ndazvinzwa. [**Okay.**]

MAI TAMBA: Ndizvozvo, nyemwerera – [**Okay. Smile eh –**]

THE GIRL smiles a little too brightly.

MAI TAMBA: Here she is Masta.

THE GIRL: *(Curtseying in a manner typical of a Muzezuru girl when greeting and elder respectfully.)* Harro Masta.

MAI TAMBA: She a good gir Masta, and strong to work.

CHILFORD: *(Inspecting her keenly.)* What is your name girl?

THE GIRL looks at her aunt, exasperated, not understanding his English.

MAI TAMBA: *(Fiercely under her breath.)* Zita rako.

THE GIRL: Oh, Jekesai.

CHILFORD: Hmmm…do you want to know the Lord?

> *THE GIRL looks to MAI TAMBA, exasperated.*

MAI TAMBA: Ita, 'yes.'

THE GIRL: Yes.

CHILFORD: Yes?

THE GIRL: Yes?

CHILFORD: Mai Tamba, is this of most certain?

MAI TAMBA: *(Nodding profusely.)* It is of true Masta! She has been bothering me to come end rearn [learn] from you for RONG [long] time Masta!

CHILFORD: Well then this is good. This is very, very good, very good indeed. *(Beat.)* Well, the first of things that must be done is that name must be changed, you need a name that expresses a Christian faith – Mary – mother of Jesus – is the most blessed name – but I just named another girl that this afternoon, ahh, there is Ruth – but I hate names of monosyllables so – ESTER! Yes, that is it, that is your name. Ester, she was a woman of great, great courage, saved her people in fact, second only to the Virgin Mary in Holy women in my opinion. And you look like one – indeed you do, you do.

MAI TAMBA: *(To THE GIRL.)* Hanzi waakunzi Esta manje. **[He says your name is Ester now.]**

THE GIRL: Esta?

MAI TAMBA: Unyemwerere futi uti 'thank you.' **[Yes, and smile and uti 'thank you.']**

ESTER: *(Smiling too brightly.)* Thenk you.

7

CHILFORD: You are most welcome. I must finish writing to Father Helm now I can tell him that we have another convert to report – that is great news indeed, the numbers have been on the dwindle of late, to say the most least. So, I suppose if she is of little expectation of too much pay I will retain her for now. I must see if the Colterns still are in need of a maid, she can go there perhaps and perchance on weekends so as to alleviate her payment. And she must come to my school on every day for lessons in Bible studies and math and language.

MAI TAMBA: Schoo Masta?

CHILFORD: Yes, that will be of no charge.

MAI TAMBA: Why schoo Masta?

CHILFORD: Why school? You are not in seriousness! She is sunken in the deepest deep of barbaric practices that is of why! We are trying to civilize our people Mai Tamba! How is that going to happen if she is not steeped in the most potent marination of biblical and academic studies – *(Knock at the door.)* Goodness of graciousness! HOLD ON! If she is under my roofing – she will certainly be joining my schooling. And she will be there, *every* day. Were you ever in a doubt Mai Tamba?

MAI TAMBA: No…no Masta…but ah…she is a gir masta.

CHILFORD: And what of that? The sisters are all educated, and look at Mistress Prudence! There is not a nary to be discussing Mai Tamba.

MAI TAMBA: Yes Masta. Thenk you Master.

ESTER: Hanzi chii? **[What did he say?]**

MAI TAMBA: SHHHH!

ESTER: *(Defiantly.)* AIWA! Hanzi chii?! **[NO! What did he say?!]**

MAI TAMBA: Hanzi urikuenda kuchikoro. School. [**He says you will go to school.**]

ESTER: Chikoro chevarungu? [**School like for whites**?]

MAI TAMBA: Eh ey. Like for whites.

ESTER: *(Excitedly.)* Eeeeeeey!! *(Snapping her fingers.)*

MAI TAMBA: SHHHH! Thenk you Masta.

ESTER: *(Instinctively.)* Thenk you Master.

CHILFORD: You are of most welcome. Now go on and get her settled, I have to deal with this.

MAI TAMBA: Yes Masta, thank you Masta.

ESTER: Yes Masta, thank you Masta.

CHILFORD: Yes, yes, just go now!

MAI TAMBA and ESTER scuttle out of the room nervously, CHILFORD goes to the door, finally allowing the fervent knockers indoors, they are two black men, shabbily dressed, one as a miner (we recognize him as the young man who brought JEKESAI earlier) the other appears to be very upset. The miner is thankful for CHILFORD's presence.

CHILFORD: Now, stand there…NO THERE! Now, in the first and foremost, you do understand, I am a mediator for your pagan concerns by the grace of God. So it is best for you to thank Him right now. THANK HIM!

1ST MAN: Thenk you God.

2ND MAN: *(Reluctantly and with great disdain.)* Thenk you God.

CHILFORD: Now. What exactly is the issue with the goats or whatever –

2ND MAN: That one, that gir that the maid she bring – she is mine! She is my brotha's chil Masta – now they ara trying to tek ha when she must be going to she ha new husband and be doing what she must be doing.

CHILFORD: What exactly are you –

1ST MAN: Don't let him tek ha masta – she betta with you masta!

CHILFORD: What is going on here?

2ND MAN: *(Increasingly agitated.)* They ara wanting to bring ha here and stop the goats being paid! The brideprice! Thet Gir is MINE Masta! Give ha bek!

CHILFORD: How is she yours?

2ND MAN: Ha fatha die – now I am the fatha – she is mine Masta!

MAI TAMBA bursts through the kitchen door, screaming at the man.

MAI TAMBA: KANA! KANA!!! She is NOT! LIAR! Haasi mwanawako, Kunyepa!// Haunyare! Hautye vakayenda! SHAME! **[You liar! You liar! Have you no shame? She is not your child! Do you not fear those who have parted?]**

2ND MAN: //UCHAFA! UCHAFA NHASI! **[TODAY YOU ARE GOING TO DIE!]**

CHILFORD: NOW HOLD ON!! WHAT IN THE EARTH IS HAPPENING HERE! *(They all rush to speak at once.)* NO! Mai Tamba, bring the girl to speak.

MAI TAMBA rushes out to get ESTER, who walks in fearfully.

CHILFORD: Now, what is going on here. I want to hear from Ester herself. No one else.

UNCLE: *(Shocked at the disrespect of a girl speaking before him.)* AHHH!

MAI TAMBA: She can't in Engrish Masta.

CHILFORD: We will make an exception. She can speak the vernacular. You speak it back to her in English, she can begin learning right away.

MAI TAMBA: Hanzi taura neShona. **[He says speak in Shona.]**

10

ESTER: Chokwadi? **[Sure?]**

MAI TAMBA: *(Agitated, with urgency.)* Chokwadi, TAURA KA! **[Yes! Speak!]**

ESTER: *(In Shona, with defiance and animation. MAI TAMBA interprets.)* Baba vangu vaindida kupfura vamwe vana vese, ini ndiri musikana. Vaida kunditsvagira murume akakosha, wandaida inini futi. **[Saka, my father, he favored me best, even though I was the girl, so he wanted to choose a special suitor for me that I also choose first and that I loved.]**

MAI TAMBA: My father loved me more than all, even though I was a girl. He wanted me to get a good husband that //I loved also.

ESTER: //Kangani varume vaida kunditora se mukadzi, Baba //vachiramba. **[So many times these older men would come for me, wanting me as their third or fourth wife, then my father would refuse.]**

MAI TAMBA: // Other men would come and my father// refused.

ESTER: //Avamanje – Babam'diki *(Pointing at UNCLE with disdain.)* Vakavengana nababa vangu nenyaya yokuita zvisina musoro. Vari kutamba kundirooresa neChembere, kuti vatore mbudzi yeroora. **[Now he is dead, his younger brother, this one who my father he never even like him because he is always getting in bad stories – he is wanting to betroth me to a very, very old man and to take the goats for his needs. The brideprice.]**

MAI TAMBA: But now, this uncle since my father didn't even like him because to do mad things and now have me marry a very old man for goats for his needs, the brideprice.

ESTER: Ini ka HANDIDI, NDIRIKURAMBA!!!// Ndosaka ndauya pano naMai Tamba. **[And me, I DON'T WANT**

THAT!!! So that is why my aunt and cousin have brought me here.]

MAI TAMBA: //And me I DON'T WANT THAT. So I have been brought here by my aunt and cousin.

CHILFORD: *(Indicating 1ST MAN.)* This is your son Mai Tamba.

MAI TAMBA: Yes Masta.

CHILFORD: *(Indicating UNCLE.)* And this is your brother.

MAI TAMBA: Yes Masta.

CHILFORD: *(To UNCLE.)* What do you have to say for yourself?

UNCLE: *(In slow authoritative deliberation.)* I am now the head of the famiry. I do not have to answa to E-N-Y-O-N-E. Not to this one *(Indicating MAI TAMBA.)* Or to you. This girl is always trying to cause a problem, thinking she is too much betta than others, YOU ARA NOT! And I say she must behave like a propa girl. Eh EH! STOP shaking like that to me! *(To ESTER who is shaking her head at him defiantly.)* Hauna tsika iwe! **[You are too rude you!]**

CHILFORD: Continue to be speaking to ME!

UNCLE: She want to be TOO rude – this one. I am saying – she is my child and I say where she go and not go and she is comin bek to Mazowe with me TODAY.

MAI TAMBA: KANA!

ESTER: *(Bursting out.)* KANA ARIKUNYEPA! Kana nechirungu zvinonzwika, Haasi Babavangu. Kachunhu kasinabasa, pasi //pegonzo chaiyo, Vakadzi vake nevanavake havamufarire. Ini ndingato mupfura semurume! **[KANA! He is LYING! EVEN IN ENGLISH I CAN SEE IT! He is NOT the fatha of me! He is a small thing, even less than a rat!// Even his children end his wives ara not liking him! I can be a betta man than him!!]**

TAMBA: *(Trying to restrain her.)*//Ahh AHH! Jekesai! Jekesai!

MAI TAMBA: //Nyarara mwana! Nyarara mwana iwe!!
[Be quiet my child, be quiet!]

UNCLE: //AHHH AHHH!! *(Advancing towards her.)*
Ndichakuratidza kutindiani murume. Betta man than
me! I show you today who is betta than who! Wati chii?
Kundipfura inini semurume. Kundi pfura inini?

CHILFORD: BE OF SILENCE! *(Jumping between them.)* You!
RECLINE YOURSELF PRESENTLY! RECLINE
YOURSELF!! I WILL NOT TOLERATE SUCH
BEHAVIOR IN MY HOME. UNDERSTANDING?
*(UNCLE and ESTER back away from each other, both
smoldering.)* Now, Mai Tamba, this man, to whom she is
betrothed, has he wives in the present?

MAI TAMBA: YES!!! Many, many wives Masta. More then on
my hends. *(Holds up all her fingers for inspection.)*

CHILFORD: Ha! And you do not wish to become a wife?

MAI TAMBA: *(Rapidly translating.)* Haudi kuita mukadzi here?

ESTER: KWETE! NO.

MAI TAMBA: It is as the gir has said Masta. This man, he is my
younger brother, I am knowing him VERY well. He is not
honoring the spirit of my brother, this is not what he would
be wanting for Jekesai…eh Esta.

CHILFORD: And you wish to become a member of Christ's
Church?

MAI TAMBA: Eh ye.

ESTER: *(Mimicking MAI TAMBA.)* Eh ye, YES.

CHILFORD: Well then she cannot return.

UNCLE: *(Shocked.)* You cannot do that. This is not our way –

CHILFORD: We are currently in Salisbury, a city under British
juridiction, and not a village, your 'way' has no jurisdiction
here. I have jurisdiction. You came to me, an employee of

13

the Native Commission, with authority through Sir Rhodes directly from Queen Victoria herself to settle your familial dispute, I now see it was a dispute with Ester.

UNCLE: Esta? Ndiani Esta? – Who is that?

MAI TAMBA: *(Smugly, pointing at JEKESAI/ESTER.)* SHE is the one!

CHILFORD: BE OF SILENCE! Where you failed to find an understanding, is that not only am I a mediator of native affairs – I am a man of God. I will not be on the stand by and release allowance to you to practice polygamy and the selling of a young woman's body and soul under my very nostrils. You picked the wrong one my man. These are the VERY aspects of our ways that must die if we are to advance. It is not of WONDER the white speaks of our savagery. Dispute settled.

UNCLE: AHH – Ayewa! **[No!]** He has already paid some of the brideprice! You cannot do this!

CHILFORD: Your pagan debts are of no concern of mine. I will write up a report and have it filed by the Native Commissioner. Be of leave. NOW.

UNCLE: *(Utterly shocked at CHILFORD's lack of sympathy.)* AHHH AHHH!! YOU! YOU ara NOT one of us! You are BAFU!! Asi tirikuita zvinhu uchaona. **[But we are doing things.]** You shall see! Pane NGOZI ichakuvinga! When revenge is taken, I will be sure to let YOU know!

CHILFORD: Spare your threats. Do leave before I am forced to notify authorities of the commission.

UNCLE: Uchaona! **[You shall see!]**

UNCLE reluctantly retreats and leaves.

ESTER: Eeeeeey!

ESTER's eyes brim with tears of gratitude, her relief is palpable. She stares at CHILFORD with a deep admiration.

ESTER: *(Still in disbelief to MAI TAMBA.)* Eeeeey! Saka Babam'diki vaenda? [So Uncle is gone?]

MAI TAMBA: *(To ESTER.)* EHey! GONE *(She dances a bit in glee, singing a short Shona chorus.)* Thenk you chokwadi [surely] Masta. *(Quickly.)* AND JESAS!

CHILFORD: Please Mai Tamba, what am I telling you about all of these histrionics? If you are in such a mood of thanks perhaps you could teach Ester 'Hail Mary' *(Pointing at crucifix on wall. MAI TAMBA's face falls, grudgingly, heavily, she takes ESTER to the crucifix.)* And please do not ever allow such an ambush upon me in the future near or far. Ever. Understanding?

MAI TAMBA: Yes Masta. *(To ESTER, pointing at crucifix.)* Hanzi uchadzidza miteuro waJesu. [He says you must learn the prayer of Jesus.]

ESTER: *(Eagerly.)* Ndiye Mwari akadzinga Babam'diki, Ndiye Jesu? Mubvunzei, Mubvunzei!!! [Is this the God that he use to chase away Uncle? This Jesas? Ask him, ask him!!!]

MAI TAMBA: Eh eh! Mira! [Wait!] Masta, she is asking if Jesus help you chase away her uncle.

CHILFORD: Yes he did indeed. He gives me the authority to stand up for the weak, to protect the downtrodden. Indeed he did. She *is* clever Mai Tamba.

MAI TAMBA: *(Translating.)* Ndiye eh he.

CHILFORD: *(Observing the girl keenly.)* I see your strong will young girl. Very useful in Christ's army.

TAMBA: Ndakuenda Amai. [I am going mother.]

MAI TAMBA: Famba zvakanaka mwanawangu. [Okay, bye my child.]

ESTER: *(Runs to him.)* Waita zvikuru mukoma! [Thank you so much older brother!]

TAMBA: Eh ey. Chisarai zvakanaka. [**You stay well here.**]

He smiles at her as they hold each other's gaze for a moment, it is clear they are very close. Finally he exits.

ESTER: *(To her aunt, pointing at the Crucifix.)* Ngatidzidze munamato. [**Let's learn the prayer.**]

MAI TAMBA: *(Surprised at ESTER's keenness.)* Chiita wakadai. [**Do like this.**] *(Crosses herself.)* Ita…Hair Mary fur of Ghost –

CHILFORD: *(Who had turned to his now cold meal jumping up.)* GRACE, MAI TAMBA, GRACE!!!

SCENE TWO

Early evening, months later. ESTER cleans the room, now dressed in an oversized maid's uniform, an obvious hand-me-down from her aunt. She polishes the furniture clumsily, placing large amounts of polish on the floor and furnishings and does not rub them in thoroughly, leaving large shiny clumps everywhere. She sings merrily to herself. CHILFORD enters with CHANCELLOR GWENDO, a fellow member of the Catholic Church and Interpreter for white mine owners, they grew up together at the Catholic Mission in Bulawayo. A bit of a scoundrel, he is an African opportunist, the beginnings of the black upwardly mobile, his interest in his Christian God is a nominal one, whatever is needed to garner the white man's trust, study his mechanisms of power and control and exult his learnings upon his own people, to his own capitalistic ends. He, like CHILFORD, speaks strained and malapropism-ridden English; though his is perhaps a touch less strained. ESTER rushes out of the room to return shortly with a tray with a tea pot and cups.

CHILFORD: But you must share this newfound wealth man! I have not had a piece of meat in a week!

CHANCELLOR: I have a herd of connections my brother, a HERD!

CHILFORD: Of course, you always do!

CHANCELLOR: If you are looking for the usual supply from the usual resources you will be ridden with disappointment. But you must always be in awares, with the right amount of monies – all is available, always! And why were you inquiring about maize meal earlier?

CHILFORD: It is finished, I am in need of more.

CHANCELLOR: Chilfy – you CANNOT be telling me in honestys. What did you do with it? It was near twenty pounds!

CHILFORD: I shared it with the children and the families at the mission –

CHANCELLOR: AGAIN! What is this in you Chilfy? To be parting with such coveted commodities with common folk, WHY? Are they your kins? Are they?

CHILFORD: These people are in the most needs of dire. Jesus commands we care for the poor! I cannot sit upon my loins and witness it when food is in my possession. Now let me be spared all your learnedness, I just need some meat man!

CHANCELLOR: Let us consider it done. I will save you of your hunger. AGAIN.

CHILFORD: Thank you brother.

They drink tea.

CHANCELLOR: You must really deepen your thoughts about joining me in more interpretating and trade – this devotion to the church is of nobility but the monies –

CHILFORD: Of yet again brother? I have told you many a time – I am not of the slightest desire to do anything BUT work for the Lord my God in His holy church. I am already strained and distracted by this additional Native Commissioner employment – your suggestion by the by –

CHANCELLOR: I am helping you grow on the ladder of prestige – we are still a rarity – African and highly educated – you best be in obedience to my wise ideals or die a pauper!

CHILFORD: Considerable exaggeration as of always. Look at my home. *(Gesturing.)* How many Africans can boast of such an accommodation –

CHANCELLOR: An inheritance from British missionaries.

CHILFORD: In the exact!

CHANCELLOR: Chilford Ndlovu: the Church's favorite savage. *(Sips his tea.)* Though on that front – you may have some competition. I just read in the morning Chronicle that Herbert Mhuloyi in Cape Town was just ordained into the Jesuit Priesthood!

CHILFORD: NOT NEVER!!

CHANCELLOR: Yes! The very first African Priest, in Cape Town!

CHILFORD: I…I…am very disturbed by that! I was told we weren't allowed to be considered for Priesthood –

CHANCELLOR: I am knowing; you have been in a rants about being the first native priest and heading a church since we were…?

CHILFORD: TEN – or near abouts. And they were always saying that wasn't possible right now because that level could only be attained in Europe! I am talking to Father – first thing. What is that <u>smell</u>? *(Sniffing the air suspiciously, CHANCELLOR shrugs and lights a pipe.)* An African priest! *I* have grown a congregation, Father Bart is not of the most sharpness you know! Without me there would be not a nary to report! Yet *he* is the priest! I started a *school,* albeit a small one – *(His arm making contact with a large amount of polish on the chaise.)* NOT AGAIN! ESTER!!

ESTER comes forward fearfully.

ESTER: Yes Masta?

CHILFORD: WHAT have I most constantly told you of rubbing wood polish on cloth? This is for the FLOOR and the WOODEN DESKS! Things of wooden and cement making, do you understand? You are ruining this furniture!

ESTER: *(Quickly cleaning off the polish.)* Sorry Masta.

CHILFORD: It must never be done again.

ESTER: Yes Masta.

CHANCELLOR: *(Chuckling in disbelief.)* Ahh…savages. Direct from the village?

CHILFORD: Yes.

CHANCELLOR: Well what else are you to be expecting? I heard of a maid at one of the mine owner's homes, she built a fire in the middle of their wooden panel floored lounge. Broke up the wood with an ax and made use of it for firewood.

CHILFORD: Goodness of graciousness. And the house?

CHANCELLOR: Burnt to the ground of course.

CHILFORD: GRACIOUSNESS!

CHANCELLOR: Yes, yes, yes.

CHILFORD: You will never do such a thing will you Ester? Thanks be to God this floor is made of cement. Though that still seems to bear befuddlement upon her – she is of course accustomed to cow dung floors, I have caught her sniffing at it a few times.

CHANCELLOR: *(Laughing.)* Of course. She, I am certain, had never seen it in the priors.

CHILFORD: But I have explained. *(To ESTER.)* You know it is cement, not cow dung now yes?

ESTER: Cement! Ey ye! Ahh…yes!

CHILFORD: Good. *(To CHANCELLOR.)* Now –

ESTER: But Masta, why is it?

CHILFORD: Why is it what?

ESTER: A cement end not a cow dung?

CHILFORD: Because we do not want the excrements of a bovine in our homes when we can use a sturdy permanent substance.

ESTER: What that it is?

CHILFORD: What?

ESTER: Pemanant.

CHILFORD: Permanent is meaning it will stay forever.

ESTER: Foreva?

CHILFORD: Yes.

ESTER: Rike Jesas?

CHILFORD: No. Not that long, it will as you can see, start to chip away and crack and need replacing –

ESTER: Rike with cow dung Masta, I reprace it verrry nice. This one it not be rooking as nice –

CHILFORD: Yes, but –

ESTER: So it is the same, it need repracing too?

CHILFORD: Yes but – NO! Not as much. Cement is superior. *(Beat.)* Are you in understanding?

ESTER: *(Unsure if she can answer honestly in the affirmative.)* Ahhh…

CHILFORD: Just say 'yes' Ester.

ESTER: Yes.

CHILFORD: Good.

CHANCELLOR: *(Bemused.)* She is an inquisitive one eh?

CHILFORD: Yes. It is in general, a thing of goodness, but at times I feel we run in the circular.

CHANCELLOR: Ahh…savages. *(Beat.)* Oh, that gives me a reminding. You cannot be out brandishing your Holy Church ways to the kaffirs just nows; what you did out there – must not be repeated.

CHILFORD: And why ever not? You mean the natives I addressed on the road to come to mass?

CHANCELLOR: Yes!

CHILFORD: How is that different from what I am always doing? Bringing the natives out of darkness and into ligh –

CHANCELLOR: Were you not of the hearing of the latest lingos?

CHILFORD: What?

CHANCELLOR: It is of the apparents, that we are now referred to as *Bafu*, it was shouted to us as we walked away from them into the Commissioner Office, did you not hear?

CHILFORD: Oh, yes I have heard it in the prior. So what, and I ask, with a full heart of trepidation is a *Bafu*?

CHANCELLOR: A traitor – a white man's native. And they are killing us.

CHILFORD: What? That is considerable exaggeration!

CHANCELLOR: Eh, eh brother!? There is a bloody uprising in Bulawayo – Matebeleland man! Maids killing white families in their sleeps! Do you think the hesitation wills arise to knock your black block off?

CHILFORD: Ahh….the Matebele man. Beasts.

CHANCELLOR: Those are your peoples.

CHILFORD: *Were* my peoples. Now my peoples are any and all who embraces Christ as Lord.

CHANCELLOR: What I am telling you is be of care. It is best you not do any saving of black souls for a whiles. Just for safetys.

CHILFORD: Is it not under control as yet? In Bulawayo?

CHANCELLOR: *(Brimming with admiration.) Rhodes*, Sir
Cecil Rhodes, he's quite a man eh! He quickly arranged
reinforcements; they are hanging savages in Market
Square! But even stills we better be in hopes it stays there –
we are not safe.

CHILFORD: Are you in seriousness with this? Bulawayo is
more than two hundred miles away! Here? The Shona?
Oh, cometh.

CHANCELLOR: Don't be putting it past these Shona here! They
just addressed you as a traitor! When a man comes into your
house and takes it over, and you are a man – there is no way
you can takes that lying down! And with the white mans, he
is not just taking over the house, he is saying – this should
be over here and this looks better there and this floor must
be made out of wood and not cow dungs and here is where
you release your bowels and here is where you lie with your
wife – only ONE wife by the bys! It is as if to say, what we
did before was somethings of a mess.

CHILFORD: What is your preference Chancey? Are you
wanting to go back to your father's ways?

CHANCELLOR: Not even a jotting! *He* is a good samplings
of the very problems of our peoples! He was a FOOL
and I can be telling you why – there he is – a chief in the
Karanga area –

CHILFORD: I know and he refused to submit when they came –

CHANCELLOR: Not only did he refuse! He rebelled. And
where is he now? Many other chiefs still enjoy their
sovereignties, why? Because they think like myself. They
embraced and accommodated. He went and broke the
laws they set up, sent his mens to steal the cattles back
that they had taken. When they came to talk to him man
to man what did he do? Refuse to meet them – send his
mens out with their little spear and shield. Foolish. Of
course the white man returns with his guns. I was there,
with my father in his *kraal*, about ten years of age, but

who really knows, and there he sat, on his little throne of lion hide. I had spent my whole life with such respects for him, I thought he was God. I thought if he was to tell the sun – today it would not be shining, it would obey. But that day, hmmm, I saw my father was just a small, powerless African man, resisting a tide TOO much biggers than him. I watched those men destroy EVERYTHINGS. Baba and his mens were powerless against their guns, and they had African men helping them to the boot! Would we have white mens helping us if we were fighting white mens? Ha! Of that one I am in doubts. *(Beat.)* Anyways. That day I saw fear on my father's face, I saw it and I knew who I was to be paying attention to – and it was not the African. My father, died like a coward, begging for his life. After that I asked these white mens if I could go with them. I wanted to learn their ways, I could see ours were of no use. They laughed but they took me as their servant boy for a time and after that –

CHILFORD: After that is when we met at Father Helm's.

CHANCELLOR: So keep your shirt buttoned, we are in understanding as to why the African will never succeed, but they *will* fight, I am just saying, just saying. *(Beat. CHANCELLOR puffs on his pipe and pulls a bottle of whiskey out of his coat. To ESTER.)* Girl, go get glasses. *(ESTER rushes out.)* Ah, in fact – *(He proceeds to pour whiskey into CHILFORD's tea.)*

CHILFORD: Ahhh!

CHANCELLOR: Oh have some living! *(He pours some in his own cup, swirls and drinks.)* But the white man, huh, the white man will never wholly befriend us of course. *(Chuckling.)* Their utter holy fears of our touching their womens. Even when they jump on ours without a thoughts!

Chilford: …Well…

CHANCELLOR: *(Chuckling.)* You know it is true old boy. *(ESTER returns, with glasses on a tray, she stops, confused as she sees CHANCELLOR pour more in his tea cup, she retreats with glasses.)*

Drink up! I got this in exchange for some translating I did at Beatrice Mine, don't of dare waste a drop!

CHILFORD: *(Finally drinking.)* Yes… Well, it does take the edge off a rather rough day… Herbert Mhuloyi, HA! Cannot believe it. And I had only four pupils today. FOUR!

CHANCELLOR: Change is a kind of a tricky business my friend.

CHILFORD: Well it is a must! Ester was at school weren't you? What did you learn today? Tell Master –

ESTER: *(Stepping forward, happy to take the stage after the mortifying polish incident, she recites.)* I believe in God the Fatha Armighty, creata of heawen end eth. I believe in Jesus Christ, his onry son oura Rord. He was born of the vegin Mery, He suffered unda Pontius Pirate, was crucified, died and buried, He decended in hero, on the third day he was rose agen, He accented into heawen and was sitted at the right hand of the Fatha. He will come agen to judge the riving and the died.

CHILFORD: Dead.

ESTER: Dead.

CHILFORD: Isn't that to impress old boy? Look what she can absorb in one day, one day! Now we still have some trouble with the consonants, VVVVV my dear, keep working on the VVVVV sound! *(ESTER proceeds to imitate CHILFORD's facial movements in an attempt to accomplish the sound. She fails and proceeds to pronounce V as W.)*

CHANCELLOR: And the Ls.

CHILFORD: Yes, the Ls are still elusive to her; look at my mouth, my girl – *(CHILFORD proceeds to over enunciate the L sound with his mouth open wide and the tip of his tongue touching the roof of his mouth.)* LLLL, see what my tongue is doing? LLLLL.

ESTER proceeds to copy him, though her tongue keeps rattling at the roof of her mouth, producing a reverberating RRRR sound.

CHANCELLOR: It's of a damn nuisance that rattling R in the vernacular.

CHILFORD: *(To ESTER.)* Practice, practice! *(To CHANCELLOR.)* I know but she is doing so well! She is my best pupil ever!

CHANCELLOR: Where are you from girl?

ESTER: Mazowe.

CHANCELLOR: You are Muzezuru – Shona?

ESTER: Yes.

CHANCELLOR: Muzezuru…hmm.

CHILFORD: What man?

CHANCELLOR: Proceed with cautions.

CHILFORD: Oh I do! Ever prayerful that she is the real thing.

CHANCELLOR: DO you understand that the things your family teaches you are things of pagans, that they are in darkness and now it is your calling to draw them into light?

ESTER: Yes. I am to bring them to Jesas! Jesas is so good! He make so I can not be marrying an old man end now going to school end learning to be reading end writing end staying in a NIIICE house. JESAS! He is the mosting High God!

CHILFORD: *(Pleased.)* Yes! He is the MOST High God. I ask her that daily in fact, just to be of sure, you know what has happened in the past!

ESTER: Masta, I am real, for sure Masta!

CHILFORD: Yes, we shall see of it Ester we shall see. But, I have had her but for some months and look at the progress! – I may just have, I dare say too soon, a PROTÉGÉ! Finally! *(Almost bursting out of his skin.)* Oh, oh! And Ester – sing the song – sing the song I taught you.

ESTER: *(Proudly, her chest pushed out, begins to sing 'Amazing Grace', her voice beautiful and melodic. CHANCELLOR is slowly*

drawn in and more and more impressed, CHILFORD beams
proudly and conducts her with his hands.)

Amazing Grace, how swee the sound
Thet save a rench rike me!
I once was rost, but now I found
Was brind but now I see!

CHANCELLOR: Well that is quite alright!

CHILFORD: Isn't it! She just has an unbelievable ability to
absorb, it is almost afrightening! If I were to fall down to
our people's ways of thinking I would think her a witch!

ESTER: *(Terrified.)* I not witch Masta,//NO!

CHILFORD: //Settle down old girl, I am just talking. But
really, I cannot wait to be showing her to Father Helm! I
was beginning to think you and I and the few others true
anomalies, but look, here she is, a testimony to all the
others out there, wading and wallowing in the bushes; we
can be ironing out all the traditional creases and create a
state similar to the Great Britain itself with a whole new
culture and peoples! Go draw my bath girl.

ESTER: Yes, Masta.

She leaves.

CHILFORD: And she is a hard worker for the boot, she
commenced working at the Colterns a few weeks ago, they
are speaking highly of her as well.

CHANCELLOR: Indeed. *(Beat.)* So you are really wanting to be
a priest old boy?

CHILFORD: Of course.

CHANCELLOR: You do know what is alls involved in
Priesthoods?

CHILFORD: What? The Eucharist, Confessionals, catechism, I
am ready for all of that. I was born –

CHANCELLOR: Don't be a daft, I means the other thing.

CHILFORD: What? Celibacy?

CHANCELLOR: *YES!!*

CHILFORD: Oh, please, what possible problem could I have with that one? I have been practicing that anyhow!

CHANCELLOR: OH COME COMES!

CHILFORD: What?

CHANCELLOR: You are meanings to say, that you have never once had a little rompings with that plumped bottomed thing *drawing your bath*?

CHILFORD: *(Jumping up.)* You must have fallen off of your wits old chap! What in the earth! Do you really imagine – really – really – to start with – the sin involved – not to be mentioning how it is quite impossible for me to be finding – such primitiveness attractive – and –

CHANCELLOR: Oh come, comes brother. Really, really. Even the Dukes and the Earls have a few a rompings when they comes to inspect the new colony! Haven't you noticed the light browning children running around with the loose coiled hairs?

CHILFORD: *(Unnerved.)* I have no interest to be in pursuit of this conversation one inch further.

CHANCELLOR: Be steady! Just asking. She is an attractive little things. I wouldn't mind a goes if you don't object.

CHILFORD: I DO object, I am trying to bring her to GOD you imbecile, so have your GO somewhere else. Have you not a fiancé?

CHANCELLOR: Ah…yes…and so…?

CHILFORD: *(Disgusted.)* And so. Pru deserves better Chancy, she does, she really does.

CHANCELLOR: Oh for goodness, curb your loving affections for her. She is made of the toughest stuff, tougher than you and me to be in honestys! She knows me for what I am.

CHILFORD: *(Perturbed.)* Do leave man. I need to write my daily report to Father. And leave out the front. Don't go near my potential protégé.

CHANCELLOR: Settle down chappy, she is just a common girl. But on that one, you are right, I bests be having a movement. *(Getting up, checking his pocket watch.)* We were to go to that wretching marriage lessons on these hour. *(A knock at the door.)* Oh of goodness, that mights be her.

CHILFORD gets up and answer the door, PRUDENCE enters.

PRUDENCE: Chilfy! Is Chancey about? He was not where we were to meet – CHANCEY! Father Bart awaits!

CHANCELLOR: I knows, I knows my wifes to bes. Chilfy held me ups with all his chatterings. You knows how he gets!

CHIFLORD: Ahh!

PRUDENCE: I know how You get! Ohh, is that tea, God I would Love a cup, but No, we haven't a moment, Chancey! You must take this with all seriousness! It causes me distress when I must come looking for you so!

CHANCELLOR: My darling dears, Never be within distress on my front, I will Never lets you downs. Let us be gone.

PRUDENCE: *(Enamored.)* Chancey! *(Noticing ESTER who has returned and is staring at her with deep curiosity.)* Ohh! A new one! Hello! I am Mistress Prudence! What is your name?

ESTER: Esta.

PRUDENCE: Ohhh! Ester! 'If I perish I perish.' Love it, Chilfy! Okay let us be gone Chancey. Cheerio Chilfy!

CHILFORD: Yes, goodbye.

CHANCELLOR: *(Following her out, to CHILFORD.)* Stop all the soul saving eh! We must be of cares, we MUST be of cares! I will see you in the morning, His holiness.

CHILFORD: Be of leave Chancellor!

CHANCELLOR: *(Chuckling.)* I am gone, I am gone!

They exit. CHILFORD closes the door behind CHANCELLOR and goes to his desk, and commences reading his letter.

SCENE THREE

Evening, several months later. MAI TAMBA paces the room looking anxious, she checks a few times for CHILFORD's arrival. She replaces the indiscernible objects from their hiding places with fresh ones. She sneaks a little snuff out of her pouch. Finally he enters, with ESTER in tow; her gait now more formal, she has visibly become more like CHILFORD in poise and manner.

MAI TAMBA: *(Nervously.)* Good evening, Masta.

CHILFORD: Good evening Mai Tamba, I will have my supper in the present. *(To ESTER.)* What I am in an attempt to explain is that you may NEVER be doing that in the future.

ESTER: But Master –

CHILFORD: But Master what? Are you in understanding of what I have said?

ESTER: In honesty?

CHILFORD: Of COURSE in honesty!

ESTER: I am not in understanding.

CHILFORD: How is that?

ESTER: You told me that we must never be in the tolerance of a misquoting of the Bible in our presence.

CHILFORD: Yes but –

ESTER: You told me that under that circumstance we must be quick to correct, to be of certainty that the Lord's word is never in distortion – that is what I am in belief that I did.

CHILFORD: Yes but NOT to Father Bart!

ESTER: May I be asking why?

CHILFORD: Why? Is it not in the obvious? *(They stare at each other for a couple of beats, she does not answer.)* He is a white!

ESTER: He is.

CHILFORD: So you MAY NEVER correct him.

ESTER: This is because//he is a white.

CHILFORD: //Because he is a white. Yes.

Beat.

CHILFORD: Be in belief, it is for your good. You can correct our people in all times and any. *(Softening.)* You were in the right, it was Jacob and not Esau who wrestled with the angel; I am in disbelief that he was in the ability to confuse this. But that is neither in here or in there. I hope you never do that to the Colterns. Your ability to work in the Church goes in the hand of getting along with the white. They are the ushers of the Lord's word. Without them, where is it you and I would be? It brings on a shudder to be imagining.

Beat.

ESTER: So never am I to correct them or admonish them as Saint Paul instructs?

CHILFORD: NO, never. We must learn from them and teach their ways to our own. Respect them Ester, and trust them, they bring much to be learning. Are you in understanding?

ESTER: I am not Master.

CHILFORD: Ester!

ESTER: Master, according to the word of the Lord my God in the Holy Scriptures we are to admonish one another, there is no Greek, no Jew, no male, no female in Christ –

CHILFORD: It is not – it is not so simple as –

ESTER: 'Be ready in season and out of season. Convince, rebuke, exhort, with all longsuffering and teaching.'

CHILFORD: Ester! I am aware what the Scriptures say! But, you will learn in time – *(Searching as to how to appease her.)* It, it is as the scriptures say, Longsuffering – Longsuffering. Allow the Lord to speak on how to handle these whites and their ways, and not be quick to correct them. That is it, meditate on it, LONGSUFFERING.

ESTER: *(Thinking deeply.)* Alright. *(Beat.)* Yes Master.

CHILFORD: *(With great relief.)* GOOD, good, good, good! Now you may go settle for the evening.

ESTER: Thank you Master.

MAI TAMBA: *(Whispers to ESTER.)* Usaende kure gara muKitchen. **[Don't go far – stay in kitchen okay?]**

ESTER: *(In English.)* Yes Aunt. *(She exits.)*

MAI TAMBA: Oh-ahh…ahhh, I have something to tell you Masta.

CHILFORD: *(Put upon.)* What is it?

MAI TAMBA: Can we have time to go to the virrage Masta?

CHILFORD: Who?

MAI TAMBA: Myserf end Jeke – ahhh Esta Masta.

CHILFORD: What sort of time?

MAI TAMBA: A week Masta.

CHILFORD: A week! How am I supposed to manage on my own for a week?

MAI TAMBA: We can send someone to come and herp [help] from Masta Chancera Masta.

CHILFORD: Why do you need to go for so long?

MAI TAMBA: *Kurova Guva.*

CHILFORD: And WHAT is that?

MAI TAMBA: *(Shocked.)* You don know what *Kurova Guva* it is?

CHILFORD: NO! I have not lived among – the people since I was a small boy, how am I supposed to know every backward ritual's name?

MAI TAMBA: It is when the relative they have been dead a year, then they do ceremony so that he can return to the famiry.

CHILFORD: Who? Who can return? The dead relative?

MAI TAMBA: Yes Masta. Not him dead, but his spirit Masta.

CHILFORD: You must be joking. You still in belief of that rubbish Mai Tamba? After all our time together? After all those masses with Father Bart? You still believe in communing with the dead?

MAI TAMBA: *(Distressed.)* It is our way, Masta, we must be treating the dead propery.

CHILFORD: Oh Holy Mother. WHERE did she go?

MAI TAMBA: She is in the back.

CHILFORD: Bring her here in the immediate.

MAI TAMBA exits, distressed. CHILFORD looks equally disturbed, MAI TAMBA re-enters with ESTER in tow.

CHILFORD: Ester. *(Beat.)* You read so beautifully in mass on Sunday.

ESTER: Thank you Master.

CHILFORD: Did you believe what you were saying?

ESTER: Of course Master.

CHILFORD: What were you saying?

ESTER: I was reading from First Samuel fifteen verse twenty two. *(Reciting.)* 'But Samuel replied: "Does the Lord delight in burnt offerings and sacrifices as much as in obeying the voice of the Lord? Because you have rejected the word of the Lord, he has rejected you as king."'

CHILFORD: Very good. So are you rejecting the word of the Lord like Saul now Ester?

ESTER: *(Firmly.)* No I am not.

CHILFORD: So why do you wish to go to participate in a pagan ritual Ester?

ESTER: I...I...Master, it is our way.

CHILFORD: IF you participate in pagan acts you are a pagan. Are you a pagan Ester?

ESTER: No! I am a Roman Catholic. But –

CHILFORD: BUT WHAT?

ESTER: I have duties, to my family, I –

CHILFORD: HAVE you taken Christ as your Lord and Savior?

ESTER: OF COURSE!

CHILFORD: SO why is it you are going to do this?

ESTER: Christ does not instruct me to abandon my family; my mother, she, she needs me Master –

CHILFORD: NO SHE DOES NOT! 'Let the dead bury the dead and follow me.' WHO SAID that eh? ANSWER ME!

ESTER: Jesus.

CHILFORD: IN THE EXACT! I cannot believe you are doing this, like all my other converts! How can you think it is that you can function on both of the fence sides? You CANNOT! I chose to go with Father Helm when I was nine years old and I haven't looked back SINCE! Do you have ANY knowing of what I have forsook? Things beyond my imaginings. The storytelling at the feet of my grandmother – my brothers and sisters of my blood – who KNOWS what has become of them! I left them for my call – embracing all who respond to the name CHRIST JESUS as my kin in their replace. My own mother! Her, her – cookings of kaffir corn and and mixed beans – her, her kind…embrace, yet savage – but good and kind and – MY OWN *FATHER* I – *(Collecting himself for a few beats.)* There is no other way for us, Ester, there is no other way for those who are called, you must fully respond – forget it – as I have – it is in the past! What is it you want to do, Ester? What is it you want for your future? *(Beat.)* ANSWER!

ESTER: I want to translate and teach.

CHILFORD: Do you think that comes with an ease? Do you know how much I still must do to attain a position of priesthood? To arrest their fears that I will not turn and run back into the bush and grab hold of four wives? To THINK I imagined you ready to take the title Protégé!*(Beat.)* YOU MUST NOT GO, Ester. You must not. It is not what your Lord and Savior is wanting of you. *(Beat.)* But the Lord sayeth 'I placeth before you life and death, blessings and cursings, therefore choose life.' Deuteronomy 30 Verse 19.

MAI TAMBA: Uhh Masta WHY? Why you no just ret her GO Masta? She can come beck end sing to Jesas.

CHILFORD: *(To MAI TAMBA, not taking his eyes off of ESTER.)* BE OF SILENCE! Ester what is it you are going to do?

Silence ensues for several beats as ESTER decides, her face is still but her eyes betray her state, she is distressed and torn. She finally speaks, her voice is deep and still.

ESTER: *(Slowly.)* I will stay.

CHILFORD nods his head profusely and falls back in his chair, his eyes still locked with hers.

MAI TAMBA: *(Lamenting.)* Aaaaah ah, Maiweee, Ndoti chii kuna Mai? Usadaro Jekesai! Unodiwa na Maivako! Ndiwe ani manje iwe? Who are you now? **[What will I say to your mother and grandmother? What do I say? Ahh my God, you can't do this Jekesai! Your mother needs you!! Who are you? Who are you now?]**

ESTER: Aunt//I must, I must heed to my calling. I am a new creature –

MAI TAMBA: //AIWA! Taura neChishona! KIRI-CHA Kuitasei!? Haunyare?! HAUNYARE!! SHAME. **[No! Speak in Shona! CREATURE! Have you no shame, have you no shame!!]**

CHILFORD: STOP NOW Mai Tamba, we will send you with supplies for her mother, I will make sure of it, but Ester can no longer participate in this type of thing. Ester, you have saved the money you have made working for your mother have you not?

ESTER: I have.

CHILFORD: Be sure to be passing it on to your aunt. I will send some of my own supply of mealie meal and greens, and that last cut of meat Mai Tamba, be sure to take it along, allow that to make it clear that Ester is, here, with me now. That will be all, Mai Tamba, I will be taking dinner at my leisure, I must write this letter to Father immediately.

MAI TAMBA: *(Thoroughly distraught.)* Yes Masta. Eeeee azviiti, Chokwadi. It is NOT Good for sure.

ESTER turns and walks out abruptly, MAI TAMBA follows heavily behind her. CHILFORD goes to his desk and begins his usual ritual, his hands are shaking however. He stops and after a moment reaches under his desk for some whisky, grabs a glass and takes a long drink. He slowly seems to calm as he leans back in his chair and closes his eyes.

END OF ACT ONE

ACT TWO

SCENE ONE

Weeks later. ESTER and her cousin TAMBA sit in the lounge, a large Bible open before them on the coffee table. At points in the beginning of this scene TAMBA will speak in Shona and ESTER will respond in English.

ESTER: *(Both are snapping their fingers at each other like ten year olds.)* //Eeyy, chokwadi, its true! I wasn't even *liking* those mangoes ka!

TAMBA: AHH! *(Jumping up.)* Kunyepa! Kunyepa! *(Motions eating with hands.)* Maidya muchidya muchichema *(Pretends to cry and squats as one moving their bowels.)* 'Oh! Oh! Amai! Amai vangu! Ndakufa. Daidza n'anga chokwadi!' **[You lie, you ate and then you would cry, Oh! Oh! Mama, mama! I am dying! Call the traditional healer surely!']**

ESTER : Ah?! You were the one eating too many!

TAMBA: Aiwa, Ndakamatora kukupai imimi *(Pointing at her emphatically.)* chete chete – **[No, I got them to give to you. Only.]**

ESTER: *(Quick to object.)* Eeeeeey, getting them for me! *(Snapping her fingers.)* Tambaoga ewe!

TAMBA: Ichokwadi! Ndakatiza imbwa yemurungu! I was happy to bring you mangoes. **[I outran the white man's dogs!]**

ESTER: Yaah! Well Thank God the white man's dogs were never catching you – Jesus be praised!

Beat. TAMBA stops laughing.

TAMBA: Hmmm. So. This your Jesus – *(Indicating Bible.)* I am hearing you are bringing many people to the church.

36

ESTER: Ya, God is to be praised! We baptized Mai Tatenda on
    Sunday!

TAMBA: Mai Tatenda! Ichokwadi? **[For sure?]**

ESTER: Ey ye! Ah...Yes! I started talking to her one day at the
    market, gave her my testimony, now she is a believer, her
    name is now Abigail, after a virtuous, wise wife of King David.

TAMBA: Ohhh ohhh.

ESTER: Yes. I wish to bring you and all of my family to Christ also.

TAMBA: Ohhh nai. And who is this Christ you want to bring
    me to?

ESTER: *(Her voice resounding with sudden power and authority.)*
    There is so much power we can be having through Christ,
    these way of our people, he has come and brought the
    white man as our teacher to guide us from those ways.

TAMBA: Ohhhh. What is it that is wrong with our ways?

ESTER: Look at what happened to me, the bondage I was in.
    I was freed by the Lord my God. Now I can choose what
    I do, I go to school, I follow the Lord as my guide and he
    empowers me.

TAMBA: Doesn't Mwari empower us also? Doesn't Mwari
    protect us and guide us?

ESTER: Cousin, this is the same Mwari who says I can be
    married off by my drunken uncle without a choice? This is
    the same Mwari who says that we must kill babies if they are
    born as twins? This is the same Mwari who says we must be
    married to our brother-in-law when our husband he die –

TAMBA: But he guides our paths, he shows us how to take care
    of our family. He give us something to stand on, something
    strong – so we can have an order.

ESTER: What order is that brother? An order that has us
    worship the dead? Even relatives we did not like or even

trust? Christ came to earth and proved himself to us in the flesh, in character.

TAMBA: The ancestors look down on you, to protect you, to care for you to –

ESTER: NO Cousin! If they are dead, they are dead.

Beat.

TAMBA: So this Jesus of yours is dead.

ESTER: Jesus ROSE from the dead, BECAUSE he was clean of sin; he died for us, he went through that for you and me Cousin. He Loves you Tamba, he created you and he LOVES you so much.

TAMBA: Ooooh oh? *(Beat.)* So what is it this Jesus he want of me?

ESTER: He want you to accept Him into your heart, to have relation with Him.

TAMBA: *(Ponderous, looking deeply into JEKESAI/ESTER's face.)* Ooooh oh? So what is it I must do now?

ESTER: *(Excited.)* Yes! Indeed! Foremost, we must put a change to your name.

Beat.

TAMBA: Oright.

ESTER: What do you think of Phineas? You look like one, you do, you do.

TAMBA: Eh he.

ESTER: *(Looking heavenward.)* God be praised! That is your name then: Phineas. Now, Phineas, you must take Jesus Christ as your Lord and savior – I will speak the profession of faith and you speak it after me and –

TAMBA: I can't do that.

ESTER: What? Don't be of worry, He is a God of great grace, it is not at all hard Phineas, I will further explain who He is and –

TAMBA: I know who He is –

ESTER: No you do not as yet, but as I explain –

TAMBA: I KNOW who he is. He is the one who make you a *Bafu*, a lover to the white man.

Beat.

ESTER: What is this now cousin?

TAMBA: *(Explosively.)* YOU KNOW WHAT YOU DO! How ken you not go to your own fatha his *kurova guva*?

ESTER: Cousin –

TAMBA: NO! You want to be a white now and do rike they be doing. But you are NOT!

ESTER: Cousin, I know I am not a white – but I am a Roman Catholic and that is of the first and the foremost –

TAMBA: MARARA! **[RUBBISH!]** You are a muzezuru of the first and the foremost. The daughter of many lines of vazezuru, but you want to sit in this *BAFU* idiot's home acting rike you ara a white; telling my motha to call you this *BAFU* name of yours! And when was the last time it is you see *your* motha?

ESTER: I send her monies.

TAMBA: She no want your monies – she wants to see who it is she has born in her face! We should have ret babam'diki give you to the old man.

ESTER: How dare you say that?! It is not only for those who bore me that I live! I do good for our people every day, teaching AND feeding them EVERY DAY and that is more than I would be doing as some old goat's tenth wife!

TAMBA: MARARA!!! At least then you would know who it is you are. Now you are lost. Forgetting the ways of your peopo. Loving on the whites. What good ara they doing, eh? Bringing, this Jesas. You say he give and give till he die. What ara they giving eh? They ara teking end teking and you want to love them for that? I work in Beatrice mine, EVERY DAY they mek me work for little little money for what? Before they come, we neva work like this, for this thing, digging end digging rike our arms they are not of our own. Onry digging for food for our families. Now we do what they say because we need these monies they bring to GIVE BEK TO THEM in the hut tex to live in a smar hut and they ara riving in the BIIIIG houses they mek US buiud. Then they say – 'Oh – here is this God who is coming from they sky to mek you crean from a sin – you love on him end be heppy. Oh – and onry one wife for one men.' End you love them? You ara a bafu end a fool cousin. End YOU, you must rememba who it is you are before too late. End I will NEVA want this. *(Picks up Bible and throws it to the ground.)* It is the poison of the white man. It kill the spirit of your forefather inside you. So now you ara empty and they can fir [fill] you with anything they want. NEVA. My name is Tambaoga Chiangawa Murumbira. CHETE. [Only.] *(Turns to leave.)* But you must watch yourself Jekesai – the people are not taking the white man's poison ENYMORE end you don't want to be with these ones when it come.

ESTER: When what come?

TAMBA: Ha. *(Beat.)* Just hear what it is I say.

PRUDENCE stands at the door as TAMBA opens it, she is poised to knock.

PRUDENCE: Oh! Maswera sei youth? **[How are you?]**

TAMBA: *(Hurriedly.)* Ndaswera. **[I am fine.]**

He leaves.

PRUDENCE: *(Entering with an air of regality.)* Well he seems to have a couple bees in the bonnet! *(Noting ESTER's state.)* Are you alright?

ESTER: *(Attempting to collect herself.)* Yes, thank you, I am fine. How are you Mistress Prudence?

PRUDENCE: I am…quite well. Who was that?

ESTER: My, my relative.

PRUDENCE: Oh yes, family, they are always cause for distress, that is at times their sole design! 'If I perish, I perish'… ESTER! Yes?

ESTER: Yes.

PRUDENCE: Yes! That is how I keep trying to remember your name, I love that story! Ahhh! The Market is a bloody madhouse today. It better settle down, or I don't know how we are to get all the provisions for the wedding! There is some unbearable tension in the air, I can truly FEEL it! Most of the stalls aren't even open! People just milling about. Is he here by the slightest chance?

ESTER straightens out the room, she moves with methodic precision.

ESTER: Master Chancellor? He is not.

PRUDENCE: Ahhk man. I was sure he would be, he is nowhere to be found! He was to meet me at the wretched Market an hour past. Now heavens what!

A couple of beats pass.

ESTER: Would you be liking some tea?

PRUDENCE: Why yes, that would perhaps take a bit of a load off.

ESTER exits. PRUDENCE sits and picks up the Bible, she smoothes out the pages absentmindedly.

PRUDENCE: *(To ESTER offstage.)* We are to meet with Father Bart every week for this marriage lessons and he keeps disappearing on me! I don't know at this point if Father will marry us at all! Chancey better have some lovely thing for me to replace my distress that's all I can bloody say! He is probably – oh! Never mind. *(ESTER enters with tea tray.)* Oh! That was rather speedy!

ESTER: I had it prepared for Master Chilford's return.

ESTER pours and serves the tea.

PRUDENCE: *(Sipping a cup of tea.)* Not too bad, you must not put so much milk, it completely suffocates the essence of the tea, and more sugar. *(ESTER jumps up and brings a sugar basin to PRUDENCE, who places three large heaps into her tea.)* Mmmmm *(Sipping tea.)* that's much better, I can grab hold of my bearings again. Mmmmmm.

Beat.

ESTER: So…the market is in disturbance?

PRUDENCE: Or something! God only knows! Even Mai Gwatiro, I go to her for my vegetables, she was truly off, glaring at me, acting all strange! It better not be that Bulawayo uprising stuff, I have been very good to everyone, very good. *I* still speak the bloody vernacular, unlike Chilfy, the Great Black Tragedy.

ESTER: You still speak it?

PRUDENCE: Of course, do you not?

ESTER: Not, not too much. Master doesn't like me to speak it too much, only when converting others.

PRUDENCE: And how do you feel about that?

ESTER: It fits in well with my goals.

PRUDENCE: Which are?

ESTER: I want to learn how to speak English very well, so that I can teach and preach like Master. I want to do what he has done for me, for others, to bring our people out of darkness into light, as Master says.

PRUDENCE: Oh yes, I know what *Master* says, of course, he must seem like the brightest spark you have ever perceived I am sure! Let me let you in on a little secret – I have Far more schooling than him.

ESTER: You do?

PRUDENCE: Oh yes! I went to Natal to the Ndana school for girls, I was such an impressive student that the sisters got me a place there. The boys will never ever tell you this, but I am far more educated than both of them. In black or white terms.

ESTER: *(Snapping her fingers.)* Maiwee!

PRUDENCE: HA! See, there is still some native left in you somewhere!

ESTER giggles bashfully.

ESTER: Eeeey, so your family, they let you go all the way to Natal?

PRUDENCE: My family! Oh dear, my family disowned me Long ago!

ESTER: *(Disturbed.)* They disowned you?

PRUDENCE: Oh yes, like you, forced betrothal, Catholic church conversion blah and blah, so boring to relate, yes, they disowned me. But! I am and will always be a Matebele, a daughter of warriors, and proud of my people –

ESTER: Proud of the Matebele? But they do evil things, they killed settlers// and –

PRUDENCE: //Oh mercy. Do you think we are not also being killed by the whites? Do you suppose there is any good that can come from how they have taken the land? I am not defending murder, nor do I advocate an eye for an eye, but my dear, justice must come to pass – and it will be brutal, and it will be very, very ugly.

ESTER: But Master says our people need to heed to the settler! They are worshipping dead ancestors// and heeding charlatans –

PRUDENCE: //Indeed if they are ancestors they must be dead. Do you have anything to say?

ESTER: Matii? Ah…ah – I beg your pardon. What do you mean?

PRUDENCE: I mean I am SO disappointed! Though I saw Chilfy clearly at work on you I always thought I saw a little fighter in you, an independent spirit. But ALACK! I have sat here with you for a good many minutes and am yet to hear *you* speak.

ESTER: I am not in understanding.

PRUDENCE: Thus far, I have heard Chilford, 'Masta this and Masta that' I have heard Biblical ideology in its least synthesized form, but I am yet to hear *you.* I cannot wait! I am fascinated to finally meet you. I really, really am!

ESTER: I…

PRUDENCE: Yes? *(Reaches into her bag and brings out a pipe, and match and proceeds to light it.)*

ESTER: *(Aghast.)* Maiwee! Munoputa mbanje?!

PRUDENCE: It's not *mbanje* my dear, ha, wish it were, it is merely tobacco, something I picked up from an American Sister, Sister Alice, she was quite a rebel. I like rebels. Course I am not really much of one, if I was, I would never marry. *(Smokes.)* I am still waiting…

ESTER: *(Truly stumped.)* Ahh…

PRUDENCE: Really? Nothing? Oh my!

MAI TAMBA is heard entering from the back, she walks in with a bag of maize meal.

MAI TAMBA: Ah. Harro Mistress Prudence.

PRUDENCE: Yes, hello Mai Tamba, Makadini? [**How are you?**]

MAI TAMBA: Ndiripo! [**I am fine.**]

PRUDENCE: Mamboona mukomana wangu? [**Have you seen my man?**]

MAI TAMBA: Aiwa handina kuvaona! [**No! I have not surely!**]

PRUDENCE: Varume, these men, vanonetsa. [**Ahh, and these men, so trouble/rude!**]

MAI TAMBA laughs.

PRUDENCE: Well, let me be off then, I should get back to the mission before dark and inform Father of some other colorful reason for Chancellor's absence. *(Gathers herself.)* Thank you for the tea Ester dear.

ESTER: Most welcome.

PRUDENCE: We shall speak again I hope! *(To MAI TAMBA.)* Amangwana Mai Tamba!

MAI TAMBA: Amangwana!

(PRUDENCE exits. A tangible tension rests in the air between the two women. Finally –)

MAI TAMBA: Tamba ayenda? [**Tamba left?**]

ESTER: Yes. Tamba left some half hour ago.

MAI TAMBA: Ahh, sei? Ndaida kumupa upfu. [**I wanted to give him mealie meal.**] *(Holding up the small sack. Looking out the window MAI TAMBA drops the sack and pulls out some snuff from her bosom, she proceeds to sniff it, ESTER watches her distastefully.)* Ataura newe here? [**Did your cousin…did he talk to you?**]

ESTER: Yes he *talked* to me. *(The women sit and stand in strained silence.)* Aunt I –

MAI TAMBA: *(Objecting.)* Mmmm, Ah Ah Ah ! 'Aunt' Chiichocho? [**What is that? Aunt?**]

After several strained beats, MAI TAMBA begins to sing and sway gently.

MAI TAMBA: Ini ndiri Jekesai   [I am Ester
         Anenge achindi tevera   Those who follow
         Achazova naJekesai   I am the light
         Jekesai wepasi   The light of the world
         Jekesai wekupenya   The light of life.]

ESTER, very distressed crosses herself, goes to the crucifix and begins to pray 'Hail Mary' in repetition, with quiet intensity.

ESTER: Hail Mary, full of grace, the Lord is with thee, Blessed art thou among women and blessed is the fruit of thy womb Jesus Holy Mary, mother of God, pray for our sins, now and at the hour of our death.

MAI TAMBA and ESTER sing and pray more and more fervently. They appear to be in some sort of existential battle. Suddenly the door opens and CHILFORD enters, they notice him and quickly adjust, MAI TAMBA grabs her bag of maize, mumbles a quick –

MAI TAMBA: 'Good evening Masta'

CHILFORD: What in the earth? Whatever histrionics Mai Tamba?

MAI TAMBA: No, no histras Masta, no histras. *(She hurriedly leaves the room.)*

CHILFORD: Graciousness. What was it you were doing?

ESTER: I was praying to the Virgin Mother.

CHILFORD: Right. Good, good. What ever was that?

ESTER: It was nothing Master. She was just singing a song of… of my childhood.

CHILFORD: Of your childhood.

ESTER: Yes. Nothing of harm Master, nothing of harm.

CHILFORD: Well, I will grab hold of your word on that one.

ESTER: How…how was your day Master? Mistress Prudence –

CHILFORD: Yes, yes I just saw her. *(Beat.)* My day went very well, very well indeed. In fact I have some news of wonder. *(Brandishing a letter.)* Father Helm is coming! I received this letter today! He is traveling as we speak to inspect our work here. This is most thrilling.

ESTER: Oh! That is full of marvel!

CHILFORD: Most indeed! Do be sure the home is most clean, I am in hoping he will make a stop here.

ESTER: Most certainly Master.

Beat.

CHILFORD: I will share this with only you Ester. I am most hoping to be bracing my desire to be pursuing Jesuit Priesthood –

ESTER: Oh! To be asking Father Helm?

CHILFORD: Yes! I have been most fearful of doing so thusly but now he is walking into my very footstep, well, it must be being a sign. *(Beat.)* Am I in wrong?

ESTER: No! Never in wrong Master! I am thinking that is most right, and to speak in most honesty, most deserving.

CHILFORD: Thank you. *(Beat.)* I am, I am also in the hopes of telling him that I have, indeed, and finally found my first, true protégé.

ESTER: *(Deeply touched.)* Master, this…this brings me great, great joy…I…am of deep thanks…I…

CHILFORD: Yes, you are most welcome. You have worked so well with the new students, I marvel at what you did with those natives by the market – there you were, a woman at that, getting them to promise attendance to mass! It is nothing, nothing short of a marvel.

ESTER: Thank you Master.

CHILFORD: Thanks unto you, for fighting the good fight.

Beat.

ESTER: Master?

CHILFORD: Yes?

ESTER: I am wanting to ask you – how did you manage – ?

CHILFORD: How did I manage what?

ESTER: What happened with you and your – without your family…and to leave, how – ?

CHILFORD: How *what?*

ESTER: *(Cowering.)* It is nothing. It is nothing.

A few beats of silence.

CHILFORD: Do tell Mai Tamba I will have my dinner at my leisure.

ESTER: Yes. Of course. *(She turns to leave.)*

CHILFORD: And Ester?

ESTER: Yes Master?

CHILFORD: In time, you will learn whom your true family it is. For myself, Father Helm is my father, my family here on earth. God giveth us that right, to pick our Earthly family, as Jesus did with his disciples. I picked. That is *how.* Are you in understanding?

Beat.

ESTER: Yes Master.

She exits.

SCENE TWO

Late at night, the room is dark. ESTER is on her knees, praying before the crucifix. She has not changed for bed. A ferverent knock on the door. ESTER jumps up. CHILFORD enters in his night robe, holding a torch.

CHILFORD: Who is there?

CHANCELLOR: *(From outside.)* It's Chancellor old boy, open!

CHILFORD: Oh for goodness graciousness man, it's rather late.

CHANCELLOR: Open up, good man!

CHILFORD: Alright. Goodness Graciousness.

CHILFORD opens the door, CHANCELLOR enters looking frazzled, CHANCELLOR's brow is covered in sweat, he has a large wound on his temple and is very out of sorts.

CHILFORD: What happened old boy? Ester obtain him a cloth.

ESTER: Yes Master.

ESTER exits.

CHANCELLOR: Things are not good brother.

CHILFORD: What happened to your head man? Have a seat man!

CHANCELLOR: The rebellion: it has spread – now it is certain, to us in Mashonaland.

CHILFORD: The Shona? Never! They are too docile! That cannot be of truth.

CHANCELLOR: IT IS, the first white family was already slaughtered. By a maid in Hartley.

CHILFORD: Great goodness! Never!

CHANCELLOR: Yes! And I was out drinking and in hearings of an attack on the road between Umtali and Salisbury, the Shona rebelling have taken over that road, just as what occurred in the south and –

49

CHILFORD: The road – OH GREAT GOODNESS, Father! He is on his way on that road –

CHANCELLOR: I am knowing, that's why I am rushing here. I went to the station and, please, Chilfy, you must sit for this –

CHILFORD: NO, Chancy please!

CHANCELLOR: Father Helm was on the road attacked by savages and//

CHILFORD: //NO! NO! No, no, no, no, no, no –

CHANCELLOR: //the police arrived but not in time to save him –

CHILFORD falls to the couch – crumbling at the very words, sobbing into his hands, CHANCELLOR paces around the room, ESTER stares at CHILFORD with pained sympathy.

CHANCELLOR: *(Finally.)* Girl go get some whiskey and glasses.

ESTER exits.

CHILFORD: *(Sobbing, reaching for CHANCELLOR.)* Can it be possible? Can it really be possible man? CHANCELLOR! Answer me?

CHANCELLOR: *(To CHILFORD.)* It is. You have to be strong, this is not seeming behavior, and in front of the womens.

CHILFORD: Seeming for what? For an African man? I swear, if I could shake that signifier off right now I would!

MAI TAMBA enters, wailing out and physically expressing traditional mourning behavior.

MAI TAMBA: Oh Maiwee zvangu ini! Toita sei! Toita sei shuwa! Ahhhh….musandidaro kani! Baba Hem, //Baba Hem musandidaro shuwa kani! [**Oh my God! What must we do! What can we do! AHHH….don't do this to us surely! Father Helm, Father Helm, how could you leave us sure!**]

CHILFORD: //What are you doing? Do you even know what happened?

ESTER: I told her.

CHILFORD: You didn't even know him! What are you flailing yourself about for?

CHANCELLOR: Settle down Chilford. It is a cultural way to mourn with those who mourn.

CHILFORD: Silence! I can't bear to hear about this culture. This culture that nurtures barbarians, that culture? *(Refusing the whiskey being offered, near hysterical.)* We have to get his body! We must tend to it as Chuma and Susi with Livingstone, salt it and cure it in the sun so we can get it back to Great Britain as they were doing – get it to his people, away from this land of Barbarians! What are we going to do? What are we going to do without him? What? This is *his* work, *his* mission! //Oh Father, Father, Father!

CHANCELLOR: //Settle old boy, settle, settle, settle.

Several beats pass, CHILFORD eventually settles enough to observe CHANCELLOR.

CHANCELLOR: *(He attempts to dab the wound with a cloth.)* Ahhh.

CHILFORD: *(Between tears.)* Did these barbarians come after you as well?

CHANCELLOR: They are on the turn, turning into some types of primal beasts. This was my warning – anymore work with the white devil and I am a gone; I am a known Bafu. And you my friend, best stay in the deeps until this goes away – there are some who are looking for you.

CHILFORD: Who could that on the earth be?

CHANCELLOR: *(Angrily.)* Who? All the many you have angered with your brimstone fires! I was warning you of this! This wound on my head is more of yours than of mines.

CHILFORD: Eeeyy, what is this?

CHANCELLOR: You listen to nothing I am telling you! You were proceeding to convert and impose the Bible against traditions in the street with that savage protégé of yours were you not? Were you not?! Now LISTEN TO ME! Bernie Mizeki is also a gone.

CHILFORD: What, man? The Anglican catechist? Dead?

CHANCELLOR: He was dragged out from his hut in the middle of the night and stabbed.

CHILFORD: NO!

CHANCELLOR: Yes – they are killing – us. They are killing anyone who they feels threaten their senses of pagan order.

CHILFORD: WHO has dare done this?! Who in the earth is THEY?!

CHANCELLOR: Paramount chiefs! Lomagundi, Makoni, Mapondera, Mashayamombe – he is the big one – and of course the spirtual mediums, it appears they have been planning this since word of the Matabele got outs. *(Indicating the wound on his head.)* And now it is free for one and alls. I am going perhaps to Bechuanaland, they always need translators. No need to be letting these kaffirs have any more of a go at me. *(Beat.)* So. What are you going to do now?

CHILFORD: What now? What now is… *(Cracking.)* I don't…I don't know.

ESTER: We continue.

CHANCELLOR: *(Mumbling.)* Huh, you people want to die –

CHILFORD: *(Not hearing him.)* What? What do you mean Ester?

ESTER: We continue to do the work Father Helm put in our hearts and trained us to do, to bring people to Jesus so they never do this sort of thing again, and are not looking to the sword as a freedom source. You live by it, you die by it, and we can teach that and be appeasing their heathenism through Christ.

MAI TAMBA: You wirr [will] neva.

ESTER: Pardon Aunt?

MAI TAMBA: You wir neva mek the peopo do something different. That is why him his head it is breeding. You can't.

CHILFORD: What is this you are saying Mai Tamba?

ESTER: Aunt// – please, *don't* –

MAI TAMBA: //Peopo feer [feel] that the white man – he tek e-v-e-r-y-th-i-n-g end they want those things, they want those things beck. They see this white man God and say 'Oh, this is why we rose [lose] everything' – so they don't want that God.

ESTER: Jesus Christ our Lord and savior not 'that God' –

MAI TAMBA: You can say it many ways, but to the peopo that is the white man's thing. It not for us. If you take a – what do you say – shumba –

ESTER: *(Reluctantly.)* Lion.

MAI TAMBA: Ya, if you take a rion from its mother and make it to play among peopo does it start to think it is now a person? One day it will rook at its refrection and become a rion again and it wir tear those peopo to pieces who made it forget who it is. That is why I say...you wir neva.

Beat.

CHILFORD: When was the last time you went to confession? *(MAI TAMBA does not respond.)* Answer! I say, when was the last time it was you went to confession Mai Tamba?

MAI TAMBA: I neva to go.

CHILFORD: And why is that so?

MAI TAMBA: I don know what that it is. To talk to a white man about this and that things of me – for what? So, I neva to go.

CHILFORD: SO that's what you think is it? That is what you have been believing by and by! You never really converted did you Mai Tamba? I never ONCE saw you pray unless I INSTRUCTED you. You SLEEP during church – don't think I don't notice, nor have you converted ONE of your fellow village folk. And… come to be thinking on it… you have been…oh MY GOD! You have been sniffing that stuff haven't you? That witchdoctor snuff stuff? Is that where you go? You go to the witchdoctor do you not? DO YOU NOT?

MAI TAMBA: She is a *n'anga* – not a witchdocta, end yes…to her I go.

CHILFORD: HA! SO you ARE a pagan, and seemingly proud! WHAT else? What is that smell? Now I am SURE you are responsible for it! *(Sniffs the air fervently, jumps off of the couch, and pulls back the cushion, one of MAI TAMBA's concealed objects drops to the floor. Now fully revealed, it is a snake carcass.)* God of goodness. *(Stopping to examine the object, holding it up.)* What is IT??! *(MAI TAMBA does not answer.)* You have been bringing witchcraft INTO MY HOME?!

MAI TAMBA: It not witchcraft. It *muti*, medicine. It protect from bad spirit.

CHILFORD: *(Aghast with anger.)* God of goodness. You SAVAGE! SAVAGE! GET OUT OF MY HOUSE!

ESTER: Master!

CHILFORD: Get! Go! You are the very reasons we don't advance, you pretend to walk into the light but you are still in frolicks without a care in the pits of darkness. *(Advancing towards her.)* GO! I can't bear to look into your face!

MAI TAMBA: *(Rising slowly and exiting.)* Honai honai, ndobasa revarungu. Kutaura zvakadai nevakuru vako. Zvakaoma chokwadi. [**Look at this, the work of the whites. To talk like that with your elder. It is a shame for sure.**]

ESTER rises and follows after MAI TAMBA, distraught.

ESTER: You cannot be speaking to her like that, Master, please –

CHILFORD: DO you wish to leave me also? I CANNOT have heathenism under my very nostrils! Not in my home! What are *you* Ester? Do you attend to witchdoctors as well?

ESTER: Master, no of course I do not but she is a mother to me, an elder –

CHILFORD: Not in the spirit! Do you wish to be going somewhere?

ESTER torn, looks over at MAI TAMBA who has stopped and is looking back at her, caught between these two places she looks back at CHILFORD and finally decides.

ESTER: Nowhere Master. *(She sits slowly.)*

MAI TAMBA: Ahh! You are lost. Marasika shuwa. [**You are surely lost.**]

CHILFORD searches the room frantically looking under rugs and between cushions for more objects, he finds another snake, a wildebeast's horn and a monkey's mandible, complete with teeth.

CHILFORD: GOD OF GOODNESS! AHHHK! GOD OF GOODNESS! YOU SAVAGE!

MAI TAMBA: Was not your own fatha a 'witch docta' as you say? Was he not?

CHILFORD: *(Stunned into silence for a beat, with carcasses in hand, finally, chillingly.)* Get. Out.

MAI TAMBA: *(Clapping her hands in pained acceptance.)* Maiwee. Zvakawoma, shame.

MAI TAMBA exits.

CHANCELLOR: *(Shaking his head.)* Ya ya ya ya ya…kaffirs…full of nonsenses, perhaps you should be keeping her in the handys however – times are quite afeared and she may help –

CHILFORD: They will never be changing! Savages! Beasts! HAI WENA!! SUKA! HAMBA! HAMBA!!!

CHILFORD breaks into Matebele, his native tongue, yelling at the sky as though silencing demons, he starts to hyperventalate, and attempts to catch his breath, his knees give under him as he begins to collapse, CHANCELLOR and ESTER run to catch him.

ESTER: Master!

CHANCELLOR: Steady Brother, BREATHE, BREATHE.

SCENE THREE

CHANCELLOR re-enters first, followed by ESTER. Realizing he is not making to leave she speaks.

ESTER: He is in sleep now, he should feel far superior in the morning I pray.

CHANCELLOR: Yes. I pray also. *(Beat.)* Your aunt made proceeds to the village?

ESTER: I imagine so, yes.

CHANCELLOR: Ohhh.

ESTER: Yes. *(Beat. Pointedly.)* So in the 'morrow – *(Gesturing towards the door.)*

CHANCELLOR: You send an ailing mans out into the wretched night all on his onesome. Why you do not be tending to me like to 'Masta'? I too have pains to be relieved, Father Helm was of a dear nearness to my bosoms – and you reject me?

ESTER: Master Chancellor as I have said in the past, I am a woman of God// so – please leave me.

CHANCELLOR: //Come comes, I am of a sureness you do not say that to Chilfy when his needs are at a height as mine are now – I am sure you are more than willing to share this ample sweetness with him. I want some now. It is my turns.

He begins to wander in her direction.

ESTER: *(Moving away.)* Master Chancellor, HAMBA! Keep away from me! *(She turns quite fierce.)* I will NOT be of your use.

CHANCELLOR: Ahh, come comes…

ESTER: *(Trying to verbally derail him.)* You, your fiancé, Mistress Prudence – what would she be thinking of you your foul behavior!

CHANCELLOR: Ah Ha! She knows, she knows me, my dears, be not of worry, she is in awares of my appetites.

ESTER: You are not the smallest amount of a man as Master Chilford is! Look at your doings! He is sick in the room adjacent and you attempt such sin!

Beat.

CHANCELLOR: *(Stops following her.)* You little savage. You think yourself somethings of a special because of *Masta* eh? 'Please leave me, I am a woman of God.' Ha! If I was wanting, I could just be having you, right here on this floors, there would be NOTHING you could be doing to stop me. *(Sits on couch.)* You are a common savage girl. Now get me some whiskey. NOW. *(Reluctantly, with eyes of fire, she goes to get him a glass, she places the glass in front of him.)* Living here in this house, acting like you are his wife or somethings, you are not my pretty, you are a savage from the bush, it doesn't matter how much English you are learnings, this cannot be changed. As if I am in dire needs of your dirty Muzezuru womanhood. I have a woman, of CLASS. And many other for leisure. I was going to allow *you* to –

ESTER, having had quite enough, turns to leave.

ESTER: Good Night Master Chancellor, I will be seeing you in the morrow.

CHANCELLOR, jumping up, grabs her and throws her on the couch.

CHANCELLOR: DON'T YOU DARES walk out on me. I will crack you like a stick! Now you TEND to me until I say you may go. Understandings?

After several beats.

ESTER: Understanding.

CHANCELLOR: Now finds a cloth and tends to this wound PROPERLY. *(She turns to go, as she does he stops her.)* AH, remove my shoes for a starter.

Painstakingly she does and then retreats to get the cloth and water, all the while CHANCELLOR speaks.

CHANCELLOR: I am sure you are servings those whites without this countenance ey? Ahh, it is quite a sadness, we are loving on them much more than ourselves eh? You should enjoy what I am lettings you dos here. Serving a true *masta*. *(She hovers above him with a cloth in hand.)* Hmmm, we are goings to have a VERY good times tonight Protégé. *(As her hand is about to make contact with the wound he catches it.)* Be of gentleness or I will crack you like a stick.

He lets go of her hand, grabs hold of her inner thigh and rubs it and closes his eyes, she freezes in horror and fear, he starts to lift her skirts as her hand and cloth hover over his wound, suddenly she lifts her fists high in the air and brings them down hard on his wound screaming –

ESTER: NO!!!!

CHANCELLOR: AHHH!!! Whore UCHAWONA NHASI!! **[You will see today!]**

She attempts to make a run for it, he quickly catches her as she is about to scream, he covers her mouth to stifle her scream, she puts up a good fight, fighting ferociously, and getting some good kicks in but she is losing fast, he soon has her pinned to the ground, he starts to pull up her skirts just as a loud bang is heard at the door. CHANCELLOR stops, lets her go and, cautiously approaching the door, ESTER runs to the passage way door, prepared to make a run for it to CHILFORD's room.)

CHANCELLOR: *(To ESTER.)* Go to the room and do not come out, lock yourself and Chilford in there until they are gone and under NO circumstance are you to allow him to exit, wanzwa? **[Do you hear?]** *(She runs out. Calling out.)* NDIANI? **[Who is it?]**

VOICE: Tipindewo! **[Allow us to enter]**

CHANCELLOR: Ndiani asi? **[But who is it?]**

VOICE: Kana *mukasandivhurira musuwo* baba, *zvinozoitika hazvina kunaka.* **[If you do not open the door, it is not good what will happen.]**

CHANCELLOR gathers himself, straightening himself out, and opens the door. TAMBA enters, sullen, menacing and seemingly intoxicated with UNCLE in tow. They are both armed with knobkerries (large, club-like sticks).

UNCLE: Ah ha! It is *Bafu* numba 2! Where is it that you ara hiding your friend ey? The Number One *Bafu*! King of the *Bafus*! Where is it he is?

CHANCELLOR: Ahhh Sekuru! Sei *muchitaura* Kudaro? **[Ahh Uncle! Why are you speaking to me like this?]**

UNCLE: AH, AH HEY YE! Now rook at him, talking with his mother's tongue now! All this while you ara talking like you were berthed from the Queen of the Whites land – what is that it is the land called *Bafu*? What is their kingdom it is called?

CHANCELLOR: Ahh…sekuru musandidaro shuwa. **[Brother don't do me like this surely.]**

UNCLE: Eh EH!! NDATI! **[I said!]**

CHANCELLOR: *(Reluctantly.)* Inonzi England. **[It is called England.]**

UNCLE: Oh yes! Ingrand! So you are the son to the Queen of Ingrand?

CHANCELLOR: Ah…kana! Ndiri *w*epano! **[Ahh…not at all! I am of here surely!]**

UNCLE: *(Slamming his knobkerrie on the coffee table threateningly.)* AIWA! **[NO!]** Today! Today we ara in Ingrand. I want you to talk to me rike you ara talking to this white men I see you with EVERYDAY!

CHANCELLOR: No problem Sir, whatever it is you are wanting.

UNCLE: *(Sitting on the couch with regality.)* Ahh…my son, see how the bafus they ara riving [living], rike Kings shuwa. Where is he, the King of the *Bafus*?

CHANCELLOR: He has left for Bulawayo, our Father Helm has died.

UNCLE: Ohhhh oh? A white?

CHANCELLOR: Yes.

UNCLE: Hmmm! And where is that *bafu* gir [girl] of mine?

CHANCELLOR: I believe she is with him.

UNCLE: Ohhhh oh?

CHANCELLOR: Yes. *(Beat.)* Would you be liking something to drink? I believe there is some whiskey somewhere here – we can indulge.

UNCLE: Ohhhh oh? Ah, ya, I would be riking that, for my boy here too.

CHANCELLOR: *(Getting whiskey from CHILFORD's desk and glasses from tray.)* I know things, ahh… things are looking hard these days, no beef, the work is not too much at the mines.

UNCLE: *(Drinking.)* Ahhh…but this…ha….this is not a probrem for you *bafu*, I see you, you ara talking to the whites rike they are your friends, you ara putting on these nice clothing, you ara not talking to one rike me when you ara seeing me on the streets in the day *bafu*.

CHANCELLOR: Ahh! Sekuru! You must be mistaking me! I am always going to get some *kachasu* with the miners and workers and having good time.

UNCLE: *(Chuckling.)* Hey hey hey hey hey... So maybe I is mistaking you. But ha, times they ara hard shuwa, you ara right, so, so hard. These whites, they bring many probrems, is it not so?

CHANCELLOR: *(Laughing nervously.)* Ah...shuwa.

UNCLE: Ya! They ara the ones bringing this rindapest, before they ara coming we NEVA have those sickness, that ara kirring [killing] ALL the cattles. Then the drought, we NEVA have this: no rains for so long. The ancestas they ara ANGRY – we ara riving rike goats on our own soil! Am I wrong?

CHANCELLOR: *(Carefully.)* Ahh...you are never wrong Sekuru...*(To TAMBA.)* brother.

TAMBA: I am neva wrong. Ya. I rike that one. I am neva wrong.

UNCLE: *(Chuckling.)* Neva wrong.

TAMBA: Hey. I am neva wrong. I wish you could have been saying that today bhudi, TODAY! Ha! Today this white devil he want to tell me I must go – he throw me away rike that from his mine. *(Snapping his fingers.)* Just rike that. Now I have NO monies to pay hut tax for my wives theya homes. Then I want to go to my mother and I see ha she walking bek to the virrage – she saying this *BAFU* has taken she her job AWAY. That is too much aren't you agreeing? In ONE day *Bafu*! The white devil and his black slave ara teking both us our job! IN ONE DAY! AHHH, hey...*bafu*...it is too much.

UNCLE: TOO, TOO much. So they must be learning a lesson TODAY. *(Gets up, starts cracking a chair with his stick.)*

TODAY! I told THAT *BAFU* what is to come, NOW, IT HAS COME! So who ara you? ARA you a son of the soil or ara you a white? WHO ARA YOU TODAY?

CHANCELLOR: Ahhhh, hey! I am a son of the soil, FOR SURE, Sekuru! And have ALWAYS been so. Indeed I can be of much help to you, I can be giving you assistance even now! *(Reaches in his pocket; his hands are shaking, however, and he cannot retrieve the money fast enough.)*

TAMBA: YA! That would be good *brotha,* you hep me, I know you ara having lots of moni-! *(Reaches in CHANCELLOR's pocket and searches impatiently.)* Ah…one shilling? CHETE? **[Only?]** Ahh! So you ara thinking that is all me I am worth? *(To UNCLE.)* This is the *bafu* with many monies Sekuru, with the MOST monies but he is thinking we ara nothing, these ones, they ara thinking we ara animals.

UNCLE: YA!

TAMBA: One shilling ere?

CHANCELLOR: Ahh…brother…don't be of worry! I can be getting more, it is good to remain tranquil –

UNCLE: Trankill, what is that? Trankill? Ahhhh, hey, ROOK AT HIM! He is just a WHITE now, having TOO, too many of these words from Ingrand ey?

TAMBA: *(Still searching CHANCELLOR.)* Ah…what is this? *(Finds CHANCELLOR's pocket watch.)*

UNCLE: *(Chuckling.)* Hey, Trankill…

TAMBA: *(Examining the watch.)* Ahh, this is betta now, this will do brother, this is rooking verry full of monies. Rike a white man thing eh? I can be takin –

CHANCELLOR: Ahh…NO not that one brother. *(Grabbing for it.)* I can be getting you many monies, but not that one, brother, please.

TAMBA: Ah! You ara wanting to be fighting me for this? I was thinking you ara wanting to help me!

CHANCELLOR reaches for knobkerrie and keeps hold of watch, a scuffle ensues, TAMBA is too strong for him and proceeds to start beating him passionately with the stick, his UNCLE standing watch.

CHANCELLOR: *(On the ground.)* Please! Please, I am begging of you! I can…AHHH…I can be giving you…ahhh!

TAMBA: Giving me what? To make me rike a *Bafu* too? You want to mek me rike a *Bafu* too!

TAMBA beats him until he is quiet. He steps back, out of breath, examining his deed, seemingly a little shocked and confused yet wired. He looks over at UNCLE.

TAMBA: Sei andibata? **[Why did he touch me?]** Why was he grabbing my stick eh? *(To CHANCELLOR.)* Ah…hye… muka ka. SIMUKA. **[Wake up, wake up.]** *(Kicks at CHANCELLOR's limp leg.)* Ahh.

UNCLE: Afa? **[Is he dead?]** *(Goes and examines CHANCELLOR, shakes his head.)* Afa. **[He died.]**

ESTER opens the door and enters, shocked, surveying the scene – .

ESTER: It *was* your voice. What have you done? Tambaoga! What is it you have done?

TAMBA: Ah! He said you –

ESTER: *(Shaking him.)* You dofo! You kill him? You kill him! Babam'diki **[Uncle]** – how could you –

UNCLE: AH AH, me I do nothing – I do NOTHING!

TAMBA: He was starting it – he was doing these stupid things, I just wanted some monies and –

ESTER: SHUT IT YOUR MOUTH! GET OUT of here now! Just be going.

TAMBA: What will you be –

ESTER: Shh SHUT IT UP! – come on – make it look like a theft – here – be taking some things. *(She pulls apart the desk and the drawers, she hands him random items.)* COME ON!

TAMBA and UNCLE slowly join in, beginning to get caught up in it, they take apart the room, tear up letters and the Bible they find, knock the crucifix off the wall.

ESTER: Now go. GO. NOW.

They proceed to the door – TAMBA looks at her –

TAMBA: You ara not a *Bafu* –

ESTER: BE OF SILENCE and go. GO. I must never be seeing you again.

TAMBA: You ara not a *Bafu.*

He leaves. She leaves the door open, goes, throws on her night gown, comes back, surveys the room and CHANCELLOR's body, crosses herself, takes a deep breath and screams in the direction of CHILFORD's quarters.)

ESTER: MASTER!!!!

END OF ACT TWO

ACT THREE

SCENE ONE

During intermission the place has been put back in order, though different from what it was. The chaise is gone, replaced by a simple wooden bench, once used as a pew, one or two basic wooden chairs furnish the remainder of the room, with the large desk replaced by a pile of wooden blocks and a simple stool. Months later, CHILFORD and ESTER rush through the door, ESTER quickly takes her seat at the desk and begins to take dictation from CHILFORD, who strolls around the room.

CHILFORD: February 10th, 1897. The prisoner was most full of fear, but not of remorse and held fast and quick to his pagan beliefs, he refused an offering of spiritual enlightenment and rather opted to consult with a witch doctor. The request was of course denied. The prisoner proceeded to the gallows having not received Christ as his Lord and Savior – what was his name?

ESTER: Chengetai Matonga.

CHILFORD: Good. Yes. Well…we can't save them all.

ESTER: You tried, you tried most hard Master. 'Many are called but the chosen are few.'

CHILFORD: Yes…yes. But you were of some success today were you not?

ESTER: Well, we will see. She is still in resistance to accepting the powerlessness of her ancestors.

CHILFORD: Ah…one of those. She thinks her Great Uncle Torororo is just as sound a route to God, I am to suppose.

ESTER: The usual, yes.

CHILFORD: Well, tomorrow the day is anew!

PRUDENCE enters from the house, she is dressed in a night robe, seeming slightly intoxicated.

CHILFORD: Good evening Prudence, how…how are you today?

ESTER: Good evening Mistress Prudence.

PRUDENCE: Ahhh, ndaneta! Waswera sei Ester? **[I am tired. How are you Ester?]**

ESTER: *(Stammering.)* Ahh…ahh…Nda…ahh.

PRUDENCE: Oh my every day! Every day Chilfy! Give her leave to speak in her mother's tongue! SAY IT ESTER!

ESTER looks at CHILFORD who nods reluctantly.

ESTER: Ndaswera maswera sei? **[I am well, how are you?]**

PRUDENCE: Ndaswera. See did that not feel nice? Some color is returning to your cheeks as the whites say. How goes it all? How is that loving white family you work for? What are they called again?

ESTER: The Colterns.

PRUDENCE: Ahh, of course yes. The Colterns. I know them. Very…condescendingly well meaning. How was the day of savage soul saving? Any conquered souls to report?

CHILFORD: Ah…not today.

PRUDENCE: And what about reports, new suspects, anything of that?

CHILFORD: No. Not today.

PRUDENCE: Hmm hmmmm. *(Beat.)* Carry on, don't mind me! *(She lights up her pipe.)*

CHILFORD: Yes, well as we were saying then, Ester, tomorrow the Commissioner told me they have captured what may be Kaguvi, they are still in search of Nehanda –

PRUDENCE: Oh! I know of them! They are the big instigators of the rebellion no? The spiritual mediums! 'The whites' bullets won't touch you' and what not! Oh shame, that stratagem did not pan out.

CHILFORD: Yes, God be of thanks it did not –

PRUDENCE: GOD be of thanks! Chilfy! Are you so mad to *still* think these whites are going to get away with all this mess? Even you cannot *still* really think GOD is on their side!

CHILFORD: Would you rather live amongst the savages Pru?

PRUDENCE: I have no desire to proceed in this circle again with you. Carry on.

Beat.

CHILFORD: Right. *(To ESTER.)* So as I was saying – we have been assigned to –

PRUDENCE: Did you know Ester, that I am the real bright spark of all of us – myself, Chancey and Chilfy, the one with the most promise –

CHILFORD: Prudence –

PRUDENCE: What? She should know! I have a sense – she might be the brighter of the two of you – she just may not know of it yet! I was so bright I was sent on to Natal for further schooling – Ndana school for girls.

ESTER: Yes, you have mentioned it in the prior.

PRUDENCE: I did? Well anyway, it appears Miss Protégé – there is no place for a highly educated African woman. I am a mere thing of oddity and suspicion. Just wait until you try to leave his side Protégé! Oh you will see! There is Nothing out there for us!// Nothing my dear!

CHILFORD: //PRUDENCE AHH!

PRUDENCE: Tell me, *how* do I repel that voice in my head that says I am not a true African because my family disowned me, because without a husband and the children we bear there will be no one to bury me when I die. No one to stay up with my body all night singing me over to the ancestors, calling them to receive me. The Whites just throw you in the ground, cross themselves and go for tea. Chilfy isnt bothered with all that though, Chilfy, The Great Black Tragedy.

CHILFORD: Prudence! If you do not stop with this –

PRUDENCE: What? What is it you will be doing Chilfy? Removing me from your home? Ha! You love me *far* too dearly. And seeing as this is the LAST place the man who I was meant to live with for the rest of my life was alive I feel it ONLY fitting I stay right where it is I am – NO? *(Beat.)* Have you found out anything? Has ANYONE been found in suspicion?

CHILFORD: Not today.

PRUDENCE: Not today, not any bloody day, isn't it? Isn't it?

CHILFORD: We must await God's timing on this Pru. What I know is true is all we do is in Chancellor's memory.

PRUDENCE: It is not his memory I am concerned about it is YOURS and Miss Protégé over yonder. I will not leave! I will not leave until I am satisfied.

CHILFORD: Pru, not again, I am pleading –

PRUDENCE: Do not plead Chilfy – so unbecoming. You are such a weaky, look at you, with those weak puppy eyes you've got. It is not at all befitting an African man you know.

CHILFORD: Prudence –

PRUDENCE: I know, I know you are not an African, you are a European in an African costume. I know dearest, I know. Might I be adding – Chancellor would not even care! Are you in your natural sense to think he, Chancellor Gwendo would CARE that you are converting souls in his honor? His only holy trinity was money, power and the member between his legs//

CHILFORD: //Ahh ahh! Prudence! Enough now!

PRUDENCE: //Just be of truth! This is for you and for your darling Father Helm – it has nothing in the slightest to do with Chancey.

CHILFORD: Prudence! I can be assuring you – everything I do – is in his honor. He was my closest friend, my brother. Please – no more of this – I can take it not. We are hoping and praying with each day to find his attacker are we not Ester.

ESTER: Yes Master.

PRUDENCE: But why don't you remember!

CHILFORD: I have been telling you this in so many times previous!

PRUDENCE: *(Suddenly with rage.)* TELL ME AGAIN.

Beat.

CHILFORD: I was //overcome with

PRUDENCE: //You were 'overcome with grief' because of Father Helm's death. And how did you not hear anything Miss Protégé?

ESTER: *(Carefully.)* As I have said in times previous –

PRUDENCE: JUST SPEAKETH!

ESTER: Master Chancellor was instructing me to go to the back when the knock it come on the door. I go then I am hearing nothing until I am hearing Master Chancellor crying out. I was too scared to come out until I hear nothing again.

PRUDENCE: And you never heard the other person.

ESTER: No.

PRUDENCE: Hmmm. *(Beat.)* I am to bed.

CHILFORD: Again?

PRUDENCE: Just be glad I am not curling up right there where he fell! That is what I do when you are out savage soul saving. Good night. Amangwana – as they say in the vernacular you both seem to have forgotten!

She exits.

ESTER: *(Desperate to move along.)* Do you know to whom we are assigned for tomorrow? The captures –

CHILFORD: *(Collecting himself.)* Yes, yes, apparently they finally captured Kaguvi – *(A person entering through the back kitchen is heard. To ESTER.)* Shhh. Go to the back room.

ESTER: *(Petrified.)* Master…

CHILFORD: Just GO. Do as I tell you to do. NOW.

ESTER reluctantly retreats. CHILFORD obtains his large knobkerrie from behind his makeshift desk and slowly advances towards the kitchen entrance as the footsteps come nearer, he lifts his shambok and is about to swing it when MAI TAMBA screams –

MAI TAMBA: *(Seeing CHILFORD.)* MAIHWEE ZVANGU INI!!

CHILFORD: *(Quickly retreating with knobkerrie.)* Graciousness, *(They both collect their breath.)* Mai Tamba! What in the earth!

MAI TAMBA: Masta. *(ESTER emerges, thrilled to see her aunt.)*

ESTER: AHH! Tete! Ahhh – Aunt! Makadii? How are you? How is…mother? *(ESTER clings to her aunt almost too tightly.)*

MAI TAMBA: *(Ushered to a seat by ESTER, she gently embraces her back.)* Ndiripo. Varipo. **[I am fine. She is fine.]** Ahh… how is it with you Masta?

CHILFORD: It has been – a bag of mixtures. We have of course had some deep tragedies here. I am not of doubt that you heard of Master Chancellor's brutal demise.

MAI TAMBA: I am in hearing. Ndineurombo. **[My condolences.]**

CHILFORD: Yes. It was horrible. Most, most horrible. Mistress Prudence is staying with us, she is afeared to live alone presently. But now, as you well are knowing the fighting is just about at end. How is it with you? I am trusting you have been in the ability of obtaining new employment.

MAI TAMBA: Ahh...hey...it has been very, very hard for me Masta. Very, very hard.

She begins to weep.

ESTER: Aunt, what...what has happened?

MAI TAMBA: Varungu, these whites, they ara coming to Mazowe Masta, and they destroying many, many things! They ara beating end kirring [killing] us, they tek the cattles and burning the kraals. Then they ara coming to me Masta! They ara wanting him – to tek him – they ara saying I must be bringing him to the court in this few days or they ara going to tek me Masta.

CHILFORD: Who? Who are you speaking of?

MAI TAMBA: Tambaoga Masta.

CHILFORD: He has been in involvement with all of this?

MAI TAMBA: Ahhh...me I don know Masta. He wirr tell me nothing. But they ara wanting him. A white man, a mine owna die then the whites, they ara thinking him he the one who do it. Now they ara wanting to tek me if I don't bring him Masta! You must be talking to them, to you they can be listening Masta.

CHILFORD: And did he do it?!

MAI TAMBA: *(Breaking down more.)* I don't know Masta! He is not telling me.

CHILFORD: Where is he?

MAI TAMBA: He is here.

ESTER visibly stiffens.

CHILFORD: You brought him here?!

MAI TAMBA: We ara needing a prace to go where they wir not be rooking for him. They ara not going to be rooking for him here Masta.

CHILFORD: Jesus be of guidance.

CHILFORD: *(After several beats.)* Bring him in. But his lips best be loose. I am not in tolerance of silence over bad deeds, he will tell us everything and all that he has done.

MAI TAMBA: Yes Masta, thenk you Masta, I wirr [will] tell him that now, now.

MAI TAMBA bustles out the door, ESTER crosses herself and walks to the Crucifix, CHILFORD sits still, bracing himself. MAI TAMBA enters with TAMBA in tow, he looks forlorn and beaten down, though he is still in possession of an aura of resistance, his eyes have a fire in them still but he is broken. A revolutionary on a failed mission. He enters with his head down. ESTER does not look at him.

MAI TAMBA: *(To TAMBA.)* Taura ka.

TAMBA: Harro…Masta.

CHILFORD: Be seated Tamba. *(Beat.)* What has been happening with you of late?

TAMBA: I have been in the Chindunduma.

CHILFORD: And what in the earth is that?

TAMBA: *(Sharply.)* It is the struggle for freedom.

MAI TAMBA: Taura ka! **[Speak!]** Rike a confession Masta, you wir hep him rike confession?

CHILFORD: *(Cautiously.)* Yes, you can look at it so. What have you done Tamba?

TAMBA: Ahhk… *(Beat.)* What is it you ara doing there at the court?

CHILFORD: We are translating for prisoners.

TAMBA: End what else ara you doing there?

CHILFORD: We are teaching them about Christ.

TAMBA: They ara doin bed bed things to us there.

CHILFORD: No, the courts have been more than fair considering what it is you – these people have been doing.

TAMBA: Some they don't even get to the court, the white devil just kill right there on the street they –

MAI TAMBA: *(To TAMBA, greatly impatient.)* AHH! Taura ka! Tell him! Tell him so he can hep you! *(Clicks her tongue. To CHILFORD.)* He come bek with this Masta, he say I can use it to pay for food end hut tex end I say – mumoyo wangu **[in my heart]** *(Holding her heart.)* I know he do bed thing. *(MAI TAMBA hands CHILFORD a pocket watch.)*

CHILFORD: *(Starring at the watch, examining it.)* What in the earth…God of graciousness…where…where did you obtain this? WHERE? You best be speaking now, or I am going to call on the authorities forthwith.

MAI TAMBA: *(Hitting TAMBA over the head.)* IWE TAURA KANI!! **[You! SPEAK!]**

CHILFORD: Ester, go call for Mistress Prudence. GO NOW.

ESTER, reluctantly and greatly disturbed exits to the back. CHILFORD grabs his knobkerrie and stands far from TAMBA, examining him closely. TAMBA glares back at him.

MAI TAMBA: Ahh…Masta…wha…

CHILFORD: Be of silence. We are to await Mistress Prudence.

ESTER and PRUDENCE re-enter, PRUDENCE in a night robe, looking disheveled.

PRUDENCE: Mai Tamba? What is going on Chilfy?

CHILFORD, never taking his eyes off of TAMBA, hands PRUDENCE the watch.

73

CHILFORD: Was this not –

PRUDENCE: Oh my God. Chancey. I gave it to him after our…after our engagement was official. Where? Where…?!

CHILFORD: Yes. *(Beat.)* Tamba. What is it you have done?

TAMBA: I…I neva mean to be *kirring* him.

MAI TAMBA: TAMBAOGA! KANA, oh Mwari baba wedu oh! Musandidaro, ndofa nhasi! SHUWA ndofa nhasi izvozvi ! NO! TAMBAOGA! **[NO! Oh God! Don't do this to me, I will die today! Surely I will die today like this!]** You KIR HIM! You KIR HIM?!!

PRUDENCE: //My God.

CHILFORD: //Lord Jesus, Lord Jesus, LORD JESUS. *(Sudden rage.)* AHHHHH!!!!! *(He breaks into his native Matabele and starts to hyperventilate, finally releasing long pent up regret and grief.)* HAIKONA! HAIKONA WENA! HAMBA! SUKA, SUKA!!!! *(ESTER rushes to his side, and guides him to sit, he refuses her help and remains standing. He weeps.)* I am sorry my brother, oh, so so sorry my brother…

Several beats pass.

CHILFORD: *(Finally.)* You dirty savage beast. You will rot, *you will rot* in the eternal fires for this.

Beat.

TAMBA: *(Cautiously, yet firmly.)* I neva mean him to die. He just want to fight so then we ara fighting and him he rose [lose].

CHILFORD: Oh, he lose is it? And the furniture? My papers? My desk they just lose too ha?

TAMBA: THAT was not just – *(Quickly, barely glimpses at ESTER, who stands petrified in the corner.)* I…I was engry. Very, very engry.

CHILFORD: At whom? At me? At Chancy? What did he EVER do to you?

TAMBA: It is him who start fighting. Me I was not going to kirr him.

CHILFORD: DON'T YOU DARE! YOU TELL THE // TRUTH!

TAMBA: //THAT IT IS THE TRUTH. I onry want to mek him be afraid.

CHILFORD: Hah!

MAI TAMBA: Oh Masta, forgive him Masta, forgive him rike Jesas. Prease! Don't ret the whites to tek him.

CHILFORD: Be of silence //Mai Tamba

PRUDENCE: //Did he beg?

CHILFORD: What?

PRUDENCE: I asked the youth – did he beg? Did he fight back or did he just let you ravage him to death? Did you just beat him down, did you catch him unawares? What happened? He better have fought – Do you have children? ANSWER! Do you have children?

TAMBA: *(Standing up, dismissing her, to CHILFORD.)* Ahhhk… what is this now? Who is she – to be talking to me like that?

PRUDENCE: DON'T YOU DARE! DON'T YOU DARE!! You see how they do – these – these BLOODY MEN!! You squander, you derail, you RUIN and then you are in the fullness of audacity to still, STILL possess a masculine bravado. You come in here – BEGGING for our help, you didn't expect to see me did you? Eh? The kaffir woman with the BIG BIG mouth. It has gotten me in much trouble before – and today I CARE not! You are at my mercy! Do you know how well I can wax poetry to these white men? They will listen to my word in a SNAP! You could be dead before the dawn! I will not show you respect you have never spent a mere moment of your life earning SIMPLY because you possess an added fixture at the apex of your thighs. I will not. ANSWER my QUESTION. Do you have any children.

CHILFORD: Answer her.

TAMBA: *(Very reluctantly.)* Yes. I am having them.

PRUDENCE: So did the man you killed. Six of them so far – and counting. The bloody bastard impregnated SIX women without my even knowing in the past ten years. They are all coming forward, begging for recompense, it is apparent they were all receiving support from him. It is not of bloody wonder he was so in love with money, he had a village to support! Now they are alone, fatherless, penniless, because of you. And never mind…never mind the one he never even knew about, the one sitting in *my* belly. NEVER MIND THAT ONE. He better have begged. Did he beg?

TAMBA: Ahhhk…me…me I am not remembering.

PRUDENCE: Of course you are not. *(Grabs knobkerrie from CHILFORD.)* SIT down. SIT DOWN. *(TAMBA reluctantly sits.)* Now you are going to tell me everything. EVERYTHING you can remember – and you are going to tell me now.

CHILFORD: Speak.

TAMBA: Ahhhk.

Several beats pass.

MAI TAMBA: TAURA KANI! **[SPEAK!]**

TAMBA: I coming, he is letting me in, then, then we ara talking, I am telling him I am having hard, hard time – that I rose my job just now rike that with no monies for foods then he is saying he want to help me, then when it come the time for him to help he no want to help –

CHILFORD: You were alone?

Beat.

TAMBA: Yes.

CHILFORD: And what of the watch.

TAMBA: He want to give me// then he say 'No' – he no want to give me anymore –

CHILFORD: //You liar. He would NEVER have willingly been parting with that watch to give you – your truth is most flawed! You came and of most probable FORCED your way in and started beating on //poor Chancey and taking whatever you could find –

TAMBA: // NO! We talk! He say he want to help me. But when he not help he jump on me –

CHILFORD: He jumped on you? And I suppose the table and the chaise jumped on you too – my Bible – //did IT attack you? What did he EVER do// to you –

TAMBA: Ahhhh!//HE WAS A *BAFU*! Me I have nothing. Him he have all these thing. They come to force me to work in the mines with a shambok and guns. I neva hev ONE choice since I hev been a man. Me I want too to feel like a man. Then I say, why he and you can go every day and feer rike men but me I can't. I want what my ancestas they want for me. But I neva mean to be kirring him. And I neva kir the white mine owna or do the things they ara saying. That one – THAT one – it the truth.

PRUDENCE: What do they say, these…these spiritual mediums, these leaders of the rebellion.

Beat.

TAMBA: They say…they say the ancestors ara angry because we have let these whites come and tek ova what they left for us. They say we ara the true daughters and sons of the soil, they say we must reclaim our rand [land], and not be slaves on it. They ara saying we must fight now. NOW, because the ancestors are terring them it wir keep being this bad and then more and more bed. But now…ah now they ara defeating us. Things ara going bed for us. Peopo ara scare, they ara turning on each otha.

PRUDENCE: How long have you worked the mines?

TAMBA: A rong time, rong rong time – since I was not even heving one child.

MAI TAMBA: He was the oldest of the grandchildren – as a boy, he was to help her father. *(Indicating ESTER.)* Then they tek him. He stirr [still] try Mistress Prudence, he stirr try to do him his duties as the one who care for the femiry, but ahhhh…this mining it hard on him.

ESTER: *(Suddenly.)* He is a good man, Mistress Prudence, he help me run when my uncle want to marry me to an old man.

PRUDENCE: Hmmmm. *(A couple beats pass.)* Let him go.

CHILFORD: WHAT?

PRUDENCE: I said let him go. What is the use Chilfy really. What is the use?

CHILFORD: But –

PRUDENCE: There is no justice to be had, no vengence. Nothing. What? You want to condemn him to these colonial brutes? Does that amend? It doesn't bring Chancey back, it won't give my child a father. Where will it end Chilfy? I am sure they scuffled and Chancey lost – he was more a lover than a fighter – I am sure he was most provocative and most probably deserved every last bloody blow. He was a bastard. We all know of this. Let him go. This is all most, most unsatisfying. We all know the true source of this problem and his skin is a lot different from our own.

MAI TAMBA: Oh THENK YOU MISTRESS PRUDENCE!!

ESTER: *(Gushing with relief.)* Mistress Prudence, great, great thanks. Great thanks. GREAT –

PRUDENCE: Yes, yes. How ever do we proceed though?

CHILFORD: How can you, Pru? He killed him like a dog! Anyway, ANYWAY, refusal to report Chancey's murder matters not! Tamba MUST be taken in; Mai Tamba cannot be free until he is reported in for interrogation over the mine owner's death. IF you have ANY makings of a man Tamba, NOW it is time for these to manifest!

Beat.

TAMBA: I can go. I will go. Even now like this.

He turns to the door.

ESTER: *(With assertive conviction.)* NO. WAIT. THIS IS WHAT WILL BE DONE. We must take him to the Native Commissioner, we will present him to them as an innocent of the thing they blame him for, we will teach them of him being a good man.

CHILFORD: Ester, you must have fallen off your wits!

ESTER: NO, I have not! Master, you know I can speak well, you talk of what a marvel I am, of how many people I have brought to the Lord, I can speak for him. Prudence and I will petition on his behalf. The courts are following the laws of the Lord, of 'His mercy, that is new every morning,' of seeking peace and loving one another. Indeed it is them who taught this to *us*. We take him, we petition for him, he will be acquitted. Are they not sparing those who submit themselves Master?

CHILFORD does not answer.

ESTER: MASTER?

CHILFORD: There are those who have surrendered and as a consequence been spared.

ESTER: RIGHT! As it will be with you Tamba. With us as your advocates. Prudence? Please? *(Beat.) Please.*

Beat.

PRUDENCE: Well, let us go then. To save Mai Tamba also, I see no other way. I will wax as much poetry as I can for you Tamba. We will see what it can do.

TAMBA: Why…why would you be doing this for me?

PRUDENCE: I may as well put all this Queen's English to use. *(Beat.)* We should move along. Chilfy? If you come with –

CHILFORD: Never. Get him out of my house. I care not what becomes of him.

ESTER: Master!

MAI TAMBA: Ahhh Masta!

CHILFORD: And for YOUR sake Mai Tamba I am not turning him in myself. But please. Remove him from my home forthwith.

They gather themselves and bustle out of the door, ESTER grabs a Bible as she goes, glancing at CHILFORD with hurt and disappointment. CHILFORD and TAMBA stare at each other with smoldering hatred. They exit. CHILFORD sits on the wooden pew.

SCENE TWO

Much later that same evening. CHILFORD sits in the same spot, having barely moved. He starts suddenly at a knock at the door. CHILFORD opens the door and PRUDENCE enters, she proceeds to the back.

CHILFORD: What? What happened? Pru?

Moments later PRUDENCE reappears, having removed her hat, hardened defeat on her face.

CHILFORD: What happened? And where are they? Where is Ester?

PRUDENCE silently searches for the whiskey, finds it behind the desk and retrieves a glass, she sits on the pew and proceeds to drink, she drinks one glass then two, then three.

CHILFORD: Prudence. Please. Stop that.

He grabs for the bottle. Unfazed she pulls out her bag of snuff from her bosom and proceeds to sniff it. CHILFORD watches her, disturbed and with great distaste. Finally –

PRUDENCE: They killed him on the spot. The second he identified himself. Mai Tamba went back to the village, Ester ran off, I have no idea where to.

CHILFORD: No. *(Beat.)* No trial, no –

PRUDENCE: It seems they have no need to try one they believe killed a mine owner. So my and Ester's advocacy was nothing short of a joke. They observed me like I was a creature designed for their amusement, this kaffir monkey speaking their language better than themselves. They commended us for bringing him to *justice.* And then they murdered him. Right in front of his own mother. *(Beat. Starts to laugh.)* I thought…I actually thought….We are damned Chilfy. Damned. I am going to the witchdoctor in the morrow. I will not bring another black soul to be damned on this wretched, cursed soil. I will not. I will not, I will not, I will not, I will not, I will not. *(She gets up and walks out, repeating herself over and over.)*

CHILFORD: PRUDENCE! PRU! YOU CANNOT – *(He gives up following her and walks to the door, opens it and shouts out rather futilely.)* ESTER!!!!

He looks around and finally he exits back into the house.

SCENE THREE

Much later that same evening CHILFORD sits on the pew, waiting for ESTER, he is asleep. A knock at the door, CHILFORD starts, grabs for his knobkerrie from its usual spot.

CHILFORD: Who is going there?

ESTER: It is me Master.

CHILFORD: Ester?

ESTER: Yes.

CHILFORD opens the door. ESTER enters, wrapped in a large zambia (African scarf).

CHILFORD: Where is it you have been? You must not be going out on your own like this, these times are of trouble you –

ESTER: You must be starting you your own church Master.

CHILFORD: Wh – what is this now?

ESTER: You your own. They will never be giving you one. They will never be letting you be priest Master. But you can be doing it. You are ready. The people they will be listening to you more than Father Bart, they will be following you better.

CHILFORD: Ester –

ESTER: Master, I would like to have a confession.

CHILFORD: What? In the here and now?

ESTER: Yes.

CHILFORD: For what end? Perhaps it is best we await Father Bart.

ESTER: No, I want to make it to you.

CHILFORD: I don't feel I am qualify.

ESTER: *(Firmly.)* You are *my* priest Master, I want to make it to you.

Beat.

CHILFORD: Alright then.

ESTER: Thank you. In the first and the foremost, I must be introducing myself to you properly. My name, it is Jekesai Wekwa Chiyangwa Murumbira. You have been giving me this name Master, Ester, and it is a good name. I have been liking it all this time, but today I must be giving you my name, Master, Jekesai, it mean to illuminate. I am wanting to make confession to you with you knowing me who I am. *(Beat.)* I couldn't be like you Master – I couldn't. All this time I have been trying and trying but it can't. It can't work. Me I am learning this the day Master Chancellor he die. I am learning that NOTHING is stronger than blood. Nothing. Blood it can make you move – it can make you be doing things you are not knowing are inside you to be doing. Tamba save me. He was always saving me – I could not let them be taking him for what he do to Master Chancellor when I am knowing what Master Chancellor was wanting to do to me. I can't.

CHILFORD: *(Carefully.)* You were knowing what happened here and you were bearing false witness – to spare your cousin.

JEKESAI: Yes.

Beat.

CHILFORD: And Master Chancellor was doing what?

JEKESAI: He…he was wanting to put his love on me.

CHILFORD: He was forcing on you?

JEKESAI: Yes.

CHILFORD: When Tamba was coming?

JEKESAI: Yes.

CHILFORD: So you witnessed the attack?

JEKESAI: No. I was in the back, in your chambers when Tamba he come – Master Chancellor send me there when they come to the door. I only come in the end – when I know that it is his voice I am hearing.

Beat.

CHILFORD: Why…why are you telling me now?

JEKESAI: I am confessing – everything. I have to tell you something now, Master. The time is not long. I…*(Beat.)*

they killed my cousin like a chicken Master. A chicken.
(Beat.) He kept, he kept looking at me – I know what it was
he was thinking. He was thinking I have this good English
and this Bible learning why I couldn't stop them like I was
saying I could. Why I couldn't save him this time. Just this
one time. And I couldn't. I couldn't do one thing. I just
was standing there with my Bible like a fool, like a dofo.
So I had to… I had to … I… *(Beat.)* They were sleeping,
Master and Mistress Coltern, when she see me, I am
thinking she thought I was just coming to be warning them
of something. I am a good one. That is what they would
always be telling me, 'You are one of the good ones Ester.'
I like being good Master. But I couldn't, I couldn't *manage.*
(Beat.) Master, you have never told me about you your
father but I want to tell you about mine. My father was a
good, good man. And today, today I meet him. And he
was angry with me. He told me to shed blood for my own.
The whites don't do what their book it is saying. I thought
they would be like Jesus, show his love, love their enemy, I
thought – *(Beat.)* I wanted to not care and spill their blood
like they were not caring and spilling mine. They killed
him like a chicken, Master. A *chicken. (Beat.)* She open
her eyes, Mrs Coltern, her eyes they were looking at me
like she know me – but she did not know me today. Amai
always called me the best with the chickens, I could do it
one time, I knew how to cut quick, how to lift the knife
just like so and drop it heavy. I just lift the knife like I do
with the chicken and drop it through Mrs Coltern she her
neck. I think if I drop it somewhere else she would have
been screaming but I was cutting the neck so she just open
her mouth and it look like the sound it want to come but
it can't. Her eyes they looking at me like she can't believe.
Him he not even wake up, I leave him like that – to sleep,
I just put it the knife in his breast many, many time. I see
it, the blood, somehow it make me to feel better. I know
their kind bleed like my cousin he bleed; their blood it
was looking like his, same color, it come out same. I was
thinking, maybe it a difference but no, we have same under